Praise for *The Mindful Carnivore*

"Entertaining and erudite. Cerulli's refreshingly evenhanded tone allows readers to judge the author's argument on the merits of his literary and personal evidence. Today's noisy media environment often consists of rigid, uninformed viewpoints passed off as the sole truth. Cerulli provides a welcome antidote to the bluster."

—*Kirkus Reviews*

"A remarkably candid, nuanced, and engaging meditation on what it means to be human. There are no prescriptions or preachy admonitions—just an honest account of the mindful unfolding of a person who has taken seriously the responsibility upon the deaths of other organisms in order to live. A bracing read."

—Jan E. Dizard, author of
Going Wild and *Mortal Stakes*

"A personal tale of how one man comes to terms with the meat on his plate and a historical look at humanity's connection to animals. *The Mindful Carnivore* delivers new insight in the too often simplistic vegetarian versus carnivore argument."

—Novella Carpenter, author of *Farm City:*
The Education of an Urban Farmer

"Bull's-eye! This coming-of-age story is right on target in equating living—and killing—with eating. Cerulli cuts through forests of argument with a thoughtful and thrilling narrative as he turns from vegan to hunter, stalking, killing and eating his first deer. We experience his growing awareness of what it means to be fully involved in the web of nature. With him we can wonder at its complex mystery and share in 'mindful eating' as a sacred act."

—Betty Fussell, author of
The Story of Corn and *Raising Steaks*

"Tovar Cerulli embarks on an unlikely journey from vegan to hunter, laying bare the complicated relationship we have with the food we eat, exposing the many myths and prejudices that pile up on our plates. *The Mindful Carnivore* is a healthy reminder that our choices matter and an invitation to vegetarians and carnivores alike to examine their paths to sustenance."

—Langdon Cook, author of
Fat of the Land: Adventures of a 21st Century Forager

"Tovar Cerulli has written the book I've been waiting for. It's memoir, adventure story, exploration and a journey into history, ethics, nutrition, ecology, and philosophy. An entertaining read—and an entertaining ride—into the human experience. A savory morsel indeed."

—Daniel Herman, author of
Hunting and the American Imagination

"Cerulli offers penetrating insights into not only where our food comes from, but what our daily dietary choices say about who we are as human beings."

—Hank Shaw, author of
Hunt, Gather, Cook: Finding the Forgotten Feat

"Within these pages Tovar Cerulli navigates our role in the cycle of life in a way that is spiritual, intuitive, and profoundly real. By witnessing his transformation from staunch vegan to thoughtful hunter, we are reminded that mindful hunting not only makes us stewards of the land, but thoughtful eaters and more awake human beings. Bravo!"

—Georgia Pellegrini, author of
Girl Hunter and *Food Heroes*

"An unflinching account of one omnivore's dilemma, drawn with psychological sensitivity and ecological sense. Cerulli treats compelling arguments on both the pro- and anti-hunting sides of the environmental divide with equanimity, while being just as equally impatient with both sides' time-worn clichés and sound-bite slogans. A nourishing read!"

—Mary Zeiss Stange, author of *Woman the Hunter*
and *Hard Grass: Life on the Crazy Woman Bison Ranch*

"Elegantly written, thoughtful, intensely personal yet universal, *The Mindful Carnivore* is destined to become a classic."

—Nicolette Hahn Niman, author of
*Righteous Porkchop: Finding a Life and
Good Food Beyond Factory Farms*

THE
MINDFUL
CARNIVORE

THE
MINDFUL
CARNIVORE

A Vegetarian's
Hunt for Sustenance

TOVAR CERULLI

PEGASUS BOOKS
NEW YORK

THE MINDFUL CARNIVORE

Pegasus Books LLC
80 Broad Street, 5th Floor
New York, NY 10004

First Pegasus Books edition February 2012

Interior design by Maria Fernandez

Portions of this book were previously published, in somewhat different form, as "Life and Death," *Northern Woodlands* 13, no. 4 (2006): 9; "Whitetails: The Ever Changing Challenge," *Massachusetts Wildlife* 61, no. 4 (2006): 9-17; "Full Circle," *Outdoor America* 73, no. 1 (2008): 18-20; and "Hunting Like a Vegetarian: Same Ethics, Different Flavors," in *Hunting—Philosophy for Everyone: In Search of the Wild Life*, ed. Nathan Kowalsky (West Sussex, UK: Wiley-Blackwell, 2010), 45-55.

Grateful acknowledgment is made for permission to reprint "The Peace of Wild Things," Copyright © 1998 by Wendell Berry from *The Selected Poems of Wendell Berry*. Reprinted by permission of Counterpoint.

Library of Congress Cataloging-in-Publication Data is available.

ISBN: 978-1-60598-277-9

10 9 8 7 6 5 4 3 2 1

Printed in the United States of America
Distributed by W. W. Norton & Company

For Willie and Mark,
for all who eat and care,
and for the living earth that feeds us.

The symbolism of meat-eating is never neutral. To himself, the meat-eater seems to be eating life. To the vegetarian, he seems to be eating death. There is a kind of gestalt-shift between the two positions which makes it hard to change, and hard to raise questions on the matter at all without becoming embattled.

—Mary Midgley,
Animals and Why They Matter

CONTENTS

1 · No More Blood   1

2 · Man the Gardener   19

3 · Trouble in Eden   37

4 · An Animal Who Eats   53

5 · Where the Great Heron Feeds   65

6 · Hunter and Beholder   85

7 · Double Vision   102

8 · A Hunter's Prayer   121

9 · Healing Ground   143

10 · Into the Woods   156

11 · Kinds of Killing   177

12 · Fickle Predators   192

13 · Blood Trails   202

14 · Hunting with the Buddha   216

15 · The Red Deer   231

16 · Reckoning   243

Epilogue · Mindful Eating   253

Notes   259

Acknowledgments   279

THE
MINDFUL
CARNIVORE

1

No More Blood

The lavish Earth heaps up her riches and her gentle foods, and offers you dainties without blood and without slaughter.

—Ovid, *Metamorphoses*

The trout, pinned to the cutting board, flared its gills for water that wasn't there. The thin blade of my fillet knife hovered above. I had been thinking about kindness.

The week before—halfway through college and full of questions—I had attended a retreat led by Buddhist teacher Thich Nhat Hanh. He spoke of compassion. He encouraged vegetarianism and said how glad he was to see tofu becoming available in American supermarkets. Most of all, he encouraged mindfulness.

Awareness.

Aliveness.

Being awake.

I severed the trout's head and felt a sharp twinge as the blade bit.

The killing hadn't bothered me when I was a boy. I remember a snapshot from back then: My father's friend Willie stands beside me on a low granite shelf at the water's edge. We're both bundled in winter jackets, his giant form dwarfing my small one, our attention fixed on the boundary between air and water and on the unseen presences moving below.

I remember how chilly it was that April day. I remember my father out on the water in the battered, oft-patched rowboat; he had his camera with him. I remember because that was the day of the salmon egg.

Willie had opened his tackle box, taken out a jar, unscrewed the lid, and extracted a small red orb, no more than a quarter-inch across. Deftly, his big hands pierced the salty-smelling egg with a tiny gold hook. It disappeared inside. The length of nearly invisible leader between hook and swivel seemed too delicate to withstand a fish of any size. Willie cast out a short distance and let the egg settle into the depths. Minutes later, the diminutive tackle struck its mark and he reeled in the biggest brook trout I'd ever seen, its sparkling bulk almost a foot and a half long.

Willie grinned, cheeks bunching up on either side of his broad face. I was thrilled. And mystified, too, that he had accomplished the feat with such finesse, with such improbably small implements.

I lost the photo years ago. But the image remains with me: the place where it was pinned up in my father's house, the intent looks on Willie's face and mine, the quarry wall behind us, the blueberry bushes and birch saplings clinging to crevices in the rock.

I had caught my first fish within twenty yards of that spot, a few years earlier, at the age of three or four. My mother had chaperoned me down to the water's edge and I'd tossed in a hook baited with bread. Rewarded by a tug on the line, I had hauled up my first scaly prize. I suppose I should prevaricate here, in the venerable tradition of fish stories both exaggerated and fabricated, by waxing lyrical about the majesty of carp—which Izaak Walton called "the queen of rivers"—and about the daring exploits of carp fishermen around the globe. There is, however, no getting around it. The carp I caught was an orange-and-white goldfish. Some nine inches long, perhaps, but a goldfish nonetheless.

When the fishing bug bit me more seriously at five or six, Willie became my mentor in all things finned and gilled. A big man, quick to laugh, he had grown up in South Carolina and Harlem, and had met my father years later when they both lived in Boston. I didn't know much of his story then. I knew he was a clever angler, knowledgeable about fish and water and tackle; I had no idea his innate brilliance had earned him a full scholarship at Boston University and, later, admission to Harvard Business School, which he attended on the GI Bill, both in an era when racial integration was far from the norm. I knew he was imperturbable; I had no idea that he'd done three tours of duty with the navy and another tour in the struggle for civil rights, sustained by a spirituality that had little to do with religion. I knew he always seemed genuinely happy—"in good humor and good spirits," as he put it; I had no idea how deep he'd dug, completing his MBA at Harvard and then turning his back on the lucrative life he could have led to start a custom furniture business and return to the craft he had learned to love in the high school woodshop at Bronx Science.

Nor did I know what it was like for him to visit us there in southern New Hampshire. The area was, like me, quite white. And

3

Willie was black. I never stopped to think about it. To me, he was simply a marvelous fisherman and longtime friend.

By the time he and I started fishing together, I was living in Vermont with my mother and stepfather. Whenever Willie's visits to New Hampshire coincided with mine, we made the most of the daylight. We stood for hours on low ledges around the quarry's perimeter. Or we drifted around those two and a half acres of water in the old rowboat, flakes of pale-blue paint peeling from its interior. My father, who didn't care to fish, left us to it.

Willie treated me like a full-fledged fishing partner. When I had questions, he listened closely and gave real answers. On the water, though, we talked little. Mostly we waited in silence, watching our spiraled lines dimple the water's surface as they went out, praying for an acceleration or pause in their movement, any sign of a trout taking the bait. As the lines straightened, all attention went to our rod tips, to anticipating a slight twitch, a sudden increase in the tension of line against forefinger. When we pulled trout from twenty, forty, or sixty feet down, we delighted in their sparkling jewel-like colors, red spots haloed in blue. Then we ate them.

We did not catch and release. Why torture your food? We caught and killed, stopping when we had enough. And we had no qualms about it. Like Willie, I enjoyed the catching: the undeniable excitement of the first tug on the line, the uncertainty of whether I would land the fish and, if I did, of how large or small it would prove to be. Not that the size of the catch mattered much: We were fishing for lunch, not bragging rights.

An enthusiastic young omnivore, I also enjoyed the eating. The killing was merely a means to an end, to putting the trout on a plate. I took no pleasure in beheading my prey. I simply did it, without thought or apology. Willie and I didn't talk about such things back then. We just fished, killed, and ate.

Willie's passion for food had, over the years, enlarged his naturally big frame. I remember him standing near the water one time, telling my father how he had lost weight. He pointed to his leather belt, at eye level for me. Curved wear lines showed that he had taken it in several notches.

"The only exercise I've been doing is pushing myself away from the table," said Willie. He demonstrated the motion with his big arms and laughed, his barrel chest heaving with a surprisingly high-pitched, nasal chuckle.

We cooked the brookies simply. Each was beheaded and gutted with my birch-handled fillet knife, then fried in a cast-iron skillet with butter. The finely scaled skin crisped to a golden brown. The delicate flesh separated easily from spine and ribs.

Between catching and cooking, each fish was measured, its length jotted in a little spiral-bound logbook that Willie had encouraged me to start: date, length of fish, lure or bait used, any special notes such as food found in the mouth or stomach. Though he had spent much of his life in cities and still lived in the Boston area, Willie observed the world with a naturalist's eye. He knew that keeping track of details would help me understand the fish we hunted and the ecology of the place. It had been years since any trout were stocked in the quarry but they—like the goldfish someone had apparently dumped there—had taken well to their new home. The big trout suggested ample insects and minnows to feast on. The constant presence of little ones indicated successful spawning.

I couldn't have found a better creature on which to focus my hungry curiosity about local life-forms. Though the old granite quarry in which they swam was hardly a natural feature of the landscape, the trout themselves were. Brook trout (*Salvelinus fontinalis*) are native to only one place on the planet: northeastern North America, from the streams of the Appalachian Mountains, up through the Great Lakes basin and New England, and northward all the way to Hudson Bay and the northern Atlantic.

Though being of the genus *Salvelinus* technically makes them char, not trout, brookies are members of the broader trout and salmon family: *Salmonidae*. Like all salmonids, they're thought to be descended from a common ancestor species that lived in the rivers and lakes of southwestern Canada fifty million years ago. That's most of fifty million years before anyone resembling you or me showed up. We *Homo sapiens* are a very recent blip. Brookies and their ancestors were here a long, long time before we got around to noticing how gorgeous they were. And how tasty.

Each summer, as soon as school was out and I had arrived from Vermont, I would begin scouting for that summer's sweet spot, relying on my rough mental map of the underwater terrain. From constant exploring and swimming, sometimes with a diving mask, I knew every foot of the perimeter: where the cliff walls plunged straight down toward the bottom, where shelves jutted out, where the rock piles were, where branches and leaves collected, threatening to snag my hook if I cast in too close. The deeper reaches remained more mysterious. My father had been down there with scuba gear once and said there was a grocery cart on the bottom. We joked that in the movies it would have been something more sinister, probably a car.

My father had a pair of grainy, black-and-white photos from the quarrying days. The men looked tiny at the bottom of the ninety-foot granite cliffs. From those pictures, taken shortly before the quarrying stopped, I could see the shape of the basin: the shallow, low-walled section and the wider, deeper end. Where would the trout be in summer? During April vacation, with the ice just melted as it was the day Willie landed that huge one, we would often see—and catch—hungry fish near the surface, as they hunted every corner for minnows and insects. Though more adaptable than other species of char, brookies prefer chillier water than do their rainbow and brown trout cousins over in genera *Oncorhynchus* and *Salmo*. By July, as the upper waters warmed, they'd be deep, especially at midday.

But logic was only part of the equation. In selecting a sweet spot, I relied on intuition, too. After a bit of scouting, I would decide on a place without knowing exactly why. Perhaps the spot didn't matter. Perhaps I would have done just as well somewhere else. It *felt* like it mattered, though, as if that was the exact place I needed to be if I wanted good luck.

One summer my spot was a deep corner under the tallest cliff. Another year, my father and I set out an old, dark-green glass buoy, anchored to the bottom about twenty feet down. I would tie the rowboat to the netted four-inch sphere and sit there over the rock pile that marked the transition from the quarry's shallow section to the deeper eastern end. On a calm, bright day I could see the rocks below, illuminated by ribbons of sunlight streaming downward like the fanned tail of some great bird. If I was lucky, I might pick out the dark shape of a trout silhouetted against the granite and have the chance to get my hook out ahead of it. In dimmer light, I would watch for narrow, white fin edges ghosting by.

There, in my little corner of the world, I was fascinated by the drama of eaters and eaten, aware that I was only one predator among many.

Under the eaves of my father's house, antlions lay in ambush, their conical pit traps pocking the dusty earth. When an ant fell in and began scrambling out—or when a curious boy trickled in a few grains of sand—the hidden lion would rear its flat, ferocious head from the bottom of the pit. If an ant was within reach, the lion would seize it in its massive jaws. If not, the lion would flick up showers of sand, destabilizing the loose sides of the pit and bringing its scrabbling prey back down. I passed no judgment on the antlion—the larval form of an insect resembling a damselfly—for killing ants. That was its nature.

Toward the end of those long summer days, as the light began to fade, I would watch trout surfacing for food. The best shows were the all-out minnow chases. A little shiner—sometimes two or three of them abreast—would leap clear of the water, a hungry trout inches behind. A few feet farther on, the minnows would break the surface again, seeking escape, the trout still nipping at their tails. A third or fourth time the chase would flash into view before vanishing toward an uncertain conclusion.

Watching these chases reminded me of more exotic creatures. I had learned about the cheetah from the box of National Geographic cards that lived on the top shelf of my bookcase, and my mother had made me a quilt with the face of that great cat at its center, striking black eye lines embroidered on yellow, running down around the muzzle like tears. I had met the peregrine falcon as Sam Gribley's companion, Frightful, in *My Side of the Mountain*. I knew that both were endangered—the cheetah by hunting and habitat loss, the peregrine by decades-long use of the pesticide DDT. This concerned me. But what seized my imagination was their raw, predatory speed.

I had seen it on Mutual of Omaha's *Wild Kingdom*: the cheetah's slow, careful stalk, the explosive charge, a gazelle leaping away, the cat accelerating to seventy miles per hour in a matter of seconds. It made my heart race. And even that stunning velocity was eclipsed—three times over—by the deadly strike of the peregrine, hurtling down in my mind's eye like an arrow from the sky.

As a young bipedal predator, I had neither great stealth nor great speed. What I had was stubbornness, augmented by luck. I also had innate cleverness and a few rudimentary skills that—like Willie's far greater and long-practiced skills—were unimpeded by allegiance to any notion of aesthetic purism.

I fished with whatever worked: lures, salmon eggs, live bait. Grasshoppers were a favorite, caught by hand among the tall grasses of a nearby field and stowed in a plastic bread bag. Minnows were a close second. A wire-mesh trap, baited with crumbs and set overnight in a shallow, sheltered corner of the quarry, would yield a dozen or more by morning.

In a pinch, if I wanted a minnow but hadn't set out the trap, I would catch them singly, on a tiny hook. One afternoon I impaled a small black ant on such a hook and, rod in hand, threaded my way down to another corner of the quarry where thick alders overhung the water. Minnows congregated there in the shade. They scattered as I lowered the hook. I thought I had startled them, but then saw a trout just cruising into the shallows. I jiggled the hooked ant. To my delight, the hunter struck and I had an eight-inch fish in hand.

Another summer, I watched one drama unfold evening after evening: a single trout hunting whirligig beetles. Each time I saw the fish, it surfaced in the same area. Each time, it appeared to be the same size. I decided I was seeing the same trout again and again. Most of its leaps missed the beetles as they zigzagged their way across the surface. The ripples would subside and the whirligig would emerge, still paddling away in its evasive pattern. But the trout was persistent. Eventually there would be a leap, the ripples would vanish, and the beetle would be gone.

The trout's tenacity gave me an idea. Though I knew little about fly-fishing, I had a rod, and I'd taken a short series of classes in fly-tying, taught by an old Vermonter who knew his stuff. The flies I had tied under his direction included a compact, dark-gray bundle of deer hair with an encouraging name: Irresistible. It floated and was about the same size as a whirligig beetle.

One evening when that trout was jumping again, I tied on the Irresistible, hopped into the rowboat, and started paying out line. For fly-fishing purists, masters of the double-haul cast, I'm sure that trolling a dry fly is an especially grievous act of sacrilege. But it worked. The trout started striking. And missing. Either its aim was poor or it was aiming to the side, anticipating that this whirligig beetle would, like all others, whirl off one way or the other just as the strike was made. A few misses later the trout connected and, looking for a meal, became one.

To me, killing fish wasn't so different from picking wild blue-berries. Both were edible parts of my world, free for the catching or gathering. Early on a summer morning, I would head to the pine and oak woods above the cliffs on the quarry's high southern side. The berries were thick in there. I'd fill a quart container with a mix of them, some small and dusty blue, others big, shiny, and nearly black. Back at the house, my father would stir them into pancake batter and drop spoonfuls onto a sizzling griddle. On our plates, their purple juices mingled with syrup from the few maples we tapped each spring. In early evening of the same day, a pair of trout might sizzle on the same stovetop and be served up on the same plates. The sweetness of gifts straight from the land.

Hunting bullfrogs was more troubling. On summer nights—lying in a bunk bed Willie had made, the clean lines and joinery crafted with the same precise, no-nonsense style he brought to fishing—I listened to the rhythmic chorus of the frogs' foghorn voices. By day, I caught them bare-handed.

The lucky ones got away or were released after I had marveled at their glittering gold-and-black eyes, their uncannily familiar hands and forearms. The unlucky I put into a long blue cotton-mesh bag. Back at the house, I killed them one by one with a quick plunge of my fillet knife down through the spine. Three frogs and I had lunch: six hefty hind legs, each measuring five inches or so after the feet were removed. Skinned, then sautéed with butter and garlic powder, they were mild as chicken. I took their bodies, along with trout heads and entrails, out to the woods for raccoons and other animals to feast on.

Catching bullfrogs by hand took time and skill. Any approach by land was nearly hopeless. The best strategy was to swim along the shore and look for the telltale yellow throat of a full-grown male. Then, slowly, I went straight in toward his nose, keeping my hands below the surface. A swift grab and I had him—sometimes.

After my father gave me a BB gun, the killing got easier. I could take the rowboat along the shore, spot a frog a few yards away, get in position so I had a side view of his head between the cattails, and then—if he hadn't skipped off already—aim for his big, concentrically patterned eardrum and squeeze the trigger.

I no longer needed to match guile against instinct, hand against leap. I no longer had to feel the fine, slippery texture of the frog's skin where my hand encircled his waist, nor the forceful push of his hands against my fingers. I no longer saw the details of great webbed toes attached to living, meaty legs. I no longer had to look at his face up close before deciding whether to kill him.

In hindsight, I realize that the gun changed my frog hunting for the worse. The killing became too efficient, too coldly distant. And there was the chance of injury. Hand-caught frogs suffered no harm in the catching; I could release them unscathed. If I decided to put them to the knife, death was instantaneous. A frog hit by a BB, on the other hand, might get away wounded, suffering needlessly before succumbing to the injury or to another predator.

I don't recall any ever escaping: I was a decent shot and made my kills at close range. What I do recall is a letter my father sent me. I was about nine. A few weeks earlier I had been at the quarry and had gone fishing and frogging. The letter reached me at my mother's in Vermont. To say I recall it is, I suppose, an exaggeration. I recall only one or two lines. My father had found a dead frog. By the time he discovered it somewhere along the shoreline, it was gray and foul. Since a BB would only make a tiny hole, he couldn't tell how it had died, but he wondered: Had I shot and failed to recover it? Even at that young age, the possibility made me sick—the frog in pain, its death pointless.

Still, hunting enticed me. I had a big-game knife of sorts. I don't know where it came from or whether it would have been useful in the field. But the sweep of the blade, the stubby guard, the antler handle, and the sheath embossed with wolf and trees all excited something primal within me.

That same atavistic spirit had been kindled the moment I stepped into my uncle Mark's room for the first time. He was living with his sister and her husband on Cape Cod's south shore. My mother, stepfather, sisters, and I had driven down from Vermont for Thanksgiving. Walking into that room was like traveling back in time. On the walls were bows and arrows, a powder horn he had made and scrimshawed, antlers from bucks he had taken, pelts from traplines he had set. Mark, whom I saw only once every year or two, was the only hunter I really knew. He made a belt for me: smooth, wide leather embellished with arrows, diamond shapes pressed in as broadheads, fanned scallop-shell marks suggesting fletching. Snapped to it was a large brass buckle, a symmetrical cross in a near circle. I wore it every day.

I had a pair of plastic recurve bows and spent hours launching a hodgepodge of wooden shafts at straw bales or blocks of old foam. My father, though he had no interest in hunting, recognized mine. I was thirteen or so when he handed me a small Christmas package. Unwrapping and opening the box, I found a double-edged steel broadhead. My little recurves were no match for this deadly looking thing. The message was clear. He was giving me a real bow. That Jennings compound, its lacquered wooden grip richly grained in reddish orange, was a huge leap from my plastic toys. It suggested real hunting.

Yet I never took to the woods in pursuit of game. I knew no local hunter who might have offered to teach me how to hunt and, besides, I enjoyed shooting for its own sake. With my bow, I shot at targets. With my BB gun—and later with my father's .22 revolver, a six-shot Smith & Wesson on a big .38 frame, and my first rifle, a Remington bolt-action .22—I mostly plinked cans.

Once or twice, at my father's utilitarian request, I did pick off woodchucks that had been tunneling around the foundations of the house.

And, once, I took aim at a chickadee perched on a low tree branch. My sights had been drawn to the bird by the challenge of making the kill. When the .22 went off, the creature dropped to the earth and I felt a burst of exhilaration, of accomplishment. I approached and picked up the bloody bundle of feathers. There wasn't much left. The meaninglessness of it turned my stomach.

One evening in early fall, we had dinner guests coming. I was in middle school and had moved back to my father's full-time. That night, there would be four of us. Fresh trout topped the menu. As soon as I got home from school, I dropped my books, hopped into the boat, and rowed, oarlocks squeaking, out to that summer's sweet spot, a short distance off the jutting granite corner we called Paul Winter Point. The musician had, I was told, sat there once, playing his sax, plaintive notes echoing off the quarry walls opposite. Half an hour before dinner, I hooked the fourth fish.

But such meals were rare. Most flesh came from the grocery store, and I gave no thought to its provenance: the chunks of beef my father sliced up for his favorite slow-simmered stew full of parsnips and carrots, the pork chops my mother broiled. They came neatly wrapped in plastic. No muss, no fuss.

Right through high school, I ate whatever was in front of me. When I had dinner with my girlfriend's family, I enjoyed their vegetarian stir-fries and salads. When I visited my best friends—a pair of brothers—I savored their mother's meaty German-style cooking just as much. If I was out with friends and we stopped at McDonald's, I would order a Quarter Pounder with cheese, never pausing for a moment to consider where the beef patty came from.

By the time I was twenty—holding that trout to the cutting board and considering Thich Nhat Hanh's words on kindness—my days of carefree carnivory were over.

I started cutting back on meat in my late teens. I had learned that excess beef and pork weren't good for my health. I had learned, too, that supermarket meat was far from pure. Looking at ground chuck in the local IGA cooler, I wondered what chemical mysteries lay accumulated inside those plastic and foam packages. How much pesticide had been on the corn those cattle had eaten? What antibiotics had been pumped into the animals, keeping them alive for slaughter day?

A year or two later, I learned that more than ten pounds of corn were used to produce every pound of U.S. grain-fed beef and that broad swaths of South American rainforest were being denuded to raise cattle for North American markets. Why should my diet harm the earth? Why should it make such wasteful use of the fruits of the land, perpetuating this pattern of First World gluttony when people around the globe were starving?

My appetite for supermarket flesh had been further dulled by what I knew about factory farming: pigs crammed into crates barely larger than their bodies, chickens stuck in tiny cages for the entirety of their brief lives. What right did humans have to treat animals so cruelly? And must not that cruelty harm humans in turn? Must not the common practice of "thumping" runt piglets—grabbing them by the hind legs and smashing their heads against concrete floors—harden people's hearts and distort their notions of morality?

The change had been gradual: these questions growing, my meals including less and less meat. Now, at twenty, the final recognition hit hard. I had killed this fish out of nothing more than habit.

Picking up my little spinning rod, I had tied a lure to the stiff, tightly spiraled line and cast out into the quarry. Soon enough the trout had struck and had come in flashing, struggling against the hook. A minute later, I had it on the cutting board, its head severed, my heart filled with sudden disquiet.

Because I had killed the fish, I ate it. But I cooked and swallowed its tender flesh with regret. Unlike a factory chicken, it had lived well, yet its death had been gratuitous. There were so many other things I could have eaten, things like rice and vegetables, things that would not have felt the hook or even the briefest slice of steel. It was, I vowed, the last time I would ever consume a fellow creature.

During my last two years of college, I lived in Brooklyn and attended classes in lower Manhattan. Practically all of my friends were vegetarians. We could see no conscionable reason to eat the flesh of other animals. No rationale could justify it. No apology could set it right. Before long, I became a purist: a vegan. I forswore eggs, milk, yogurt, and cheese. I objected to specific practices like the partial clipping off of laying hens' sensitive beaks to prevent them from pecking at each other in overcrowded conditions. And I objected more generally to the confinement of fellow animals, the bending of other creatures' lives to serve human ends.

I could walk into any New York City grocery store and find shelves and display cases brimming with bread and beans, fruit and greens. Or I could walk over to the farmers' market in Union Square, at the intersection of Broadway and Fourteenth Street, to buy produce directly from the folks who had grown it.

I still knew plenty of meat eaters, of course, including my family. Fortunately, they accepted my diet. When we sat down to Thanksgiving dinner at Uncle Mark's house and I declined turkey, no one said anything. I, in turn, said nothing about the roasted flesh on the table or about the antlered deer head on the living-room wall.

If I had paused to think about it, I don't suppose I would have known what to make of Uncle Mark and his pursuits. To me, hunting now seemed like a barbaric relic of the past. Perhaps it had been a necessity in our days as hunter-gatherers, but here in modern America that time was long gone. Mark didn't depend on wild meat to feed his family. His job as a mechanic and machinist, keeping mowers and other equipment running smoothly on a Cape Cod golf course, put groceries on the table.

The idea of hunting for trophies—anachronistic proof of Man the Hunter's machismo, his capacity to dominate nature and shoot down the largest possible animals—appalled me. So did the idea of hunting for "sport" or "recreation." What excuse could there be for taking pleasure in the act of killing? As a boy, I had read Jean Craighead George's *Julie of the Wolves*. In the novel's climactic scene, the young heroine's friend and wilderness foster parent, the wolf Amaroq, is killed on Alaska's North Slope. The men who shoot him from an airplane do so not for the sake of protecting livestock, nor for his pelt, nor even for profit. They kill solely for amusement. When I put the book down, I had no words for the grief lodged in my throat.

Yet sadistic fun wasn't a motive I could have attributed to Mark. He was tender with his wife and kids. He doted on his dog. Driving, he swerved to avoid squirrels or turtles crossing the road. And, though there was that one deer head on the wall, I couldn't have imagined Mark—who seemed quiet to the point of timidity and self-effacement—getting all puffed up about trophies. So why did he go to such lengths to pursue and kill meat on the hoof?

I might also have wondered why Willie fished. We had lost touch after my father's sudden, devastating death in an accident when I was seventeen. But toward the end of college, I called Willie and we met for lunch in Boston. He was just as I remembered him: big, warm, full of that funny, high-pitched laughter, at ease with himself and the life he had crafted. He had no vicious streak. And his custom furniture business, while not lucrative, kept him fed. Why, then, I might have asked, did he feel the need to catch and kill fish?

Repentant, I looked back on my own boyhood with a mixture of regret and sympathy, wishing I hadn't been a killer, but chalking it up to hot-blooded ignorance. I hadn't known any better.

Now, with the unassailable certainty of youth, I did know.

Peregrine falcons, well on their way to recovery, had begun nesting in New York City. But living there wasn't going to suit me for long. In my small apartment, I felt separate from nature. It was all around me—in the trees that lined the streets, in the gray and black squirrels that loped through Washington Square Park, in the grass that sprouted in the cracks and seams of the pavement—but it felt too fragmented. I wasn't touching soil. I wasn't hearing the sounds of water, of wind in the trees. Unlike the farmers whose trucks I visited in Union Square, I had no contact with the earth from which our food sprang.

Along the sidewalks of Brooklyn and Manhattan, I picked up pigeon feathers. I read and reread the Wendell Berry poem pinned to the wall of my apartment, "The Peace of Wild Things":

> When despair for the world grows in me
> and I wake in the night at the least sound
> in fear of what my life and my children's lives may be,
> I go and lie down where the wood drake
> rests in his beauty on the water, and the great heron feeds.
> I come into the peace of wild things
> who do not tax their lives with forethought
> of grief. I come into the presence of still water.
> And I feel above me the day-blind stars

waiting with their light. For a time
I rest in the grace of the world, and am free.

One evening, leaving class and stepping out onto Eleventh
Street near the corner of Sixth Avenue, I noticed an unusually
bright streetlamp out of the corner of my eye. Looking up, I saw
the full moon and realized I hadn't seen stars in months.

Two years later, I was in love. My sweetheart, Catherine, and
I were moving in together and had rented a place among New
York's Finger Lakes, an hour from her hometown.

Leaving my father's house for the last time, I sorted through
my things. I had gotten rid of my .22 and my father's few firearms
by then; guns had no place in the life of mindful compassion I
intended to lead. I still had my Jennings bow, though, and decided
to give it to a friend.

I still had my old tackle box, too. Figuring it might be useful
for some other purpose, I kept the box, and also the retractable
tape I had used to measure trout before jotting their lengths in my
logbook. Most of the rest I tossed out, including a few bedraggled
lures and a handful of rusty Eagle Claw hooks in paper-and-
plastic sleeves. They smelled of salmon eggs.

My fillet knife I sent to Willie.

Half a decade into being a vegan, I couldn't have fathomed
eating flesh again. And I certainly couldn't have pictured myself
eight years later, plunking my first freshly eviscerated mammal
down onto the kitchen counter.

2

Man the Gardener

The wolf and the lamb shall feed together, and the lion shall eat straw like the bullock: and dust shall be the serpent's meat. They shall not hurt nor destroy in all my holy mountain.

—Isaiah 65:25

Vegetarians take a lot of ribbing from meat eaters.

Bumper sticker: "Eat low on the food chain. Barbecue a vegetarian."

Wisecrack: "If vegetarians eat vegetables, what do humanitarians eat?"

Personally, I didn't get much flak. My newfound love, Cath, had been a vegetarian longer than I had—ah, domestic harmony. She had never gone as far as veganism, but once we got together she acquiesced to my dietary zeal. Mostly. She never quite gave up the occasional cup of coffee with half-and-half, or cocoa with whipped cream. Nor did I ever quite manage to say no when she offered me a sip. (A sip, I found, is a highly ambiguous measure of volume, especially when the coffee or cocoa is good.)

With only the rare gibe, our families accepted our diets and refrained from subjecting us to nutritional tirades or exasperating questions about protein. And our friends were vegetarians, or meat eaters who understood. They got it.

By and large, though, American meat eaters do *not* seem to get it.

Once, during a cross-country trip, Cath and I stopped to eat at a truck-stop diner in rural Louisiana. The vegan options were, shall we say, limited. French fries, perhaps, or a little bowl of iceberg lettuce. I asked the waitress if we could get the spaghetti without the meatballs. She looked up from pad and pen, regarding me as though she had just realized I was a green-skinned, three-fingered, bug-eyed alien.

"You don't want the *meat?!?*" Her holler was generous, inviting the other patrons to share her incredulity and turn to stare. They obliged.

There's the constant suggestion—whether made in jest or in earnest, with good humor or with malice—that vegetarians aren't quite right in the head. That a diet composed of rice, veggies, and tofu must be a notion that was hatched a few decades ago in California, the Land of Fruits and Nuts, inspired by the inhalation of something that filled Flower Children with warm, fuzzy feelings for all beings in the cosmos and also gave them the munchies.

Vegetarianism, however, isn't some recent, wacky dietary fad. You can find its roots in the ancient East, in the Indian religious traditions of Buddhism, Hinduism, and Jainism. All three emphasize teachings on compassion and nonviolence. In varying degrees, major schools of thought within each hold up vegetarianism as an ideal. Eating flesh, these traditions suggest, not only causes unnecessary suffering for animals, but also has a negative karmic impact on us, stunting our spiritual growth.

Mahatma Gandhi, for instance—though he experimented with meat in his youth—spent most of his life as a strict vegetarian in keeping with the ideals of Hinduism. "To my mind," he wrote in his autobiography, "the life of a lamb is no less precious than that of a human being. I should be unwilling to take the life of a lamb for the sake of the human body." I don't doubt the man for an instant. My powers of imagination fall short in the attempt to picture the past century's greatest proponent of nonviolence tearing into a lamb shank for lunch.

As British humanitarian Howard Williams documented in his 1883 history of Western vegetarianism, *The Ethics of Diet*, you can also find its early tendrils in ancient Greece. Today the name Pythagoras is most widely recognized in connection with the geometry of triangles. But in the decades and centuries immediately following his death—about half a millennium before Christ's birth—he was primarily remembered for his philosophical and religious teachings, including his advocacy of a meat-free diet.

Eastern and Western traditions of vegetarianism intersected in the seventeenth century, when European travelers returning from India brought back tales of a peaceable society where animals were treated with kindness, not eaten. As historian Tristram Stuart illustrates in his book *The Bloodless Revolution*, Europe had already begun grappling with the religious and moral implications of meat eating, and the introduction of Hindu philosophy had an enormous impact.

Here in North America, vegetarianism began to take root in 1817 when forty-one followers of the Bible Christian Church sailed from Liverpool, England, to Philadelphia. Before then, isolated groups—including some Quakers—had avoided meat. But, as historian Adam Shprintzen documented in his dissertation research, it was the Bible Christians, drawn across the Atlantic by the promise of civil and religious freedom, who sparked American vegetarianism as a movement.

Settling in Philadelphia—the Quaker-founded City of Brotherly Love—the Bible Christians began spreading their gospel. The

Good Book, they argued, called for abstinence from flesh foods. Meat, after all, had not been consumed in the Garden of Eden, and the commandment "Thou shall not kill" could be reasonably applied not just to humans but to animals as well. Like alcohol, which the Bible Christians also condemned, meat was said to be harmful to the human soul, evoking the violence, cruelty, and aggression that led to war and slavery.

In 1830, the Bible Christians' message struck a chord with Presbyterian minister Sylvester Graham, who had come to Philadelphia to lecture on the evils of alcohol. Graham believed that physical health was directly related to ethical development, and he soon began to preach about food, claiming that vegetables were humanity's natural source of sustenance. Though he considered eggs an important part of a balanced diet, he argued that meat-free foods made people healthier in body, sharper in intellect, and more refined in morals.

As Shprintzen notes, Graham was not primarily concerned about animal welfare. If animals were protected as a result of the diet he advocated, that was a secondary benefit. What mattered was that eating flesh was an intense sensory experience that made humans act like "the lower animals." Overstimulation of any kind—whether from eating spicy foods and meat, imbibing spirits, or seeking sexual pleasure—inspired dangerous primal urges. Successfully capitalizing on the social reform concerns of the day, Graham contended that animalistic behavior was at the root of all evils and that a plant-based diet was vital to alleviating poverty and abolishing slavery.

Overstimulation was also said to make the body susceptible to physical illness, and Graham took advantage of the 1832 cholera epidemic—which killed more than thirty-five hundred New Yorkers in less than two months—to heap blame upon "dietetic intemperance and lewdness," especially meat eating, and to recruit new converts. Shprintzen points out that there was no lack of meat eating in nineteenth-century America. One cookbook, published in 1824, identified thirteen categories of American foods—seven of them were meat. And Charles Dickens, during a visit to the United States, wrote that "breakfast would have been no breakfast unless the principal dish were a deformed beef-steak . . . swimming in hot butter."

Poor diet, Graham argued, was symptomatic of a degenerate, luxury-loving society. Making critiques that still resonate almost two centuries later, he asserted that industrialization had disconnected Americans from natural ways of living and from their food sources, and that whole grains were superior to white bread, which had become convenient and cheap. He advocated cold water and bland foods, including a coarse, all-natural wheat bread that became known as "Graham bread." Little did he know that, by the early 1900s, his name would be attached to a tasty, sweetened, highly refined product he would have abhorred: the modern Graham cracker.

By 1850, meat-free diets had become intertwined with a growing American interest in holistic, preventative health care. That year, inspired by the recent formation of a Vegetarian society in England, U.S. dietary reformers held a convention in New York City and founded their own organization, the American Vegetarian Society. Establishment of the society cemented the term "vegetarian" in the American lexicon. Though the word had been in use for at least a decade, adherents to meatless diets had also been referred to as being "Pythagoreans," "Grahamites," or followers of a "natural diet."

Present-day vegetarians would not, I think, be surprised to learn that such labels were used to ridicule more often than to praise. In 1850, *Scientific American* assailed members of the American Vegetarian Society for having "a good conceit" of themselves, and the *Saturday Evening Post* suggested that the diet would make men "weak and cowardly." From New York and

Massachusetts to Georgia and Ohio, the popular press accused vegetarians of being timid, unnatural, overly sentimental, and bizarrely obsessed with animals.

The newly formed society and its *American Vegetarian and Health Journal* gave dietary reformers the opportunity to articulate the principles and aims of their movement. Vegetarianism, they contended, was healthy, in part because meat was often diseased and overly processed. By eating a plant-based diet, Americans could assure their quality of life, wresting control back from industrialized food producers. Because meat was expensive, vegetarianism assured stronger personal finances. And it assured economic equity: "Were there no hogs," argued an 1853 article criticizing the Kentucky swine industry, "there would be a large surplus [of corn] for bread, the price would be greatly reduced, and the staff of life within the reach of all, however poor."

Though the religiosity of Graham's message had been set aside and bland foods were no longer championed—the society's convention banquets offered both savories and sweets—American vegetarianism remained committed to moral reform. At its core, Shprintzen argues, was "an unwavering moral principle that equated violence against animals with a cruel and aggressive society . . . driven by lust, rage and desire." Its proponents believed that vegetarianism was "a radical reform . . . laying, as it evidently does, the 'axe at the root of the tree.'" It naturally resulted in peaceful relations among humans. It would lead to women's suffrage and gender equality. It would hasten the end of slavery. The diet was, in short, the way to achieve all positive social change.

In the end, Shprintzen contends, this universal claim undermined vegetarianism's effectiveness. There were, after all, plenty of other movements and organizations to join, each specifically dedicated to causes such as suffrage and abolition. And as slavery drew more and more attention among social reformers, vegetarianism became unnecessary as a central organizing principle. By 1854, the American Vegetarian Society and its journal were already dissolving.

As a social reform movement, vegetarianism was dead. As a diet, however, its life had only just begun.

After the Civil War, vegetarianism was linked primarily to health and fitness and was promoted by a growing number of health institutes focused on naturopathy and preventative medicine. Foremost among these was Michigan's Battle Creek Sanitarium, founded by Seventh-day Adventist leader Ellen White. In keeping with a vision White claimed to have had in 1863—instructing Adventists to abstain from meat, tobacco, and alcohol—the sanitarium promoted meat-free living as a path to physical health and vigor. Under the direction of Dr. John Harvey Kellogg, the institute expanded rapidly, drawing guests from across the nation and inventing an assortment of new health foods, including nut butters, meat substitutes, and a cereal dubbed "granola."

In 1898, John Kellogg and his younger brother, Will, began producing these foods for mail order. By purchasing such products, Shprintzen argues, vegetarians continued to move away from social reform and toward "a fascination with the possibilities of personal empowerment through consumption." Eight years later, Will Kellogg struck out on his own to start the Battle Creek Toasted Corn Flake Company, which would, of course, become Kellogg's, the cereal giant.

By the 1890s, a new national organization—the Vegetarian Society of America—had emerged. And Chicago had become the new center of American vegetarianism, due in large part to financial support from the city's elite, who saw the diet as a way of perfecting human health, encouraging progress away from our savage origins, and creating moral, industrious, financially successful citizens.

Simultaneously, as Shprintzen illustrates, America was becoming obsessed with physical fitness, particularly the development of muscular men: rugged, hard-working individualists who could triumph in the new industrial economy. At the center of this trend was the magazine *Physical Culture*. In contrast to earlier vegetarian publications, *Physical Culture* carefully avoided politics and ideology. What it promoted was vigorous masculinity, frequently praising Theodore Roosevelt as a symbol of strength, vitality, and moral character. (The fact that Roosevelt was a meat eater and avid hunter made no difference. Like earlier public voices of American vegetarianism, *Physical Culture* paid little attention to the issue of animal welfare. Though the American Society for the Prevention of Cruelty to Animals had been founded in 1866, the humane movement and vegetarian movement remained almost entirely separate.)

Before long, the Vegetarian Society's magazine, *The Vegetarian*, caught on to *Physical Culture*'s success in linking diet with an athletic, prosperous lifestyle. Together, the two publications celebrated the physical prowess of vegetarian boxers, swimmers, and baseball players, including legendary pitcher Cy Young. Of particular interest to *The Vegetarian* was the success of the 1907 University of Chicago football team, which trained on a meatless diet. Even the mainstream *Chicago Daily Tribune* reported that the diet made the players strong, agile, and quick thinking, and also made them better sportsmen, who played with a powerful and gentlemanly discipline, far superior to the "leg breaking and ear twisting savagery" of their "beef-fed" opponents.

As the twentieth century progressed, broader societal trends continued to shape the meanings of American vegetarianism. Growing concern for animal welfare and the continued development of ideas about animal rights brought the living sources of meat into sharper focus. Rachel Carson's 1962 book *Silent Spring* heralded an emergent ecological awareness and set the stage for the publication, nine years later, of Frances Moore Lappé's landmark *Diet for a Small Planet*, in which Lappé encouraged

Americans to reduce their meat consumption, argued for a different nutritional paradigm, and challenged the economic policies underpinning the protein inefficiencies of U.S. agriculture. Vegetarianism was further influenced by the counterculture of the 1960s and '70s, with its ecological concerns, its rejection of convention, and its interest in Eastern philosophies and religions, including Buddhism.

Though unfamiliar with this history at the age of twenty-five, I had woven my convictions from many of the same threads. Abstaining from meat was part of a natural, healthy lifestyle. It would make me whole, both physically and morally, cultivating compassion in my heart and alleviating the suffering of animals. It would put grain into the bellies of the hungry and rescue the rainforests from destruction.

Vegetarianism—and, soon thereafter, veganism—became more than a mere diet. Though secular, it became a way of life, a statement of values and identity, a coat of arms for the struggle to right all that was wrong with the world. It started out being about food, but soon the beliefs themselves began to sustain me. I felt sure that everyone should be vegetarian.

My zealous certainty should have set off warning bells, but it didn't. I hadn't yet figured out that religious fundamentalism isn't the only dangerous kind.

The best food in the world would, logically, be organic vegetables, as fresh and local as possible. As it happened, I was in luck. Cath had been gardening since she was a girl.

She told me about growing up in the farm country south of Syracuse, New York, about an hour's drive from the place we had rented near Ithaca. Her father's father, who'd lived just across the yard in a second farmhouse, had been the family's head gardener. She spoke of him with such affection: his passion for flowers—the rose bushes by his front door and the mock orange nearby; the bridal veil spireas that hugged the house with their clusters of white, five-petaled blossoms; the big, round bed of phlox, lavender and pink with white eyes, salmon with a dark-pink center—and his strong, steady, limping gait, wooden cane compensating for the old leg injury; as a younger man, he had been dragged by a team of horses.

From the stories she told me, it was easy to picture her as a little girl, sitting on her beloved grandfather's knee, taking the occasionally proffered cigar. It was easy to picture him, chuckling kindly and patting her head as she coughed and sputtered at the sweet, thick smoke. It was easy to picture them together in the garden, the girl tagging along, her big, brown, earnest eyes taking in all the beauty this man had cultivated, seeing the tenderness with which he handled all the living things in his care.

At the corner of his house, beyond the rose bushes, Grandpa set aside a patch of soil a few feet square as Cath's first flower garden, all her own. And beyond that, alongside the woodshed attached to Grandpa's kitchen, towered the six-foot golden glows, topped with the double-daisy bursts she liked to pick and bring home by the fistful to put in vases.

"Why do you pick those weeds?" her mother would ask, disdaining unruliness. Roses were nice to have in the house, but weeds were weeds. Except for her once-an-evening inspection of the beds around the house, picking off a dead leaf or bloom here and there, she steered clear of gardening.

At planting time each spring, Cath and her brothers had been at Grandpa's beck and call. In the big vegetable plot out back, they would unfurl the bundles that had been stored away over the winter—two sticks in each, with a length of string in between. Cath would go to one side of the garden with a stick in hand, while one of her brothers went to the other side. When everything was lined up the way he wanted it, Grandpa would say so and the sticks would be driven in. Following the string, he would carefully mark out the arrow-straight row, hoe in his right hand, wooden cane in his left. Then he'd point to his thumb to indicate how deep each kind of seed should go: *Here, to this knuckle.*

Even there in the vegetable garden, where the soil was dedicated to the serious business of food production, Grandpa found room for whimsy. In the first section, behind the lettuce, grew a row of red, white, and pink peonies. Mom didn't like those in the house either: Ants swarmed the unopened buds, feeding on the sweet resin. Alongside the main vegetable plot—corn, potatoes and onions, carrots and green beans, cucumbers, zucchini and yellow summer squash—stood a row of tall delphiniums, pale blue and dark purple.

Cath's grandfather had gardened professionally, too, tending ornamental plantings for local estates and businesses right into his eighties. Right up until the day he finished tidying the flower beds around the funeral home in town, climbed into his '49 Ford, put the key in the ignition, and slumped over, struck by a heart attack. The undertaker found him in the driver's seat.

When we moved in together that spring, Cath still had his tools: a four-tined soil rake, an edger, a weeder, a heart-shaped hoe. And she also had his passion for forging relationships with soil and plants. For her, making a home meant building a garden.

The idea appealed to me. My time living in New York City, educational though it had been, had left me feeling estranged from nature. It had left me longing to "rest in the grace of the world," as Wendell Berry put it. Though I had never gardened much, I remembered enjoying what little I had done as a child, helping my mother with vegetables and marigolds. And I was eager to learn, to start growing my own food. With our landlady's permission, we set to it.

The tiny house—nestled along one side of a large, grassy clearing, with woods all around—had a timber-and-stucco look that made us think of a Tudor cottage. Where an ell extended from the original structure, the front door opened onto a patch of ground perhaps ten feet square, tiled with pieces of dark-gray slate, tufts of grass poking up between them. The two outer sides of the small, rough patio were bounded by the sloping lawn.

With shovels, we cut out the sod in a three-foot-wide swath alongside the slate, then started into the earth beneath. It was reluctant ground. Levered with a shovel blade, it moved in chunks, clay-laden soil packed between pieces of dark shale the size of dinner plates. But Cath and I won out bit by bit, breaking up the dense earth, extracting the rock.

To define the edges of the small raised beds—and to keep them from collapsing—we built miniature stacked-stone walls, first using the shale our digging had yielded, then hauling more from a pile we found on the opposite side of the clearing. When the edges were finished, two gently curved beds cradled the rough patio, one reaching out from alongside each of the cottage walls. We smoothed out the piles of upturned soil with Grandpa's long-tined rake and planted salad greens and flowers. Cath wanted forget-me-nots, dark delphiniums, and hollyhocks like those her grandfather had tended. I wanted orange marigolds like the ones I had helped my mother plant when I was a boy, and delicate purple irises like those that had grown in little bunches around the quarry's edge.

In summer, we extended the garden, working up the slope beside the cottage with shovels and, for one bone-jarring day, an undersized rototiller. The machine wanted no part of the dense soil, nor of the pieces of shale it locked onto. We levered out one slab the size of a coffee table. We surrounded the piles of dirt with foot-high stone walls and smoothed them out, narrow paths in between. The small terraced beds descended to the cottage, complementing it in scale and form, their stacked-shale borders lending the place an old-fashioned feel. Wild white roses climbed among the trees, their blooms filling the clearing with strong, sweet scent. A few yards beyond the back window of the kitchen coursed a little brook, low and murmuring.

In the quiet—disturbed only by the occasional whine of a speedboat on Cayuga Lake a mile to our east—we tended the garden and watched the songbirds that came to our feeders: chickadees and cardinals, finches and rose-breasted grosbeaks, a bright indigo bunting, three scarlet tanagers startlingly brilliant against the emerald grass. A turkey hen and her brood frequently picked their way through the clearing, giving us the chance to see the young ones grow from small, puffy juveniles into longer, leaner birds almost indistinguishable from their mother. On the grass we often found their broad tail feathers, barred in black and brown. We dubbed our new home Bird Cottage.

The next year was even better. Planting was easy. No rototilling, rock hauling or wall building. We had the luxury of turning soil with shovels, adding some compost, and presto: seeds in the ground. By summer the beds were happily pushing up lettuce and broccoli, nasturtiums and tomatoes. We still got many of our vegetables from the grocery store, food co-op, and farmers' market. But the garden gave us things we couldn't buy. It connected us to land and food: handling the cool spring soil, marking rows with trowel or finger, seeing young plants burgeon, inhaling the sweet musk of tomato leaves, savoring fruit still warm from the sun. Five minutes from earth to table.

It was perfect. I had achieved my goal. I was a benign herbivore, as nature intended me to be. Leaving blood and carnage behind, I had found the moral high road, the one true path to a harmonious, harm-free relationship with my fellow creatures. Alongside my sweetheart, I was working the earth, reaping the fruits of our gentle labors.

Others, though, were reaping them as well.

First, we caught glimpses of a pair of fawns venturing out of the woods and into the clearing. Then we started seeing them near the stone-walled beds. We found browsed salad greens, and neatly clipped stems where tulip buds had been the day before. Cath decided the fawns needed a talking-to.

She was, I think, uniquely suited to the task. Children gravitated to her everywhere we went. She had been a nursery and elementary schoolteacher and then a professional storyteller, performing for kids in that same age range: jobs I could not do well if my life depended on it. She had loved and excelled at both. More than a decade my senior, she had also raised two fine sons who were in high school and college by the time I was on the scene. All this is to say that she knew how to deal with misbehaving youngsters.

Walking out the front door one day, she gave the twin fawns a firm but gentle lecture. While she talked, the spotted rascals stood their ground, just a couple dozen yards away. When she was done, they sauntered off, unperturbed. We saw them less and less after that. Coincidence? Perhaps.

Yet the garden ravaging continued. Were the fawns coming at night? Entirely possible. If so, however, they weren't the only visitors. A full-grown woodchuck had begun putting in appearances in broad daylight. Here, Cath's lectures had no discernible effect. Breakfast, lunch, and dinner, our garden beds became a favorite stop on the critter's daily rounds.

"Did woodchucks bother your grandfather's garden?" I asked.

"Yes," said Cath. "We ate them."

Like me, she had grown up eating meat: beef, chicken, and pork from the grocery store her father had managed in the nearby village of Cazenovia, rabbit from the big, shedlike hutch her older brother tended out beyond the barn. And woodchuck from the garden. Cath said her brother would shoot and dress them, then take them over to their grandfather.

"Mom was embarrassed by them," she said. "She wouldn't cook or eat woodchuck, but Grandpa did. He never wasted food."

He told the grandchildren about his cavalry service in southern Italy, before he came to the States in 1904. The soldiers had been so hungry they had taken to hunting squirrels and crows.

Committed as I was to eating harmlessly, I couldn't imagine hurting our garden visitor. The animal was simply living its life, taking advantage of the easy pickings we had planted.

But one afternoon, when it came ambling across the lawn for another snack, I flung open the door and raced out, yelling. The lettuce thief turned on a dime and—with surprising speed for such a small, ungainly creature—hurtled toward the woods and disappeared. *There*, I thought. With that scare lodged in memory, it wouldn't be so eager to return.

Fat chance. The next day the woodchuck came again, trundling along as nonchalantly as before. This time I spied the animal a fair distance across the yard. From that direction, its view of the door was blocked by the corner of the cottage. Deciding a bigger scare was in order, I slipped out and flattened myself against the rough slate landing by the front door. That low to the ground, I was well hidden.

After a minute, I raised my head cautiously and peered over the nearest garden bed. There, six feet from me, was the raider. I sprang up and leapt, roaring. The woodchuck bolted, and I raced across the grass in pursuit.

In the middle of the lawn, the animal spun to face me. I was so surprised that I almost tripped over it. Caught in the open and unable to outrun me, it had done the only sensible thing: turn and fight.

There we stood, the woodchuck hissing and baring its teeth, me looming over it trying to look threatening. What was I supposed to do? I had lain in wait, pounced, and . . . nothing. I had no gun, no spear, no shovel, no rock. Even if I had wanted to kill it, I wouldn't have dared to get any closer bare-handed. Those chisel-like teeth could have torn a nasty hole in my flesh, no doubt about it.

This oversized rodent, its shoulder not much higher than my ankle, had called my bluff. Slowly, it backed away. When it got far enough to be confident that this oddly hesitant predator wouldn't catch up again, it turned and dashed for the woods. So much for Man the Gardener striking terror into the hearts of salad nibblers.

The woodchuck kept helping itself to the fruits of our labors. So be it. I would just have to chalk up a win for my furry friend and shell out a bit more cash at the grocery store. I wasn't going to draw blood over a few bowls of greens.

These days I wonder: Was that the moment when it began to dawn on me that the larger-than-human world was entirely indifferent to my fantasies of harmless eating and conflict-free coexistence? Was that when I first began to see that I could not achieve utopia by planting a vegetable garden? Was that when I first knew that nature would not bend to my will or be chased away, either by my cleverness or by the ferocity of my bluff?

By the time we built our next garden, I was sure I had the wood-chuck problem all figured out.

Cath and I had moved to Vermont and bought a house. Like Bird Cottage, it sat in a clearing, nestled far back into the woods. The first couple summers we contented ourselves with flower beds—phlox, delphiniums, and irises in the sun; hostas, pulmonaria, and lilies of the valley under the apple trees—plus a tiny patch of salad greens protected by some old fencing tacked to aspen poles. Now, though, we were ready for a full-blown vegetable garden.

On the other side of the driveway, in a circle thirty feet across, I mowed everything to the ground. Next came the shovel, chopping out the roots of grasses and wildflowers, wild raspberries and nearby aspens. Then the borrowed rototiller, its tines turning smoothly through the fluffy soil, folding in compost. The light, sandy earth is an oddity in this part of Vermont—a gift, a geologist friend tells me, from twelve thousand years ago, when this spot spent three centuries in the shallows of a glacial lake.

I knew that woodchucks would find the garden sooner or later. The sweet, juicy veggies would be a tempting buffet, and a low-risk venture—a long stone's throw from the house, with the cover of tall field grass all around and woods close by.

I knew, too, the kind of moral quandaries that woodchucks could present. The year before, I had driven up to my carpentry partner's house one morning and had seen him standing in the tall grass near his garden with something in his hand. He walked over to my truck, looking uneasy.

"You caught me in the act of murder," he said, showing me a partially empty package of anti-rodent smoke bombs. He, too, was a vegetarian. Woodchucks had been obliterating his garden. When I drove up, he had just dropped a bomb or two into a burrow, sending sulfurous smoke down to asphyxiate the unsuspecting tunnel dwellers. His dilemma—let rodents eat the vegetables or kill rodents so his family could eat the vegetables—wasn't one I wanted to face.

His mistake was in not having a fence substantial enough to keep the critters out. I was going to do it right. Around the perimeter of our new vegetable plot, a friend and I set thirteen cedar posts, digging two- and three-foot-deep holes straight down into the sandy earth with a narrow-bladed shovel. We drove in the sharpened post points, wielding a twelve-pound maul from a stepladder, then backfilled the holes and tamped the soil down hard. Standing seven feet above the ground, the ring of rough posts looked like the beginnings of a medieval palisade. I buried sheep fencing a foot below the surface to keep woodchucks from tunneling and ran it to the top of the posts to keep deer from leaping. Between two posts, I hung a Z-braced gate made of old lumber scraps and latched it shut.

Done! I thought.

3

Trouble in Eden

To live, we must daily break the body and shed the
blood of Creation. When we do this knowingly, lov-
ingly, skillfully, reverently, it is a sacrament. When we
do it ignorantly, greedily, clumsily, destructively, it is
a desecration.

—Wendell Berry, *The Gift of Good Land*

The trouble started small: holes in the leaves of our squash
seedlings.

Investigating, we discovered the little yellow-and-black-striped
perpetrators. Cucumber beetles. Perhaps, compassionate vegans
that we were, we would let them be. We could live with a few
perforations, just as we had overlooked the woodchuck's depredations at Bird Cottage and the pinholes inflicted on our salad
greens by flea beetles.

But soon the tiny squash plants—each with only a pair of
tender, rounded leaves—were being stripped entirely.

So I started making forays before work each morning. That
early, at fifty degrees, the beetles walked slowly and couldn't

fly. I would find them, usually clinging to the undersides of the seedlings' leaves, pick them up between thumb and forefinger, and squish them one by one, their exoskeletons cracking, their innards staining my skin orange. Far better, I thought, to hunt them down like this than to spray those few plants with a toxic pesticide whose indiscriminate, invisible work would save me the gory morning task.

Cabbage moth larvae, though, were camouflaged. Their pale green caterpillar bodies blended into broccoli stalks almost perfectly and, once they got munching, they decimated the plants in a hurry. Researching our options, we decided on Bt (*Bacillus thuringiensis*), a bacterium used by organic farmers to target specific pests. When cabbage moth larvae ingest it, they die. We bought a little and sprayed it on the broccoli.

Strict veganism prohibits eating honey, out of concern for bees. Beetle squishing and caterpillar poisoning were, I knew, beyond the pale. I was murdering insects.

More than a century ago, Howard Williams began his treatise on the history of vegetarianism by invoking the ancient Greek poet Hesiod, who valorized "the peaceful spirit of agriculture and mechanical industry" over "the spirit of war and fighting." But how peaceful is our tilling of the earth?

I knew enough about industrial food production to realize that it wasn't all endless acres of Edenic cultivation. Topsoil, for example, is being lost at an alarming rate. According to a 2006 study by Cornell University ecologist David Pimentel, erosion is stripping U.S. farmland of its dirt at ten times the rate of natural replenishment. And precious soil isn't all that gets washed downstream. Fertilizers also end up in our rivers, harming fish and other aquatic life. In high enough concentrations, nutrient-rich fertilizer runoff can maintain a cycle of phytoplankton blooms, depleting oxygen levels so severely that virtually nothing else can survive. Where the Mississippi dumps into the Gulf of Mexico, the seasonal dead zone had already grown to the size of New Jersey—even before the *Deepwater Horizon* oil spill of 2010 devastated the region.

And then there are pesticides. The recovery of the peregrine falcon notwithstanding, in 2000 the U.S. Fish and Wildlife Service estimated that 672 million birds are "directly exposed to pesticides" on American farmland each year. Some 67 million die immediately. Millions more die slowly. In Central and South America, where unregulated and highly toxic chemicals are sprayed and where many migratory birds go during North American winters, mortality rates are dramatically worse. Throughout the Americas alone, creatures smaller and less noticeable than birds are presumably killed by the uncounted billions.

Whatever we do to the planet, of course, we do to ourselves. As the earth loses topsoil, we're rapidly losing arable land. Windblown dust from eroding farmland pollutes the air we breathe and carries diseases like tuberculosis and anthrax. And it doesn't take an advanced degree in toxicology to figure out that pesticides don't do the human body any favors. Sixty-seven million birds make an awfully big pile of canaries in the proverbial coal mine.

Yet I knew, too, that agriculture didn't have to be so brutal. Soil erosion could be prevented by planting cover crops, such as rye or wheat. There were alternatives to chemical fertilizers and pesticides. Whenever possible, Cath and I opted for organic foods, minimizing our diet's chemical footprint. We ate close to home, buying food grown by small-scale, local farmers: no need to truck the produce cross-country, no gratuitous plastic packaging, and, thankfully, no massive combines mincing rabbits, rodents, birds, and birds' nests as they worked the fields each season. (Studies suggest that grain harvesters wipe out between 50 and 75 percent of populations in a long list of field-dwelling species.) Though much of our food still came from afar—greens and fruit in winter, tofu and other products year-round—"local" and "organic" were my watchwords. They signified harmlessness, shoring up my decade-long vegan diet, reassuring me that agriculture was, at its roots, a gentle blessing on the land: a backyard vegetable patch stretching out into those amber waves of grain.

What got my attention was the deer. I was reading Richard Nelson's *Heart and Blood: Living with Deer in America*. Deer, I learned, eat just about everything farmers grow. They eat greens and pumpkins, corn and wheat, cranberries and carrots, avocadoes and wine grapes. They have a particular fondness for soybeans, used to make tofu, soy milk, and many other nonmeat, nondairy products sold in vegetarian-friendly stores around the country. They damage apple, plum, pear, cherry, and almond crops, often killing young trees. Individual farmers can sustain tens of thousands of dollars' worth of crop damage in a year; in many states, total annual losses run into the tens of millions.

In states where agriculture is a major sector of the economy, wildlife agencies have to keep the whitetail population down to a reasonable level. Often, that means encouraging hunters to shoot a lot of deer during hunting seasons. It also often means issuing special permits to farmers, allowing them to kill deer in other seasons, day or night. And farmers do kill them. By the thousands.

This isn't just out in the agricultural breadbasket of the American Midwest. Nelson interviewed an organic farmer in northern California who grew specialty greens for upscale restaurants and grocery stores in San Francisco. A few times a year, the farmer had to shoot a deer. Because he didn't like killing, sometimes he would cut the deer open and drag it around the perimeter of the field with a tractor, leaving plenty of blood to scare other deer away. Most years, he didn't have to kill more than five. In Westchester County, just an hour north of Manhattan, another farmer gave Nelson a more startling figure: On his farm, they sometimes shoot ten in a single night. And still the crop damage continues. Nelson's summary of the situation brought me up short:

> Whenever any of us sit down for breakfast, lunch, dinner, or a snack, it's likely that deer were killed to protect some of the food we eat and the beverages we drink . . . Everyone in modern North America who lives each day on agricultural foods belongs to an ecological network that necessarily involves deer hunting.

Deer are, he reports, "a fundamental part of our personal ecology. In this sense, the blood of deer runs through our veins as surely as we take bread and wine at our table."

I tried to keep that knowledge at bay. I told myself that those were bigger farms, far away, and that we weren't getting produce from those places. I was wrong.

In the end, I had to consider Joey, the kindly organic farmer whose veggies travel less than a mile to the produce display of the crunchy local food co-op—in whose fields Cath and I have often picked luscious strawberries. You'd be hard-pressed to find a gentler, more conscientious steward of the land. Ask him about deer, though, and he'll tell you: "I've got a few guys on call. When there's too much damage, they come and plug one and we share the venison." Or ask about woodchucks: "I smoke-bomb their burrows constantly. Preemptively. A tunnel in a sandy bank right next to a kale field? Someone's going to move into that!"

Damn. I didn't want Bambi and Chuckie getting plugged and bombed as part of my "personal ecology."

Before long, though, I began to see that these deaths were among agriculture's lesser impacts, constituting only a fraction of the story. All it took was a few years working as a logger: work that grounded me in the local landscape and opened my eyes to its history.

I have always cherished forests, for their beauty—the bright, pale green of the year's first leaves, the majestic silhouette of big white pines against a summer sunset, the fire of autumn maples, the delicate bones of snow-laden twigs—and for their special places, like the spot in the oak woods near my father's house where bedrock rose to the surface. Deep, feathery moss and low blueberries grew around the edges of the bare, weathered granite, tracing an outline suggestive of an eagle in flight.

Yet I have also depended on wood all my life. It framed the houses I grew up in, as it frames this one here on the little sandy plateau above the Winooski River. In most of those houses, the tree-ness of the structure was hidden, clothed outside with asphalt shingles or peeling paint, dressed up inside with plaster and wallpaper. In others—like the low, earth-bermed solar house my father built when I was ten—the nature of the material was more evident. The big exposed rafters for that house had been salvaged from a barn near Quincy, Massachusetts. Though they had been milled clean and square decades ago, thick, sticky sap still oozed from the wood in places, reminding me of its life in a forest somewhere, long before I was born.

Most of those houses were also heated with wood, usually delivered cut and split, dumped off the back of a truck in sixteen-inch lengths. And the umpteen thousand board feet I'd handled as a carpenter all came from the lumberyard—sawn, planed, and neatly sorted by length, with only knots or the occasional pitch pocket to make me think of a spruce, fir, or oak.

I had known all along, of course, that one came from the other, wood from trees. But I'd never had a hand in its metamorphosis.

So I apprenticed to a forester-logger and set off into the woods, intent on bridging the gap between my love of forests and the necessities of shelter and fuel. As with food, I wanted to cultivate a deeper understanding of what sustained me.

My woods mentor, Paul, wore the nearly constant hint of a smile under his short, graying mustache, as if he had just thought of something amusing. My first job with him was a salvage operation, removing trees that were already down, tipped over the previous September when Hurricane Floyd ripped its way up the coast. On the next job, though, and each one after that, virtually every tree I cut was alive. That took some getting used to. With Cath, I had cut Christmas trees for our living room, selecting ones that—crowded tight together or growing up under the power lines alongside our driveway—would have had to come out anyway. Taking down a mature tree was a different matter altogether. The first time I set my chain saw to the base of a fifty-foot pine, I paused. Though I knew why Paul had selected it to come out, knew that its removal would benefit the trees around it, knew that good use would be made of its wood, I couldn't lightly kill this being. I said a silent prayer of thanks and apology. Then I unleashed the power of the saw, sending a rooster tail of chips through the air.

Over time, such fellings became habit. Regrettably, I didn't have time for elaborate acknowledgment of each death. Why, I wondered, did this bother me? Why should dropping trees seem so different from beheading stalks of broccoli or uprooting the wild raspberries and milkweed that encroached on the garden? Did killing trees feel different merely because they were bigger? Was this why I swatted mosquitoes but live-trapped house mice, releasing them half a mile away? Or was that more a matter of loyalty to my phylum—to Chordata but not Arthropoda, to vertebrate but not insect? I had, at one time, been troubled even by slapping at the latter, but eventually decided I couldn't worry about such deaths. If insects drew my blood, or threatened to, I killed them.

As I had hoped it would, logging grounded me in gritty transformation. Before long, I could glance at a tree and estimate how far it was to the first big crook, how many sixteen, fourteen, or twelve-foot sawlogs would come out of it, and roughly how many board feet that would add up to. Thinking that way, mentally converting a part of living nature to a volume of "natural resource," made me uneasy at first. True, we weren't using those calculations to make profit-minded decisions about which trees to cut. We were usually leaving the healthiest, straightest ones to grow. But, still, when I looked at a tree, I wanted to value it as a living entity, not as mere lumber. Eventually, I realized that my aim was to hold and see both: tree as magnificent being and tree as vital material.

Meeting even a tiny fraction of our physical needs directly from the forest gave me simple satisfaction. I enjoyed hauling home the coarse, raw treasure of firewood by the third of a cord in the back of my pickup and stacking it under cover, caching a small portion of the land's summer warmth for the cold days and nights I knew would soon come.

Now and then, finer treasures could be gleaned. Once, as we split wood on that first salvage job, Paul paused to pick up two pieces of maple he had rent apart with his ax. The grain had a serpentine wave to it: the figuring that woodworkers call "curly" or "flame" maple. The next year, for my mother's birthday and my grandmother's, I carved two long-handled cooking spoons. Scraped, sanded, and oiled, the golden wood shimmered with iridescent stripes, like the wind riffles on water just before a storm blows in.

Logging also taught me a lesson in appearances. When we felled a tree, we would take what we could use for sawlogs, firewood, or pulp. That left limbs and tops, and the question of what to do with them. Leaving those downed treetops intact—their branches standing perhaps five, ten, fifteen feet in the air—would closely mimic what happened when a tree blew over in a storm. Wildlife like grouse and hare would find shelter there. But Paul and I tended to work on small woodlots, often near homes or recreation trails, and most landowners disliked the messiness of whole tops. They preferred to have them lopped down into lower, more compact piles. If Paul had offered treetop removal services, as some loggers do, I suspect that people would have taken him up on it, thankful to have everything chipped and shipped. Such removal, unfortunately, prevents that material from returning to the forest floor, where it would normally decompose, feeding the soil from which it grew.

I sympathized with the landowners' preferences. Before I started logging, I bristled at the sight of brush cut and left strewn alongside hiking trails; it looked crude, careless. My image of a good-looking forest, responsibly logged, had been one of parklike tidiness. Seeing the remains of trees that had fallen of nature's accord, thrown by wind or dead of disease or old age, hadn't bothered me, but signs of human handiwork had. Though my ecological concerns had been sincere, my perceptions of logging had been underpinned by aesthetic discomforts, by an aversion to the evidence of arboreal carnage. Like the landowners I now worked for, I had preferred to stroll through woods that looked undisturbed. I had enjoyed the seductive illusion of having my firewood delivered, of selecting my building materials from orderly, clean stacks at the lumberyard, the messy work done far away. Out of sight, out of mind.

Not all logging, of course, is created equal. Done mindfully— by conscientious loggers with the financial incentive to do it right—its ecological impacts can be minimized. Under Paul's tutelage I learned that, with good planning, softer soils could be traversed when frozen solid and the land could be protected from erosion and rutted roads. With appropriate equipment, the soil compaction that harms tree roots could be greatly reduced. With appropriate techniques, the trees we left could remain free of bark damage, which invites disease. With a little thought for our fellow creatures, dead trees could be left standing, providing nesting cavities and sources of insect food for a multitude of wildlife species, including New England's largest, loudest, and most striking woodpecker, the pileated.

Perhaps most importantly, working with Paul taught me to think in forest time. In the woods, signs of a past landscape were all around us: old stone walls, rusty barbed wire, the occasional stacked-fieldstone foundation marking an old cellar hole. Bit by bit, I began to grasp the meanings of things that I had seen long ago, but not understood.

As a boy, I had seen nineteenth-century photographs of Vermont, the hills bare and stark. The pictures looked nothing like the forested landscape I had grown up loving. In combination with other images I had seen—of New England log drives, the rivers packed with wood from shore to shore—they planted the seeds of my earliest, sinister perceptions of logging. The story seemed simple: The forest primeval had been pillaged by men with axes. Like most such stories, this one was mistaken, both in its simplicity and in its narrow assignment of blame.

When European colonists arrived in present-day New England, the land was already under active management, especially along the ocean and the major rivers. The coastal forest from the Saco River in Maine to the Hudson was, in the words of environmental historian William Cronon, "remarkably open, almost parklike at times." In some places, there were no trees at all, for the native peoples of the region had pushed the forest back from the Atlantic, sometimes by miles. The site of present-day Boston, for instance, was treeless for thousands of acres and colonists had to harvest wood from nearby islands. The primary cause of this coastal deforestation? Agriculture. In these places, American Indians had established seasonal farming settlements, clearing fields and collecting vast quantities of firewood.

Parts of the inland forest had long been managed for food, too. Archaeological digs in western Massachusetts suggest that Indians were periodically burning the forest understory as much as five thousand years ago. This burning favored plants, like blueberries, that provided edible fruit, and fire-tolerant trees, like chestnut and oak, that provided edible nuts. As Cronon points out, burning also accelerated the recycling of forest nutrients back into the soil. This, along with the absence of brushy undergrowth and the increased light that reached the forest floor, boosted the growth of herbaceous plants, which, in turn, allowed deer, elk, and other animals to thrive. In his book *Reading the Forested Landscape*, ecologist Tom Wessels suggests that the fire-swept, grassy earth also made it possible for humans to stalk those animals quietly and take unobstructed shots with bow and arrow.

Farther north, in what is now Vermont, native peoples' management of the landscape was concentrated along rivers, where they cleared fields. When colonists arrived here en masse in the late eighteenth century—after the 1760 British victory at Montreal ended the French and Indian War—it was in these riverside fields, and in old beaver meadows, that they built their first settlements. When those were used up, they carved homesteads, fields, and pastures out of the forest. Trees were felled and burned where they lay, the resulting ash used to make potash, in turn used for the production of fertilizer, soap, and gunpowder.

In the late 1700s, most Vermont farms were small, geared toward producing food for farm families. And commercial logging was concentrated in areas where large white pines, long valued as saw timber and as ship masts, could be easily transported by river. That pattern would soon change, however, and the intensity of the final assault on Vermont's forests would have as much to do with the market for wool as with the market for wood.

In 1810 and 1811, taking advantage of the chaos surrounding Napoleon's ongoing attempt to conquer the Iberian Peninsula, a merchant named William Jarvis, then U.S. consul to Portugal, exported several thousand of the region's jealously guarded merino sheep, prized for their fine and bountiful fleece. He sold most of them, but reserved a few hundred for himself and brought them to a farm he had purchased in Weathersfield, Vermont, a small town in the Connecticut River valley some fifty miles north of the Massachusetts border.

With larger political and economic forces on their side— including the War of 1812 and related blockades, tariffs, and embargoes—merinos soon dominated the state. "A wool craze swept the region," wrote historian David Ludlum, "a mania as powerful as any religious fanaticism." By 1824, Vermont was home to almost half a million merinos; by 1840, 1.7 million, nearly six sheep for every person. Textile mills popped up everywhere. And Vermont's remaining forests vanished in a single human generation. Few places were spared, as even steep hillsides went from woods to pasture. By 1840, three-quarters of the Green Mountain State was treeless, most of it grazed by sheep.

To keep their sheep contained, the settlers needed fences. With wood harder and harder to come by and the invention of barbed wire still decades off, they turned to the material at hand: stone. Between 1810 and 1840, the bare hillsides and valleys of New England sprouted thousands of miles of stone barriers. Tom Wessels suggests that these walls, constructed so swiftly and containing more stone mass than the Great Pyramids of Egypt, could be considered "the eighth wonder of the world."

A wondrous feat they may have been, but within just a few years the animals they contained were already devastating the land. By the 1830s, erosion from overstocked hillside pastures was

a serious problem. The pastures themselves became less productive and Vermont's streams and rivers silted in, causing floods.

Watching their meager soil wash downstream, Vermont's hill
farmers looked west toward the deep, boulder-free earth of the
Ohio River valley. The Erie Canal was open and the railroad
was extending its reach. By the early 1860s, tens of thousands
of Vermonters had departed and the state's wool industry was
in decline, crippled by its own brutal treatment of the land, by
changing tariff laws and tumbling prices, and by fierce competition from states to the west, where production costs were far
lower. Those who stayed in Vermont began turning from sheep
to dairy cows, working the deeper soils of the river valleys.

Logging continued—for wood, for charcoal, and for potash—
but by 1900 more than half of Vermont's open land was already
returning to forest. Soon the trend would be bolstered by the
reduced need for hay as the automobile replaced the horse. Hay
fields would lie fallow, waiting to be reclaimed by trees.

A century later, with Vermont three-quarters forested, Paul and
I were working among the sheep farmers' stone fences and cellar
holes. It was dawning on me that although settlers' axes had felled
the trees that once stood here, it was farming, pasturing, and
textiles that wrought the real havoc and kept these hillsides raw
and bleeding. Freed from the yoke of agriculture and industry,
the land had returned to aspen, pine, and maple. Today, with the
great flocks of sheep gone, the forest thrived, even with loggers
still working the hills.

After a day in the woods, a day of felling trees this way and
that, leaving piles of hacked-off limbs everywhere I went, I
would drive home past cornfields. I would return to the clearing
where our house stands, to the placid scene of the flower and
vegetable gardens Cath and I had built. And I would wonder: Is

it neatness—the even regularity of raised beds and tilled rows, of summer corn and autumn stubble—that makes gardening and farming appear so much more benign than logging?

With a broader view of the landscape and our history here, I could look out across the Winooski and North Branch valleys and recognize the obvious. Every acre of agricultural land I had ever seen—every cow or sheep pasture, every wheat or soybean or vegetable field—was once forest, wetland, prairie: another kind of land. Regardless of whether the farming was done well or poorly, its initial establishment in all those places had required conquest, eviction of the creatures that lived there before, and conversion of the land to a new use. And maintaining it required constant defense against nature's efforts at reclamation.

That helped me understand something else I had seen as a boy. In the Vermont Historical Society museum, near the capitol in downtown Montpelier, is a big glass case. In the case stands a mountain lion. It is said to be the last cougar—or catamount, as we call them here—killed in Vermont, shot near the town of Barnard on Thanksgiving Day, 1881. As a boy, looking up at the big cat, I had grasped the immediate cause of its death: the man in the photograph, Alexander Crowell, sharp nosed and bearded, dressed in dark suit and hat, firearm cradled in the crook of his arm. And I had taken catamount hunting to be what extirpated the species from the state.

In one sense, I had been right. Catamounts, like wolves, were indeed killed by men with guns, men who hated large predators for the danger they posed to livestock. Yet, despite the establishment of bounties in 1779 and the popularity of organized hunts, both species persisted in the state for decades.

What sounded the final death knell was loss of habitat. As expanses of forest were broken up, these predators' hunting territories shrank. Simultaneously, their primary food source—the white-tailed deer—was being driven to the brink of extinction by the same factors: overhunting and habitat loss. It is no coincidence that Vermont's remaining populations of wolves, catamounts, and deer all plunged precipitously in the first half of the nineteenth century when agricultural deforestation was at its peak. Only a few large predators survived the height of the merino's reign. And even those few were eventually hunted down, mainly for preying on the state's remaining sheep. There were, after all, virtually no deer left for wolf or catamount to eat. The "savage beast" shot by Crowell in 1881 had, according to a local newspaper report, "killed many sheep and lambs in different parts, and the people in this vicinity greatly rejoice at his death."

No doubt predators feasted on plenty of individual sheep. But the merino population as a whole was instrumental in wiping wolf and catamount off the landscape entirely.

Hiking in the woods late one summer, I turned off a hillside logging road toward a break in an old stone wall. Almost to that breach of tumbled stones, I glanced up for some reason. Four eyes locked with mine. Fifteen feet off the ground, two house-cat-sized felines clung to the bark of a nearby maple, one on each side of the trunk: kittens, all fuzzy from ruffed necks to stub tails.

They were bobcats, the catamount's much smaller cousin. They stared. I stared back. Though not rare in Vermont, bobcats are seldom seen in broad daylight, and such a close encounter with a pair of kittens was extraordinary. I gave myself an emphatic mental kick for not having a camera in my pocket.

When the spell broke, one kitten, then the other, leapt to the ground and vanished into cover. I caught a glimpse of one as it pranced from stone to stone along the top of the wall, then paused to look around, perhaps for its mother. She must have been close by.

Only later did I reflect on the spot. Though adaptable—and apparently tolerant of the occasional untidy passage of logging equipment through that timberland—bobcats prefer forest habitat. Neither they nor their main prey, snowshoe hares, thrive amidst intensive agriculture. The kittens would not have been there if that old stone fence still divided two pastures.

The mere fact of living, I had begun to realize, linked me to larger webs of life and death. Regardless of what I did, whether I liked it or not, I had an impact. No matter what I ate, habitat had already been sacrificed. No matter what I ate, animals would be killed.

Even while gardening within the confines of our deer- and woodchuck-proof fence, innocence was out of reach. The sandy soil, which I had ruthlessly stripped of grasses, wildflowers, and tree roots, needed all the organic matter it could get, so we imported compost by the truckload, compost made from the manure of chickens, horses, and cows. Now and then—shoveling the dark, rich stuff out of the back of my pickup—I would notice a knobby, light-colored chunk and pause to examine it. A fragment of bone. Perhaps the tip of a dairy cow's tibia.

We weren't eating animals, but our vegetables were.

4

An Animal Who Eats

Try to remember that we are going after food—that we are, in a way, exploring our place in the systems of life in the universe. I grant you that our place, when we think we've found it, isn't always comfortable.

—John Hersey, *Blues*

Our doctor, a soft-spoken Buddhist naturopath, was the last person you'd expect to say, "Go eat an animal." And she didn't. It was gentler than that. She simply reviewed an analysis of my blood chemistry and suggested I could use more protein.

She did not mean more tofu.

The suggestion was corroborated by Cath's study of holistic health and nutrition. A few of her instructors—themselves former vegetarians—offered words of caution about long-term veganism. They had seen the effects repeatedly: people showing up in their offices after twenty years without any animal foods, bodies drained and depleted. They pointed out that certain kinds of protein, particular types of omega-3 fatty acids, and key nutrients such as vitamin B_{12} were difficult or impossible to get by eating unfortified plant foods.

Cath and I eased into it slowly. Local organic yogurt. Then eggs from cage-free hens. They tasted strange and rich. But I ate hungrily, and I started noticing changes. I had more energy, felt more alive. My allergic sensitivities to cats and dust mites diminished. Within a few months, wild-caught fish and locally raised chicken were also on the menu, their flavors and textures even more alien.

We could have held the line at dairy and eggs, refusing all flesh. By then, though, I knew more about dairy products: Bovines do not lactate spontaneously. Milk comes from pregnant cows, pregnant cows give birth to calves, and virtually all male calves end up as veal. Though I had no interest in eating any kind of mammalian meat, let alone veal, I recognized that yogurt production involved the killing of calves as surely as soybean production involved the killing of deer. Ethically, which was more palatable: flesh from a wild fish, or milk from a domestic cow with a calf about to be taken away to slaughter? Legs from a chicken that lived a couple of months, or eggs from a chicken that lived somewhat longer? My faith in simplistic claims to moral superiority had shattered.

Doubts about our dietary shift did linger. If I had tried harder, could I have achieved this newfound energetic health in other ways? I had read and heard so many contradictory nutritional arguments, supported by opposing references to the longevity and health of peoples around the world, their diets ranging from rice and vegetables to fish, meat, and fat. Even more confusing were the conflicting appeals to human morphology: some noting that we lack a predator's fangs, others that we lack the masticating jaws of a ruminant; some arguing that we resemble herbivores in our digestive chemistry and structure, others that we resemble carnivores; some comparing our eyes to those of tree-climbing, fruit-eating primate ancestors, others suggesting a link to broader ocular tendencies in the mammalian world—"eyes in front, you hunt, eyes on the side, you hide."

By then, though, figuring it all out by rational means felt futile. I was listening to my body.

My physical craving for animal foods made me think of a winter camping trip to the Adirondacks. A few years earlier, when Cath and I were at Bird Cottage, a friend and I had driven up toward Blue Mountain Lake for a long weekend in February. The day we hiked in, it was oddly warm, near sixty, and the crust on the deep snowpack had begun to soften. Our boots punched through in places, our legs disappearing to above the knee, until we stopped and put on snowshoes. By the next day, the weather had shifted. Even as the stream outlet near our pond-side lean-to continued to swell with snowmelt, the mercury was plummeting. As we prepared dinner over our camp stove that evening—eager for both the immediate warmth of the food and the caloric fuel— my companion added butter to the pan. I watched ravenously. Except for cream in the occasional cup of coffee or cocoa shared with Cath, it was the first animal product I'd consumed in years. Had I been alone, I might have grabbed the frozen quarter-pound stick, peeled back the wax paper, and started gnawing.

What my body wanted was to eat other vertebrates—not for their flavor, but for their substance. Emotionally, I found it unsettling. The habitat destruction and animal casualties incidental to agriculture were collateral losses, regrettable and unintended. The deaths of the creatures I was eating now weren't incidental to anything. Each fish or bird had died specifically so that I could ingest part of its body, extracting elements of its tissues and adding them to mine. While fruit and grain could—in theory, at least— be plucked from tree, bush, or stalk by relatively gentle means, and while vegetables politely declined to bleed, these individual organisms had met some intentional, violent, twitching end.

Perhaps I would have felt less conflicted if I'd had a role model. The 14th Dalai Lama of Tibet, for example, became a vegetarian in the mid-1960s, after witnessing the slaughter of a chicken, but ill health later forced him to return to eating flesh. I might have taken comfort in knowing that such a teacher of compassion had been down this path before me. At the time, though, I didn't know his story, or any other like it. Without another's footsteps to follow, I was feeling my way along, trying to integrate my shifting diet with my essentially unchanged values.

Like other ex-vegans and ex-vegetarians I have since met and spoken with, I found that eating fellow creatures made me palpably aware of my own physical presence, waking me to the obvious: I am not simply a moral, emotional, and intellectual being. I am also an animal who eats. I have a footprint here. That simple recognition grounded me. Grasping a chicken leg and tearing off the last bits of tender flesh with my teeth, I began inhabiting the world.

Meal by meal, I began to sense how indebted my life was to other lives, how inextricably intertwined. The blood of deer did run through my veins, and the blood of woodchuck and hare, chicken and trout—the blood of the land itself.

Several months after we started eating chicken and fish, I took a bus to Boston in early spring to see Willie. He greeted me with a bear hug, then showed me around his furniture shop, meticulously maintained woodworking equipment arranged across the open warehouse floor, the scent of sawdust permeating the air. When I asked, he showed me his portfolio, too, a three-ring binder full of photographs. Each hardwood piece was more stunning than the last: polished cherry tables and kitchen cabinets, baptismal fonts of walnut and oak, altar screens for a Greek Orthodox church.

That evening Willie took me to one of his favorite Vietnamese restaurants. His taste for Southeast Asian cuisine dated back to his tours of navy duty during the Vietnam War. Across the table from me, he eased back into the seat with something between a sigh and a grunt. He was ready for a satisfying meal and visit. We hadn't seen each other much since I was a kid. More than having things to catch up on, we had a new friendship to build. Together, we broke bread—or fish, rather. And we talked. About life. About work. About food.

"You know," I said, "for a long time, eating flesh didn't feel right to me. But I'm seeing things differently now."

"Yes," Willie nodded. "We're omnivores." He had obviously worked this out a long time ago.

I asked him if he still fished. He said he did. He hadn't had much time to get out recently—not like his younger years when he would have had his morning catch cleaned and in the cooler before he got to work at eight o'clock—but he still loved being on the water.

Later, back at his apartment, our conversation continued at the kitchen table.

"I'm thinking about fishing again," I said.

Willie beamed. Eyes flashing with a playful glint, he leaned forward slightly. "You remember that fillet knife you sent me?"

I nodded.

"You want it back?"

"Sure!" I laughed in surprise.

Willie was on his feet, quick for a man so large. He disappeared into his bedroom and was back in under a minute, knife in hand. When he laid it on the table in front of me, I picked it up and turned it over and over: the smooth leather sheath stitched up the back, the blond wood handle with its crackling varnish, the fine, bright blade whispering against leather and built-in sharpening stone as I drew it out. I looked from the knife to Willie's face. He was nodding, his mouth spreading in a wide grin, that curiously high-pitched laugh rising up from his barrel chest.

He'd had the knife six years, and he had never tossed it into a tackle box. He had been keeping it somewhere special, I realized, knowing I would return to the water someday. Knowing something that I, in my certainty as a vegan, had never suspected.

That night I unrolled my sleeping bag on the cushions of Willie's couch. On the coffee table beside me were recent issues of *American Rifleman,* New York State's *Conservationist,* and some fishing magazine. The hardwood frames of both couch and table were simple: no unnecessary flourishes, just crisp, elegant lines executed by a masterful hand, the kind of lines I remembered from the bunk bed I used to lie in as a boy, listening to the bullfrogs sing their echoing evening chorus.

When Willie dropped me at South Station, where I would catch a bus back north, he gave me another vast bear hug. And a promise: We'd see each other again soon, and fish together.

Willie and I kept in frequent touch by phone after that. I learned not to call on Monday evenings. He would be home early, but he'd be catching a nap, resting up for the game. Monday was Poker Night.

Wasn't there something similar, I mused, in his two favorite pastimes—fishing and cards? In both lay the challenge of honing his formidable skills, paired with the inescapable knowledge that he was up against chance, fate, forces totally beyond his control. "What magic fixes their eyes upon the point of a fishing-rod, as if it were the finger of destiny?" asked Henry van Dyke in *Fisherman's Luck.* "It is the enchantment of uncertainty."

Willie liked to win at cards. He liked to catch and eat fish. He loved not knowing how the game would play out.

We saw each other again in August, at the weekend place he and his longtime lady friend had at the southern tip of Maine.

I had been looking forward to meeting Beth. She, too, lived just outside Boston, and though I had been in the city a few times in recent years, we had never crossed paths. Willie had talked about her, of course, yet I had no clear sense of what she would be like. When we met that Saturday, their relationship made instant sense. Like Willie's, her face was friendly, her eyes frank and curious, attentive to mine. Though quieter than Willie, with a less arresting presence, she walked with a similar rootedness. Over time I would come to see that her kindness and generosity, like Willie's, were grounded deep.

Willie showed me around the house. When they'd bought it a few years earlier it had been in rough shape, in need of a crafts-man's attention. Now, it gleamed: the paint fresh, the oak floors refinished, and the deck rebuilt, the corners of the newel posts precisely beveled. The dining table and chairs, fashioned of black cherry, glowed with the soft sheen of top-quality finish, coat after coat patiently applied by hand.

In early afternoon Willie and I ran errands. As we drove, I told him about my latest woodchuck escapade. A few weeks earlier, our vegetable garden in Vermont had finally been discovered and its defenses breached. There was no warning. One day our green beans were simply half gone and, beside them, a hole had erupted from the sandy soil. The tunnel was impressive, a rodent superhighway to Food Central, origi-nating in parts unknown, coming in under our theoretically impervious fence and popping up neatly in the middle of the garden. I filled in the mouth of the burrow several times, but it was futile. No way would this infrastructure be aban-doned. The animal wasn't merely snacking. It was gorging, wiping out pounds of produce at a time. I had to either stop the critter's depredations, or buy more vegetables at the store and admit what I hadn't been ready to face at Bird Cottage five years earlier: I was farming out the dirty work to growers like Joey. They were doing the killing, keeping the blood off my hands.

Recalling my showdown with the woodchuck on the lawn back then, I didn't fancy repeating my antics. Intimidation wouldn't work this time either.

Ever so briefly, I considered digging all the way around the garden and installing deeper underground fencing. But there was no telling how deep the burrow ran, and friends had recently told us how they had watched a woodchuck climb up and over their ten-foot garden fence.

No, I was out of realistic alternatives. Chuckie's number was up.

Smoke bombs didn't appeal. Why deposit noxious chemicals in our garden soil? Just to avoid the actual moment of the kill? So I borrowed a .22 rifle from Paul, and one weekend, while Cath was away, I put a bullet through the bean-raider's skull. Ashamed that I had no idea how to make use of the meat, I buried the body. When Cath came home and asked about the garden troubles, I told her, "I took care of it." Her look said, *You? Killed?*

Willie nodded as he listened to my story.

"You remember your father's chickens?" he asked.

"Sure," I said. My father had kept a few Rhode Island Reds.

"You remember the trouble he had with raccoons?"

I did. The hens had provided eggs, but hardly ever got old enough to be retired to the stew pot. Despite the nighttime protection of the rugged henhouse my father had built of rough-sawn lumber, the birds usually met early ends. Most of their untimely demises involved happy raccoons.

"One night," said Willie, "a raccoon got into the henhouse by pulling open the little door the chickens used during the day. So your father put a heavy latch on it. He figured he could outsmart that raccoon. But I told him, 'You're going to have to shoot him.'"

My father's next report to Willie was that the raccoon had dug its way in underneath the henhouse. So he had put chicken wire down around the edges.

"I told him," said Willie, "'Look, twenty-four hours a day that raccoon is figuring out new ways to get to those chickens. You can only spend a little time here and there trying to stop him. You're going to have to shoot him.'"

Willie shook his head, smiling wryly. "But your father said no, he wanted to live in harmony with the land.

"Finally," Willie said, "your father called me and said he'd heard a bunch of noise in the henhouse one night. He went out there with a flashlight and opened the door and there was the raccoon right in the middle of the place. 'What'd you do?' I asked. And your father said, 'I shot him.'

"Mmmnnnn-hnnh!" Willie grunted, nodding his big head and grinning.

I grinned, too. When, as a kid, I heard my father's version of this story, he seemed matter-of-fact about it, showing me the skull with its small hole, saying he had made raccoon stew instead of chicken. I never guessed that he had tried so hard to stave off the inevitable. Though it seemed to me that a henhouse should be easier to secure than a garden, I shook my head and chuckled with Willie—at my father, at myself, at the futility of our parallel efforts to segregate domestic and wild, to impose our rules and fantasies upon the world. And I wished again that I had known how to gut, skin, and cook that woodchuck.

Later that day, when Beth went to Saturday evening Mass, Willie and I went fishing.

Down the road a few miles, we parked his station wagon by a bridge and carried rods and tackle box to the middle of the span. The tide was high and would soon be falling, sweeping small fish from the Spruce Creek inlet out toward the sea. Predators would be prowling there for an easy meal. Among them would be our prey: striped bass.

Stripers, named for the dark stripes that run down their silvery bodies from gills to tail, are popular with anglers all along the Atlantic coast of North America. Like salmon, they're anadromous—from the Greek *anadromos*, "running up"—meaning that they live most of their lives in the ocean, but return to rivers and head upstream to spawn. They can weigh fifty pounds or more, though most are far smaller. And they are, Willie attested, delicious.

Hefting the rod he handed me—far heavier than anything I had used as a kid—and inspecting the tough, braided line, I wondered what I was getting into here on this bridge, fishing for the first time in a dozen years. What if I hooked into something big?

I need not have worried. We got no bites that evening. As the sun set, we just stood, sometimes talking, sometimes silent, watching our parallel lines run out toward the open ocean, entranced by the uncertainty of what fate had in store.

We were back at the bridge early the next morning, again fishing the falling tide. On the second or third cast, a sudden tug ran through my body like an electric charge. What I hauled in, though, was not a striper, but a darkly mottled fish of a pound or two, bristling with fins and spines.

"A sculpin," said Willie, as he removed the hook and dropped the creature back into the gently outflowing tide. The rugged fish darted off vigorously. "They're bottom-feeders. Not good eating."

Boyishly, I was thrilled to have caught a fish again, yet I disliked the idea of putting a creature through such struggle to no end.

Even as a kid, twenty-some years earlier, hooking fish solely for the fun of it had never occurred to me, and Willie had never suggested I throw a fish back. We hadn't spoken of it. We just didn't play with our food.

The sculpin proved to be our one and only bite. By afternoon, I was headed back north.

A few weeks later, Willie walked me to the altar: a small table covered with lace, roses, and sprigs of cedar. After seven years together, Cath and I were formalizing what we had long known in our hearts.

In a grassy clearing, surrounded by family and friends, white birches and dark-green softwoods, we exchanged vows. And rings, too: simple gold bands, circumscribed by a dark, finely cut line, tracing the contours of the hills and valleys we had come to call home.

That night, after the festivities had subsided, Cath and I wandered into the dining room of the barn-turned-1950s-ski-lodge we had rented for the occasion. It was empty, except for one table tucked back in a low corner alcove. Eight or so people sat around it, playing poker. Willie—having divested himself of suit and tie and crisp white shirt—presided. He was explaining the rules for yet another variation of Black Mariah, a kind of seven-card stud.

I grinned. My best man took his fun seriously.

The next weekend, when Cath and I went to sit by a pond and watch the sun set, I brought along a lightweight rod and reel that Willie had helped me pick out in Maine.

I didn't know the place well enough to fish it seriously. I needed casting practice, though, so I tied on one of the silvery oblong lures Willie had suggested I buy, added a few sinkers to the line for extra casting weight, and flicked the ugly conglomeration out into the shallow water. When spoon and weights slapped the surface, I reeled quickly to keep from snagging among the rocks there in the shallows. There was no subtlety to it. None of Willie's practical finesse. Certainly none of a fly fisherman's panache.

And yet, on the second or third cast, just as the lure hit the water, the surface exploded. Stunned, I whipped the rod tip up, cranked the reel, and a sleek trout came splashing to shore.

In a motion both foreign and familiar, I reached out and grabbed dinner.

5

Where the Great Heron Feeds

We have labeled and separated the moose and the wolf,
and in so doing we have lost sight of their essential
unity. We also have misunderstood ourselves, for the
biggest separation we have imposed on the world is
between ourselves and nature.

—Paul Rezendes, *Tracking and the Art of Seeing*

The question now wasn't whether my eating inflicted harm,
but what kind of harm.

The inevitable in-the-moment price exacted by every living,
breathing, eating animal on the planet? Or the gratuitous suffering and long-term destruction at which we humans have
proven ourselves uniquely adept? Perhaps it simply came down
to respect and restraint, to how we treated soil, water, plants,
and animals, to whether the tilling was prudent and the killing
clean.

Looking out our living-room window, I occasionally caught
sight of a ruffed grouse feeding high among the branches of a
nearby aspen. The bird—perhaps eighteen inches long from stout

beak to barred gray-and-black tail—would pluck the tree's buds one by one. The tree, I imagined, did not particularly appreciate this depredation. The late wildlife ecologist and grouse expert Gordon Gullion speculated that aspens may defend themselves against birds and insects alike by producing chemical compounds that make their buds less palatable and nutritious.

The grouse, likewise, would do its best not to become food. But eventually it would, in turn, be plucked from the air by hawk or owl, or from the ground by bobcat or fox.

The costs incurred were fleeting: the aspen buds nipped, the grouse struck down and devoured, food always coming in the form of other living things. Collectively, nothing was lost. Grouse droppings and owl pellets—eventually even the body of the owl itself—all returned to the forest soil, to aspen roots.

I knew that industrial food systems, in contrast, took a lasting toll on the land, giving little or nothing back. They were linear, not cyclical.

Agricultural production of grains and vegetables alters entire landscapes, and the ecological arguments against industrial meat production have, if anything, gotten stronger since I went vegan. An estimated 30 percent of the planet's land surface is now dedicated to livestock. Of the earth's current pasture and rangeland, one-fifth has been degraded by overgrazing, erosion, and soil compaction. Livestock operations contribute heavily to water usage and pollution, with concentrated animal feeding operations (CAFOs) compartmentalizing animals from the land, often making toxic cesspools of their manure rather than allowing it to fertilize and build the soil. Livestock production is also a driving force behind deforestation in many parts of the world, particularly Latin America. It has even been implicated in climate change. Related greenhouse-gas estimates encompass the felling and burning of forests to make way for grazing, the manufacture of chemical fertilizer for feed corn, and the transport of feed, livestock, and meat, not to mention the methane from cattle burps and farts.

I knew that our food systems took a toll on animals, too: birds poisoned by pesticides, rodents maimed by grain combines, livestock brutalized and confined until the day of their inevitable slaughter. And I had no doubt that these creatures, like the chickens and fish I was now eating, had the capacity to suffer. This, as British philosopher Jeremy Bentham pointed out two hundred years ago, was the ethical heart of the matter: "The question is not, Can they *reason?* nor, Can they *talk?* but, *Can they suffer?*"

I owed these creatures compassion. I had an obligation to ask how they lived and died. To remember Thich Nhat Hanh's teachings on kindness. To eat with my eyes wide open.

It was not, Cath and I concluded, so much *what* we ate that mattered—tofu or trout, chard or chicken—as *how* that food came to our plates.

Not that we were purists. If someone served us barbecued chicken, we didn't ask where it came from. But we paid attention to what we brought home to our own kitchen.

We felt reasonably confident buying poultry through food co-ops: The sources were local and the co-ops' concerns about animal welfare and ecology matched our own. We felt even better when we could buy direct. It was reassuring to know the people who raised our chickens, to stop by and see the birds pecking away in the grass, to return later in the season and walk out of the farmhouse kitchen with a paper grocery bag full of meat.

We were less sure about seafood. Pamphlets and websites told us which fish species were showing high concentrations of mercury, PCBs, and other toxins. They told us which were being fished sustainably, without overburdening populations, damaging the ocean floor, or resulting in excessive "bycatch": the wasteful killing of all manner of creatures, from turtles, dolphins, and sea birds to fish species that boats and crews didn't happen to be after. And they told us about the impacts of various fish-farming practices, from the massive harvesting of wild fish as feed to the buildup of nitrogen-rich waste and the resulting deoxygenation of areas surrounding in-ocean operations to the parasites and diseases that thrived among overcrowded fish and could spread to wild populations.

There was, I realized, only one way to know exactly what harm was inflicted in the procurement of the fish we were eating: by catching and killing with my own hands. When, near dusk, I went to a deep pool in a nearby stream, tossed in a small hook I had decorated with bits of red and white yarn, and enticed a pair of brook trout to strike, I marveled at their jewel-toned beauty. And then at their delicate flavor. When I took our canoe out on a lake one afternoon and a big rainbow went for a silvery spoon, I considered how lightly it was hooked: one steel point barely lodged at the edge of the mouth. Such a fine line between life and death, between continuing-life-in-one-form and feeding-life-in-another-form.

Now that I was fishing, the water had come alive. Ponds and lakes were no longer mere scenery. When I walked along a brook or drove over a bridge that spanned a river, I wondered what fish lived there. Did a brookie or a rainbow lurk behind that big rock, waiting for hapless insects to swirl by? Water was no longer just a surface to glance at or paddle across, but a living depth to participate in.

Fishing—like gardening—provided sustenance I could not get from grocery-store foods, the circumstances of their production unknown and unreal, a gaping chasm between field and table. "The supermarket," wrote Richard Nelson in *Heart and Blood*, "is an agent of our forgetfulness." Pulling a trout from water, like pulling a carrot from soil, reminded me of the origins of all nourishment in earth, water, and sun. Each was an antidote to forgetfulness. Each reminded me that glossy boxes and cellophane wrappers were illusions that divorced me from nature.

And there was something else, too, something in the killing itself. If I was going to eat flesh foods, I needed to be brought face to face with living, breathing creatures, to look directly at them. "Behind every meal of meat," argues feminist and vegan Carol J. Adams, "is an absence: the death of the animal whose place the meat takes. The 'absent referent' is that which separates the meat eater from the animal and the animal from the end product." That was an absence I could not stomach. I couldn't go on eating without any real sense of what it meant, keeping the truth at bay just as I did in my vegan days, eating tofu and rice—and Joey's greens and strawberries—without seeing, or wanting to see, the whole picture. I couldn't go on killing by proxy.

In his autobiography, the 14th Dalai Lama comments on Tibetans' relationship with meat. He notes that, in the 1960s, at least, very few Tibetan dishes were vegetarian. Alongside tsampa— a kind of barley bread—meat was a staple of the local diet. This, however, was complicated by religion. Buddhism, the Dalai Lama writes, doesn't prohibit meat eating "but it does say that animals should not be killed for food." And there lay the crux of what he calls Tibetans' "rather curious attitude" toward meat.

Tibetan Buddhists could buy meat, but they couldn't order it, "since that might lead to an animal being killed" for them specifically. What, then, were Tibetan Buddhists to do? How could they eat meat without being involved in butchery? How could they consume flesh, yet prevent themselves from being implicated in killing?

Simple. They did what I, as an American shopper, was already doing. They got someone else to do the killing for them. In the Tibetan case, writes the Dalai Lama, much of it was left to local Muslims.

I understood the comfort we find in not knowing, or in knowing and not looking or thinking. But I could find no virtue in it. If there was some kind of cosmic accounting system at work, it seemed to me that such willful ignorance should accrue extra bad karma, not less.

My fishing, however, wasn't yielding much food.

Even if it had been, I would have been leery of eating it in quantity. The Vermont Department of Health Fish Consumption Advisory—displayed on bulletin boards at public boat ramps and printed in the back of the state digest of hunting and fishing laws—informed me that our local freshwater fish were, like many ocean fish, toxic. Mercury, released upwind of us by the combustion of fossil fuels and the incineration of household garbage and medical waste, gets deposited in surface water, where it interacts with anaerobic organisms, resulting in the formation of methylmercury: a toxin that accumulates in fish. Though coldwater species like brook trout were rated as safer than bass, pickerel, pike, and walleye, I felt uneasy. And saddened, too, that even here, in free-flowing rivers and remote ponds, nothing could escape the poison threads we have woven into the web of life.

If I wanted to take firsthand responsibility for more of our flesh foods, I would have to look somewhere other than our local waters.

One Saturday morning in May, the spring after my return to fishing, I noticed a pickup truck parked partway down our driveway, where a path led into neighboring woods. *A turkey hunter*, I thought. In years past, I would have been irritated. Now, I was mainly curious. I left a polite note on the windshield, requesting that the vehicle's owner ask permission to park there in the future. Around noon, the truck pulled into our yard.

The driver—a man I judged to be in his sixties—apologized for not asking first. He hadn't planned that morning's outing far enough in advance.

Not a big deal, I assured him. Was he hunting turkeys? I asked.

He said he was, though he hadn't seen any.

Did he know these woods well?

Not as well as he once did, he said. He hadn't hunted here in some years.

We stood and talked for the better part of an hour. By the time he turned his truck around and headed off, I was thoroughly impressed by his friendly manner, his knowledge of the outdoors, and his affection for the natural world. I watched him go, an idea tickling at the back of my mind.

What about hunting? The thought came quietly, furtively, like an unwelcome stranger.

My first objection was simple: With the exception of turkeys and the occasional grouse or woodcock, the creatures I could hunt in these woods were four-legged, and we still weren't eating mammals. Not as a rule, at least. At Thanksgiving—when Cath's older brother lifted the top off a dish of his homemade *braciole*, releasing a plume of steam redolent of pork and parmesan, basil and parsley, garlic and tomato—it would be silly to insist, presidentially, that we didn't inhale, or that we wouldn't be spooning some of the tender, slow-simmered meat onto our plates and savoring every bite.

But we were not buying beef, lamb, or pork. Such meat seemed unpalatably alien, and perhaps unpalatably familiar, too, in its mammal-ness. The deaths of birds and fish were easier to contemplate, their pale flesh easier to consume. Was this mere habit, though? Or prejudice?

I had begun to grasp that cows and sheep, like chickens, could be raised not only humanely, but ecologically. Cattle didn't have to erode the topsoil of the pastures they trod. Their manure could fertilize and build it instead.

If ecology was one of my measures of merit when it came to food, wouldn't it make more sense to eat meat from a locally pastured beef cow than to buy salmon shipped in from Alaska or processed blocks of tofu made from soybeans grown a thousand miles away on industrially farmed land where diverse prairie habitat once thrived? If humaneness was another of my measures, wouldn't it make more sense to shoot a deer who had lived a truly free life than to buy even the happiest, most local, backyard chicken? What meat could be more ethical than fifty or more pounds of venison resulting from a single, quick death?

I wanted the creatures I was eating to have lived well and died swiftly. As much as possible, I wanted their journeys to my plate to resemble the workings of nature: the grouse snatched from the air by a great-horned owl, the minnow plucked from the water by a kingfisher. I did not want them to be mere product, churned out by an economic machine remarkable mainly for its heartless efficiency and ecological myopia—a system in which a single beef patty is often composed of assorted parts from dozens of cows processed in multiple slaughterhouses and even in multiple countries.

But *hunting?* I pushed the idea away.

The more charismatic mammals of farm and forest weren't on my plate, but they were on my mind. And the more I considered them, the more aware I became of the warped lens through which I had grown up seeing them.

On the one hand, we picture such creatures as adorably cute. Think Bambi and Thumper, or Wilbur in *Charlotte's Web*. As cartoon caricatures, they are entirely disconnected from reality.

Miraculously, Thumper and Friend Owl are buddies, and we are spared the discomfort of imagining the meaty—and often rabbity—meals enjoyed by real owls.

On the other hand, we consume animal flesh at an astonishing rate, only distantly aware of the millions of incarcerated creatures who feed us, or of the conditions in which they live and die.

I wondered, though: Might not these apparent extremes—dewy-eyed infantilizing and callous disregard—have common roots? Is there not, in both, an echo of the late cultural historian Thomas Berry's observation that we have become "autistic": deaf to the voices of nature, unable to perceive the larger-than-human world with anything resembling clarity?

In the extreme of anthropomorphism, we project human personalities, typically those of children, on to characters like Bambi. On the flip side, in the extreme of anthropocentrism, we deny animals any semblance of value as beings, treating them as nothing more than "live stock"—living, fleshy commodities. In grocery-store coolers we do not see "animals" but "meat," prepackaged, even preprepared for our convenience. In both extremes, we remain self-absorbed, caught up in our own fantasies. Stuck there, how can we hope to understand animals, or even respect them? "Respect," after all—rooted in the Latin verb *respicere*, to look back at, to regard, to consider—requires seeing beyond ourselves.

Doesn't this echo the way we see the rest of nature, too? Collectively, we and our multinational timber corporations lay waste to millions of acres of forest habitat, treating the planet as a mass of "natural resources" to be commoditized and exploited at will. Yet, often in reaction to such damage, we also invoke the notion of "wilderness" as a place off-limits to human activity and habitation. (Ironically, notions and reality often don't match. The creation of many of America's national "wilderness" parks required the eviction of local residents, both white and Indian.)

Are not both extremes rooted in the illusion that we are separate from nature, in what environmental historian William Cronon has called "a dualistic vision in which the human is entirely outside the natural"? If we imagine ourselves as essentially separate from nature—perhaps as the unseen evil presence of man in *Bambi*—how can we possibly imagine a place for ourselves within it?

When we do think of humans as part of nature, we usually imagine ourselves standing at its pinnacle. As the T-shirt states, "I Didn't Claw My Way to the Top of the Food Chain to Eat Vegetables."

It's quite a fantasy, this linear food chain with *Homo sapiens* at its apex. It neatly avoids the cyclical truth of our own mortality, glossing over the fate we share with the large carnivores, which are, as environmental scholar Paul Shepard once wrote, inevitably "pursued by microbes, fungi, and plant roots." Maybe the T-shirt should read, "I Clawed and Clawed But Couldn't Escape the Food Web—Soon I'll Be Feeding Vegetables."

There's beauty here, when you stop to think about it. If I am buried in a plain pine box, the nutrients of my body will return to the earth. Of the water molecules that reside within my veins and arteries when I die, perhaps some will be drawn up into a growing tree. Perhaps some will find their way up into clouds, come down in a spring rain, and course through brooks where trout feed and spawn. Of the calcium atoms in my shoulder blades, perhaps a few will end up in the leg of a frog or in a falcon's wing. Inevitable reincarnation.

Picturing ourselves in league with the large carnivores—or with the owl who plucks the grouse from the air and who must, in the end, return to the forest floor—has its comforts. Though death may be disturbing, most of us can make our peace with the idea of a gentle demise in old age. Being violently transformed into food—being the grouse struck down by the owl—is a less appetizing prospect.

As a boy, I read stories about human encounters with grizzly bears, encounters that didn't always end so well for the human. And I occasionally took out the bundled python skin my father kept in the closet: an oddity he had inherited from some great-aunt who had traveled overseas. I would take it out and unfurl it, fold by fold, until I had the entire skin—some twelve to fifteen inches wide and twenty-plus feet long—stretched out on the ground. The desiccated skull, still attached, smelled faintly of stale decay. I was fascinated by the sheer size of the thing. I knew that snakes this large could eat pigs. Why not a small boy?

Such events are, of course, exceedingly rare, even in grizzly or python country. Growing up in New England, long ago swept clear of wolves and cougars, I never feared that an animal would try to eat me. I never even glimpsed what such a threat might feel like, until one night well into my third decade.

The scream came at midnight.

Cath and I, still living at Bird Cottage among New York's Finger Lakes, were getting ready to move to Vermont. We had pitched a tent behind our friend Dierdre's house, not far from Syracuse. Her front yard along a main road was a perfect location for the garage sale we'd be having in the morning, jettisoning cargo in preparation for the move. We would have slept inside like regular houseguests, but Dierdre had cats and I—still vegan and still seriously allergic to them—preferred not to wake up bleary eyed and wheezy. Besides, Cath and I liked camping out. It would be fun.

"Keep the woodchucks out of my garden, will you?" said Dierdre, as we headed out back to sleep. "I've been having trouble with them." I didn't mention my track record in that department:

the woodchuck at Bird Cottage staring me down just two months earlier. Chuckie: 1, Tovar: 0.

Inside the lightweight tent, it seemed like the perfect summer night: a gentle breeze, nothing but mosquito netting between us and the stars.

When the scream came, Cath and I were both awake in an instant. What had we just heard? Yanked out of dream time, we weren't quite certain. It had been a loud, nasty sound. But what made it and where had it come from? Minutes later, the scream came again—the most frightening animal sound I had ever heard. It wasn't merely strange, like the wailing bark of a fox. It was angry, a full-throated, snarling yell. And it was close, maybe thirty yards off.

"What *is* that?" whispered Cath.

"I have no idea."

We listened. Heard nothing.

"When Dierdre asked us to protect her garden," Cath whispered again, "I didn't think it would be this hard!"

"Don't worry, honey," I said. "The garden's safe. Whatever that thing is, it doesn't eat plants."

Again the scream, closer still. Now the animal had to be under the trees at the lawn's edge, about twenty yards off. It occurred to me that I had stood right there a couple hours earlier, taking my before-bedtime pee. Had I offended this creature's territorial sensibilities? In the faint starlight I thought I caught a flash across the grass fifteen feet away, something the size of a large terrier but fluid in its movement, entirely undoglike. The mosquito netting around us seemed pathetically insubstantial.

We listened and watched, wired on adrenaline. Nothing more.

Finally, Cath said she needed to pee. In the house, of course. We unzipped the tent door and crawled out cautiously. No snarl, no silent pounce.

Once inside the house, we relaxed, solid walls on all sides of us. Cath wasn't keen on going back out to the tent. I wasn't keen on staying inside and breathing cat dander.

"Why don't you sleep in here and I'll go back out?"

"No way!" she said. "I won't be able to sleep knowing you're out there with that thing."

She decided to go with me, but wanted to bring along something for self-defense. She looked around and came back with a hockey stick belonging to Dierdre's son.

"Oh no," I said, laughing. "That's not coming into the tent with me."

I had visions of trying to swing a full-length puck slapper in the confines of a space only six feet across. In the end, we compromised. She brought the stick and leaned it against the tent beside the zippered door. I got a heavy steel flashlight from the car and set it beside my sleeping bag, more as a club than as a source of illumination.

All was quiet as we snuggled into our bags.

It was ten or fifteen minutes later, as we both began to drift softly down into sleep, that the heart-stopping scream came again. That was the last we heard of our night visitor. But we lay there a long while, listening, before finally dozing off.

In the morning, we told Dierdre about the night's events. She had woken at one point, thinking she'd heard a noise. But inside, buffered by the walls of the old farmhouse, the sound was faint and she couldn't be sure. When Dierdre's teenage daughter joined the conversation, she mentioned that she had spotted a large bobcat nearby a day or two before.

Yes, I imagined a bobcat could scream like that. And the fluid form I had seen flash across the grass definitely could have been feline.

"Oh, and I spread some dried blood fertilizer around the garden," said Dierdre. "I was hoping it might scare off the woodchucks."

Chum, I thought wryly. *Bait.*

I had never seriously believed that we were in danger of being attacked. My rational mind knew better than that. No wild animal in upstate New York was likely to attack a human, unless it was rabid. Yet my body had been in overdrive, heart racing, limbs tingling. Was this what it had been like to be human for most of the past couple hundred millennia—not only predator, but prey as well?

In her essay "Being Prey," about the crocodile attack she survived in 1985, ecofeminist philosopher Val Plumwood wrote of Western culture's "strong effort to deny that we humans are also animals positioned in the food chain," a denial she sees reflected in our revulsion at images of human bodies being consumed by predators, or by worms, for that matter. Hence our penchant for tightly sealed coffins. We imagine ourselves as "outside and above," she wrote, "not as part of the feast in a chain but as external manipulators and masters of it."

At the time of the crocodile attack, Plumwood was a vegetarian, not because she considered predation "demonic and impure," but because she objected to "the reduction of animal lives in factory farming systems that treat them as living meat." Being attacked gave her another level of insight. It was, she wrote, "a shocking reduction, from a complex human being to a mere piece of meat." Reflecting on the experience, she came to the conclusion that "not just humans but any creature can make the same claim to be more than just food. We are edible, but we are also much more than edible. Respectful, ecological eating must recognize both of these things."

Again I thought of hunting. And I thought of Uncle Mark.

We had never seen each other more than occasionally, usually for a couple of hours at Thanksgiving dinner, roasted bird on the table between us. Those visits to Cape Cod, where Mark still lived, fished, and hunted, had dwindled in frequency to once every few years. When I abandoned vegetarianism, though, I had written to him—curious about his relationships with forest, ocean, and food—and we struck up an e-mail correspondence. At family gatherings, he had always seemed contained, his full, expressive lips pressed firmly together. In writing, though, he was downright chatty.

Back and forth we went, mostly sharing experiences we'd had outdoors. I would tell him of the fox I had seen, or of the pileated woodpecker that had hopped among the trees near where Paul and I were working in the woods. Mark would tell me of his unusual daytime sighting of a pair of flying squirrels—they are typically nocturnal—or of the deer he had encountered over the past week.

Now, reflecting on my conversation with the turkey hunter who had parked alongside our driveway, I wrote to Mark again. I expressed my hope that we could visit in person one of these days, despite the busyness of our lives. Perhaps we could walk in the woods together. Perhaps we could fish. Perhaps we could talk about hunting.

I recalled the Wendell Berry poem I had pinned to the wall of my Brooklyn apartment, "The Peace of Wild Things." A vegan at the time, I had recited the poem like a mantra. I imagined reconnecting with nature, lying down, as the author does, "where the wood drake / rests in his beauty on the water, and the great heron feeds." I imagined the stillness of the heron, standing in the shallows, peaceful, tall, and majestic. I did not imagine the heron actually "feeding": the sudden, violent stab of its beak. It didn't occur to me that the heron's stillness was the stillness of a hunter.

For years, I had been glossing over the killing that surrounded me: birds, bugs, fish, amphibians, reptiles, and mammals, one feasting upon the other. The incessant eating—which I could now more comfortably acknowledge without boomeranging to some bleak Tennyson-like vision of "Nature, red in tooth and claw"— had been easy to forget, for I rarely witnessed such nutritional transactions.

When Cath and I lived at Bird Cottage, we had watched the songbirds that came to the feeders we hung, and thought little of the other visitors that were, in turn, attracted to the clearing. One afternoon I saw a cardinal dart for the trees. The sharp, taut shape of a small hawk streaked after it. The cardinal zipped back and forth, the raptor in fierce pursuit, carving tight, full-speed turns among the branches. In seconds, they were out of sight and the illusion of peacefulness returned.

Our midnight encounter with the bobcat had been similarly fleeting. The next morning, Dierdre's backyard looked tame. Mowed grass, lilacs, the vegetable patch with lettuce in rows. The tranquil scene gave no hint of the hunter who had been there a few hours before. It offered no reminder of the larger, older, wilder world beyond, creatures helping themselves to each other's very lives. All eaters, sooner or later, one way or another, being eaten.

Even in my most devout vegan phase, predation among animals had never bothered me. Unlike Cleveland Amory, founder of the Fund for Animals—who once described how, in his vision of a perfect world, "prey will be separated from predator"—I had no wish to impose my morals on the affairs of nonhuman creatures. Their actions might not meet my standards for human kindness and compassion, but it never occurred to me to interfere.

Well, almost never. I did intervene once, in boyhood. Among the cattails along the quarry's edge, I had found a full-grown bull-frog with a garter snake attached. The dark, yellow-striped reptile, less than two feet long, had grabbed hold of one of the frog's hind feet and started swallowing. It had worked its way up to the top of the thigh and was stuck there. The frog couldn't get away. And the snake, unable to get the other leg into its small jaws, couldn't get its meal. The stalemate was pointless. Wondering if digestive juices had already set to work on the hapless foot, I picked up a stick and gently pressed on the snake's back, just behind the head. Reluctantly, the reptile disgorged the leg and both parties fled the scene. That, however, had been an extraordinary circumstance.

Predator-prey relationships were, I knew, essential to the workings of nature. The temptation to judge those relationships—to delude ourselves into thinking that predator and prey could be disconnected—was just another manifestation of human hubris.

Yet I had been certain that I shouldn't participate in the bloodshed. Moral interaction with animals required nonviolence. Humans had done enough harm already: building shopping malls where forests once stood, disrupting entire ecosystems, driving species after species to extinction. It was time we let nature be.

Now, I was reconsidering.

A few months after my conversation with the turkey hunter, Cath pointed out an impressive photo in the newspaper. A local angler had hauled up a new state-record lake trout from Lake Willoughby, a deep, fjord-like stretch of water an hour north of us. The fish was more than thirty-five pounds and most of four feet long. A state biologist estimated it was more than thirty years old. When I mentioned the fish to my youngest sister, she replied, "Too bad it didn't get to die naturally." I thought I knew what she meant. A creature that venerable has earned special respect. I wouldn't begrudge it the chance to die of old age.

But I wondered: Why do we distinguish ourselves from "natural" predators? Surely it isn't just because we use synthetic fishing line, flashy lures, bullets, and arrows, rather than tooth, beak,

WHERE THE GREAT HERON FEEDS

and claw. Humans have been part of the earth's ecosystems for hundreds of thousands of years. Though we have proven ourselves uniquely capable of damaging and altering those ecosystems, we are not aliens. Why, then, do we consider our predation "unnatural"? How far have we gone in accepting the dangerous illusion that we are separate from the rest of life?

On the other hand, I wasn't sure that the "naturalness" of predation—the fact that it occurs among animals—had much bearing on the question of whether humans should hunt. Plenty of animal behaviors, after all, are proscribed by human moral codes. No one tries to justify infanticide by pointing out that other creatures sometimes eat their young: mice and rabbits, for example, and various species of fish and insects.

I wasn't sure that the ancientness of human predation had much bearing on the question either. We reject traditions all the time: the treatment of other human beings as property, for example, or the denial of voting rights on the basis of gender or skin color. Why, then, should the ancientness of hunting traditions provide a meaningful justification for its practice in modern times?

Had I—in adopting veganism and morally setting myself above the predator-prey relationship—lost sight of my unity with other animals, with nature as a whole, and with my heritage as a human? Or was I now—in fishing and in entertaining the possibility of hunting—losing sight of the very thing that made me human, the ability to reflect on my own needs and instincts and to make moral choices?

If I simply wanted a face-to-face reckoning with my meat, I could volunteer to help a chicken-raising friend on slaughter day, wielding the knife and seeing how it felt. If I wanted to experience the whole process from beginning to end, I could raise chickens myself. Had I lived in a suburban or urban setting, I might have gone that route, as many Americans have in recent years. Here in the hills of north-central Vermont, though, with the woods just a stone's throw from our front door, this disconcerting notion kept stalking my thoughts: hunting.

When I imagined Uncle Mark hunting, I did not think merely of the killing. I knew, in fact, that he spent most days and weeks afield without taking a shot. Only once a year, on average, did he drag a deer out of the woods.

I thought mainly of Mark's relationship with the land, his knowledge of the places he had hunted, his familiarity with the habits of the creatures who lived there. I recalled walking into his room when I was a boy, marveling at the bows and arrows, the powder horn and pelts and antlers. Would hunting teach me to see these wooded ridges and valleys differently? Would it sharpen my attention to the nuances of terrain and breeze, of vegetation patterns and animal behavior, the way fishing had attuned me to the interplay of current, stone, and sunlight? Would hunting help me feel more like a participant in nature and less like a spectator? Would it give me some sense of belonging, of communion? Would it remind me of the largeness and wholeness of the world, and of my tininess within it?

To be honest with myself, I had to admit something else, too. I had been glossing over the presence of predation not only in nature, but in my own psyche.

The year after we moved to Vermont, on opening weekend of rifle season in mid-November, I had dreamed of a deer. And of a cougar, watching intently. Predator and prey circled each other, round and round, until finally the deer brushed by within inches of the great cat. Not yet hungry, the cougar let the white-tail pass. Still a vegan, I woke, jotted the dream in a notebook, and thought of it no more.

Two years before that, in what little snow we had gotten at Bird Cottage, I had once found deer tracks in the woods on the far side of the brook. I followed them, slowly at first, then faster and faster, running, weaving through the trees as the deer had done, pursuing the hoofprints for the sheer fun of it, feeling like the boy I had once been: fascinated with the ways of wild creatures, delighted to find signs of their passage and to have the chance to make plaster casts of their tracks. At the time, following those tracks near Bird Cottage, the feeling seemed nothing more than excited curiosity, the thrill of tracking and not knowing where the chase would end.

But was it not a hunter's excitement?

6

Hunter and Beholder

When men and women put on blaze orange hunting vests or camo, they temporarily lose their individuality beneath the layers of symbolism loaded on the image of *hunter*.

—Jan E. Dizard, *Mortal Stakes*

Who would I be if I hunted?

After so many years of sticking to veggie burgers, could I really picture myself striding into the woods with a lethal weapon in hand, intent on shooting down a wild animal and dragging its bloody carcass home for dinner? Who would I become in my own eyes? Who would I become in others' eyes?

Where Cath's views were concerned, I was fortunate. Though my return to fishing had surprised her, as it had me, she could relate. Just as I could conjure memories of spring outings with Willie when the quarry was still half covered with ice, or of dropping my line into its cooler, shadier corners in midsummer, she remembered fishing with her brothers when they were kids, catching suckers in Rippleton Creek, the little waterway that ran near their house. They fed the small ones to the barn cats and brought the big ones home for their grandfather to cook.

Though Cath had no interest in angling now, she took mine in stride. She knew how enjoyable fishing could be and understood my desire to have a hand in procuring the flesh foods we were eating.

And though hunting was alien—except for her brother's pursuit of the occasional cottontail, no one in her family had hunted, and the regular dispatching of woodchucks in the garden had been a simple extension of agriculture—she was keeping an open mind. If the vegan she had fallen in love with eight years earlier wanted to learn to stalk his own meat on the paw or hoof, she would adjust to the idea. For that, I was grateful. In an e-mail, Uncle Mark mentioned that his wife, who now looks forward to venison each autumn, was an anti-hunter when they first met. "Things were kind of stressed when I brought something home from the woods," he wrote. I could well imagine.

In Cath's eyes, then, my hunting would not precipitate a catastrophic fall from grace. Nor would my mother, sisters, aunts, uncles, or grandmother see it that way. Though Mark was the only hunter in my immediate clan, his annual pursuit of wild meat was well respected, and no one but me had ever taken up veganism.

I was less sure about our friends. My return to angling—the idea of me tossing flies and treble-hooked lures to unsuspecting trout or bass—had been a bizarre enough surprise. The image of me in a blaze-orange vest with a deer rifle slung over my shoulder would be far worse.

But why? Why should fishing, a thoroughly predatory activity, be so much more socially acceptable than hunting, and so much more popular? Nearly 30 million Americans fish each year, while only 12.5 million hunt.

Is it because we see fish as "other," but perceive mammals, and to a lesser degree birds, as kin? As the late anthropologist Susan Kent noted, in traditional hunter-gatherer and hunter-farmer societies, "animals are classified as intellectual beings. They are therefore placed in the same macro-category as humans, whereas plants and fish are not." Here in the modern West, we tend to make sharper distinctions between *Homo sapiens* and other animals, often claiming that humans possess something that animals do not: typically a capacity for reason, or a soul. But don't we still identify more closely with hairy, warm-blooded fellow mammals than with scaly, cold-blooded fish? More with Bambi than with Nemo? (Ironically, the average American eats well over a hundred pounds of beef, pork, veal, and lamb each year, and less than twenty pounds of fish.)

Or is our greater discomfort with hunting rooted in its violence, so much more sudden and final than that of fishing? For the individual angler wielding rod and line, killing is not essential to successful fishing. Whatever we may say about the practice of "catch-and-release" angling—whatever praise we heap upon it for conserving fish populations, whatever criticism we level at it for causing pointless suffering and unintentionally killing some fish—we can agree on the simple fact: It can be done. We can fish, catch, and then decide the fate of our prey. We can even snap a quick photo before the rainbow, brown, or largemouth swims away. In hunting, our predatory implement is not a hook that can be removed, but a bullet, or a blast of shotgun pellets, or a razor-tipped arrow: a projectile that captures by killing. If a hunter shoots, there is no throwing the animal back to live another day.

Differences can also be heard in our idiomatic uses of the words "fish" and "hunt." When we say someone is fishing for something—information, perhaps—we evoke an image of a line dropped quietly into water, or a net cast out, a subtle gesture toward an uncertain end. The fisherman waits, receptive, not knowing what, if anything, will take the bait or lure, or appear in the net. Hunting for something—a job, perhaps—is different. Pointed and aggressive rather than patient and fluid, the hunter doggedly pursues his or her goal. If Simon and Andrew had been hunting along the shores of the Sea of Galilee, rather than casting a net, Jesus could hardly have said unto them, "Follow me, and I will make you hunters of men."

If I really thought about it, I had to admit: My problem had never been with hunting itself.

Oh, in my most righteous vegan phase, I *had* been certain that hunting, like other forms of animal murder, was wrong. Yet, at the same time, I had mourned the extermination of indigenous hunter-gatherer and hunter-farmer cultures around the world. If someone had pointed out that contradiction—the fact that I wished for the survival of traditions like those of the Kiowa and Cree, and of the Yupik I had first read about in *Julie of the Wolves*, all of which involved hunting—I probably would have argued that such cultures, like ours, could make moral progress away from slaughter and meat eating. (It's frightening to think that I might have made a good missionary.) If pressed on the point, however, I suppose I would have conceded: I didn't object to human predation in all times and places.

Shortly after our move to Vermont, Cath and I borrowed David Attenborough's series *The Life of Mammals* from a local public library. The final episode depicts an ancient form of hunting, the persistence hunt, as traditionally practiced by the San people of the Kalahari Desert. In the show, three hunters find the tracks of a group of kudu. When the animals are spotted, the pursuit begins. Alternating between walking and running, the three men focus on a single bull. Where tracks are visible, the hunters follow them. Where they are not, the men attend to subtler signs, in places relying on little more than their imagination, their ability to see the terrain from the kudu's perspective and know where he would have gone.

Hours later, when the kudu begins to slow, the final stage of the hunt commences: the chase. One man runs in the blazing heat, pursuing his prey. But for the sneakers on his feet, the plastic canteen he carries, the steel of his knife and spear, and the unseen presence of a camera crew, the scene—man chasing animal—could be from ten thousand years ago. For hours, they run, the hunter's expert tracking skills keeping him on the trail, his extraordinary stamina gradually overcoming the kudu's.

Evolutionary biologists Dennis M. Bramble and Daniel E. Lieberman have speculated that this method of hunting—historically used to take deer and antelope in North America, kangaroos in Australia, and a variety of species in Africa—may, along with competitive scavenging, have influenced the evolution of the human body. Though we lack the speed of large quadrupeds, we have astonishing endurance, due to the musculoskeletal specializations of our bipedal form and our unique capacity for evaporative cooling.

Eight hours after the hunt began, man closes in on animal. Both walk slowly. Finally, the great antelope's legs give out, and he lies on the ground, unable to rise, head up and alert, watching the hunter. From only a few yards away, the man launches the slender spear, striking the animal just behind the shoulder.

When the kudu lies still, the hunter scatters handfuls of sandy earth over the body, like a priest sprinkling holy water. Crouching, he caresses the animal's face, looks into its eye. With his finger, he scoops saliva from the corner of the kudu's mouth and rubs it into the skin of his own legs to relieve the pain of the long run. He gives thanks for the life he has taken, for the meat that will feed his family.

In watching that extraordinary segment, I saw the hunt as natural. Despite the artifice of film editing, the piece expressed something elemental, something true. The man was undeniably a part of nature: an intelligent, highly developed predator, to be sure, but only one among many. The moment of the kill—and the sorrowful, respectful moments just after it—made my heart ache.

No, my problem wasn't with hunting. It was with hunters.

On one hand, for me the word "hunter" conjured images of the San's reverence for the kudu, and of Uncle Mark. As a boy, I had grasped that Mark was gentle and sensitive. Now, as we corresponded about hunting, that perception was confirmed. "Killing," he wrote, "is not something to be taken lightly." Even after four decades as a hunter, he felt a wave of conflicting emotions at every kill: sorrow mixed with elation and gratitude. I imagined him crouched beside a fallen animal, touching it gently, as the San hunter did. He was glad to hear of my curiosity about hunting, but didn't push me in that direction. Hunting wasn't for everyone, he knew. "Everyone has to do what they are comfortable with," he wrote. As a young man, he had sometimes felt the need to apologize for his affinity for hunting. Now, though, he embraced it. Hunting felt deeply right for him—a kind of spiritual pursuit.

On the other hand, the word "hunter" conjured other scenes.

It made me think of *Julie of the Wolves*: the shots fired from airplanes, the animals killed for entertainment.

It made me think of the young buck Paul and I once found near a small brook, while logging a suburban woodlot. The whitetail had taken a bullet in the chest but was never recovered by the hunter. The tail appeared to have been torn out by dogs or coyotes, perhaps as they ran the wounded animal down.

It made me think of the deer parts unceremoniously dumped along our road each autumn, pushed over the steep embankment above the brook where I had been catching trout. Finding those bones and scraps, I would silently curse the slobs who had discarded them, typically in garbage bags. Twice I carried a doe's head home, left it in an anthill until the flesh had been stripped away, then set it in the woods, at the base of a spruce where I sometimes went to meditate.

"Hunter" made me think of shooting mishaps, both those that have ended in tragedy and those that might have: the Wisconsin woman killed in 2001 by a neighbor who thought he saw a deer, and the stray bullet that Cath told me had come through a window in her girlhood home and lodged in the wall of the upstairs hallway. Though such events are relatively rare, they make an indelible impression. As sociologist Jan E. Dizard notes in his book *Mortal Stakes: Hunters and Hunting in Contemporary America*, "even hunters themselves are not all that trusting of other hunters."

And "hunter" made me think, too, of the one autumn Cath and I had spent at Bird Cottage. The driveway connected to a trail that led back into the woods. When deer hunters armed with shotguns started walking down the driveway, passing within forty yards of us, we put up a no-hunting sign. A week later, we found Cath's car slouching to one side, two tires slashed.

Hunters, it turns out, have occupied a complicated place in the Anglo-American psyche from the very beginning.

In seventeenth-century Europe, as historian Daniel Justin Herman documents in his book *Hunting and the American Imagination*, the New World was said to be a land of plenty: full not of the gently flowing milk and honey of a new Canaan, but of elk and deer, turkeys and waterfowl, and pigeons that darkened the skies with their uncounted millions. Such a wealth of wild meat appealed to the investors who were funding commercial explorations of North America. It also appealed to commoners, for the privilege of pursuing European game had long been reserved for the elite.

The New World's wild plenty was matched by its wild terrors. One English sailor reported on its "many Tygers, monstrous and furious beasts, which by subtletie devoure and destroy many men." As historian Andrea Smalley has noted, most reports about the New England and Virginia colonies downplayed these dangers, so as to avoid discouraging colonization. But longtime residents were aware of the impression the continent made on newcomers. What could they possibly see upon their arrival, asked William Bradford in his account of the early days of the Plymouth Colony, but a "hidious & desolate wildernes, full of wild beasts and wild men?"

As European colonists established a foothold along the eastern shores of North America, they took advantage of the abundant wildlife. Birds and mammals of every shape and size—from pigeons and ducks to beavers and deer—were netted, snared, trapped, clubbed, and shot. For those who did the killing, wild animals provided food. They also provided the opportunity for economic profit, as meat and hides could be sold at market.

Yet hunting stories are remarkably rare in colonial lore. Herman draws our attention to New England as an example. "How was it," he asks, "that New England could be so full of game at the outset of colonization and yet produce so few tales of hunters and hunting?"

In some areas, perhaps colonists simply did not hunt much. At Plymouth, some twenty-five miles north of where Uncle Mark now hunted deer each fall, the archaeological evidence suggests that the Pilgrims were, in Herman's words, "lackluster hunters."

Though they apparently consumed a fair number of wild ducks, they ate few wild mammals and almost no turkeys. In 1621, at the feast now commemorated as the first Thanksgiving, the main course was apparently venison, supplied by Wampanoag Indians.

More generally, colonists simply did not think of themselves as hunters. There was ample reason for them not to. With a few notable exceptions, such as the Finns who settled in the Delaware Valley, they had not been hunters in their homelands. For generations, they had primarily eaten the fruits of the field and pasture, not of the chase.

Nor had they come from hunting religions. Take the Puritans, for instance. In seventeenth-century England, they campaigned against hunting and cockfighting because they believed that such activities, like drinking, gambling, and pagan celebrations, were unchristian. In the words of British historian Lord Thomas Babington Macaulay, Puritans hated bear baiting—a form of entertainment in which bears were chained to posts and tormented by dogs—"not because it gave pain to the bear, but because it gave pleasure to the spectators." In England, the Puritans had seen hunting as evidence of the gentry's moral corruption. In the New World, they saw native peoples' hunting in a similar light. "They believed," writes Daniel Herman, "that Indians, like English aristocrats, were gamblers, fornicators, and ardent hunters, men who repudiated steady work habits and godliness."

In stark contrast to American Indian religions, which placed humans within the complexities of life's web, Puritanism cast us as radically separate from nature. Distinguishing *Homo sapiens* from other species—and the spirit from the body—was an obsession for ministers like Cotton Mather, who apparently couldn't even pee without a fit of theological apoplexy. In 1700, foreshadowing the deep-seated fears of animality that would be articulated by vegetarian evangelist Sylvester Graham more than a century later, Mather wrote in his diary,

> I was once emptying the cistern of nature, and making water at the wall. At the same time, there came a dog, who did so too, before me. Thought I; 'What mean and vile things are the children of men. . . . How much do our natural necessities abase us, and place us . . . on the same level with the very dogs!'. . .
>
> I resolved that it should be my ordinary practice, whenever I step to answer the one or other necessity of nature to make it an opportunity of shaping in my mind some holy, noble, divine thought.

Herman points out that religious doctrine also provided a cornerstone for colonial expansion. In Genesis, after all, God had commanded humans to subdue the earth and to eat the plants of the field, earning their food by the sweat of their brow. Though the native peoples of eastern North America planted crops around seasonal settlements, few were full-time farmers. As hunters, they had not "subdued" the land on which they lived. Therefore, the colonial argument went, they were not really using it. According to the logic of *vacuum domicilium*—"vacant abode"—land became the rightful property of the men who farmed it.

Roger Williams, convicted of sedition and heresy for his many "dangerous opinions" and banished from Massachusetts, pointed out one major problem with this logic: Indians, like English nobles, managed their land to increase the availability of deer and other animals. Did not the former use and own that land as much as the latter? Not according to most colonists.

The dominant view held that it was permissible, even godly, to occupy North American soil and put it to "proper" use. This politically convenient religious concept of hunters' and farmers' different relationships with land complemented contemporary ideas about the development of civilization, particularly the "four-stages theory."

Propounded by scholars such as Adam Smith, the Scottish author of *The Wealth of Nations*, this theory contended that human societies progressed through four stages: hunting, herding, farming, and commerce. For many four-stages theorists, Herman notes, "the third stage, or a mixture of the third and fourth stages, was ideal," for farming was seen as the foundation of both virtue and prosperity. "Those who labour in the earth," wrote Thomas Jefferson, "are the chosen people of God."

For most colonists, hunting was secondary to farming. It might be necessary, as a way of providing food and eliminating pests and predators. And it could be enjoyable, as a diversion. As a way of life, however, it was barbaric and indolent, posing a threat to the industrious foundations of agrarian civilization. Hunting-based lifestyles made the frontier socially and morally dangerous, leading—in the words of Charles Woodmason, an Anglican who preached in the Carolinas—to "one continual Scene of Depravity of Manners . . . being more abandoned to Sensuality, and more Rude in Manners, than the Poor Savages around us."

Herman suggests that the frontier presented more complex problems as well. What if degenerate whites joined Indians in resisting government authority? And what if a large number of whites chose a life of subsistence hunting? Could white farmers take land claimed by white hunters by invoking the logic of *vacuum domicilium*, arguing that they—like Indian hunters—weren't really using it? Or would the absence of racial distinction between white farmers and white hunters bring that logic to its knees? Disturbed by such perils, colonies enacted legal reforms to curb them. In 1745, for example, North Carolina required that every deer hunter either possess "a settled

Habitation" or produce written proof "of his having planted and tended Five Thousand Corn-hills . . . in the County where he shall hunt."

At the time, the white backwoods hunter was seen as repulsive and dangerous, evoking in the colonial imagination, Herman argues, "images of man fallen to a state of nature, the condition of savagery . . . to the level of American Indians."

What a difference a century makes.

By the early- and mid-1800s, Americans were enthralled by stories about hunters. Daniel Boone stood tall in popular imagination, his real life dramatically embellished and ennobled in print. Alongside him, in the rapidly growing mythology of American hunting, stood the wilder, more reckless figure of Davy Crockett, and also that of Natty Bumppo, the fearless woodsman hero of James Fenimore Cooper's *Leatherstocking Tales*. As folk and literary heroes, Herman contends, these men represented a radically new kind of ideal American. Where the model citizen of the colonial era had been the industrious community-minded farmer, these were rugged individualists. They were not, however, slovenly frontier hunting rabble, the kind North Carolina had forced to plant corn hills. Portrayed as daring adventurers rather than native savages, these men of the wilds stoked the imaginations of a growing number of middle- and upper-class American hunters.

The hunting stories that appeared in magazines of the day were accompanied by lessons in natural history. As Herman illustrates, science and hunting were fast becoming intertwined. Like Lewis and Clark's turn-of-the-century expedition, during which the men had hunted both for meat and for scientific specimens, American hunting was framed as a pursuit both informed by, and performed in the service of, scientific knowledge. This melding of hunting and scientific discovery is embodied, for example, in the figure of John James Audubon. Though now remembered as a painter and as the father of American ornithology, the French-born Audubon was a passionate hunter who idolized Daniel Boone.

As a nineteenth-century cultural icon, the American hunter-naturalist celebrated wilderness. Yet he also conquered it. Despite Bumppo's protest in *The Pioneers* that settlers had "driven God's creatures from the wilderness," most wilderness hunters—including Boone—were seen as the spearhead of empire, making way for Euro-American science and settlement.

Likewise, Herman argues, the iconic American hunter celebrated American Indians and appeared to "take on the aura of the indigene," yet he also led the westward conquest. Though the fictional Bumppo—also known as Hawkeye, Pathfinder, and Deerslayer—grew up among Indians, and though men the likes of Boone were revered for their supposed knowledge of Indian lore and woodscraft and were consistently pictured in buckskin hunting shirts, wilderness hunters were also styled as ferocious Indian fighters.

By the early 1970s, when I was born, the mythology of American hunting had permeated the culture for 150 years. Though I grew up reading J. R. R. Tolkien rather than J. F. Cooper, I recognized coonskin caps, Kentucky long rifles, and the partial adoption of Indianness as vital elements of our national origin story.

Herman offers compelling explanations for the dramatic nineteenth-century shift in the American hunter's image. One factor was the hunter's association with the increasingly important field of natural science. Another was the popular image of backwoods hunters—including Ethan Allen's Green Mountain Boys from here in Vermont—as Revolutionary War heroes.

A third likely influence was the nature-oriented religious philosophy of Deism, to which several of the Founding Fathers

subscribed, and the Deist-influenced thinking of Romantic philosopher Jean-Jacques Rousseau, for whom all of God's creation—
including humankind—was good, until sullied by society. In
Rousseau's social theory, the hunting societies of American
Indians were idealized, for they allowed people to maintain their
natural virtue and egalitarianism.

The shifting economy was a factor, too. The eager readers of
the Boone and Bumppo tales were members of a growing middle
class. The wilderness-hunter identity appealed to them as a way
to escape their urban lives and, at the same time, provided an
apt model for the kind of resourceful and manly individualism
necessary for success in the expanding commercial sector. More-
over, warned sports writers the likes of Henry William Herbert,
America's wealthy classes were afflicted by "the demoralization
of luxury" and "the growth of effeminacy and sloth." Hunting,
these writers claimed, would revitalize the country's morality
and masculinity. (Hunting and vegetarianism have evidently
been shaped by the same cultural forces and concerns: Herbert
penned his words in the 1840s, just a few years after Sylvester
Graham condemned the American diet as excessively luxurious
and degenerate, and just a few decades before *Physical Culture*
magazine began promoting a meat-free diet as a path to muscular
and moral manhood.)

Throughout the nineteenth century, the buckskin-clad hunter
ascended in our national imagination. Despite our agrarian roots
and the critical role played by farming in justifying our claim
to the continent, we came to believe, as Herman puts it, that
Americans were "a hunting people and that it was hunting that
made [us] American."

During my years as a vegan, I had seen North American hunters
as authors of destruction. And hunting can, alongside habitat loss,

be justly blamed for the decimation of the continent's wildlife. Following the Civil War, the railroads expanded, taking more and more market hunters west. Birds and animals of every kind were relentlessly pursued, their meat, fur, and feathers often shipped to urban markets back east. Many species, including the American bison, were pushed to the brink of extinction. Others were driven over it.

By the early- and mid-1800s, passenger pigeons—the birds that had long darkened the continent's skies with their multitudes— were being killed en masse. They were shot, netted, and clubbed by the tens of thousands, then sold as food for humans, as food for hogs, and even as crop fertilizer. By 1890, they were all but gone. Their final demise was eloquently mourned decades later by twentieth-century hunter-naturalist Aldo Leopold: "The feathered lightning is no more."

There is another chapter in this history, however, one of which I had long been ignorant. When the direness of the situation became clear, hunters sounded the call for conservation. It was an avid hunter, Yale-educated naturalist and *Forest and Stream* editor George Bird Grinnell, who, in 1886, founded the National Audubon Society, aiming to halt the slaughter of wild birds for sale as food and for the making of feathered hats. The next year, it was again Grinnell who— along with Theodore Roosevelt and others—founded the Boone and Crockett Club, intended to promote hunting ethics, champion wildlife conservation, and eliminate market hunting in favor of regulated sport hunting. (Ironically, Herman points out, Boone himself was a market hunter who, with just one partner, once took seven hundred beavers in a single season. Yet, when he saw wildlife populations dwindling, Boone also spoke out against wanton killing.)

If Grinnell could see the twenty-first-century versions of the institutions he founded and worked for, he might be surprised by what they have become, and by the fault line that has fractured the ideological landscape of American conservation, splitting his legacy in two. Today, the Audubon Society is popularly associated with conservation, while *Field and Stream*—which absorbed *Forest and Stream* in 1930—is associated with hunting, and the Boone and Crockett Club even more narrowly with its system for scoring big-game trophies. In the late-nineteenth and early-twentieth centuries, though, conservation and regulated hunting were unified.

I knew that the era's hunter-conservationists could be fairly charged with excesses of their own. In *The Wilderness Hunter*, Roosevelt—who, more than any other U.S. president, made conservation a national priority—wrote of how his hunting party once killed three bull elk in a matter of minutes; when the animals were dead, the men took the heads, the hides, and the best cuts of meat, then headed back to camp. He wrote, too, of his "exulting pride" at having "procured a trophy such as can fall henceforth to few hunters indeed"—one of the continent's few remaining bison.

I also knew that they could be fairly charged with self-interest: Their desire to preserve the hunted stemmed in no small part from their desire to preserve the hunt. Yet self-interest itself is no crime. If a group of canoe and kayak enthusiasts worked to conserve a network of lakes and rivers and, in the process, protected entire ecosystems and benefited countless species, I would not object to their self-interest. Unless I objected to paddling in the first place.

Whatever I thought of hunting, I knew that these hunters had left a legacy of undeniable importance. In alliance with non-hunting naturalists like John Muir and members of the rapidly growing movement for the humane treatment of animals, they condemned market hunting and championed wildlife protection. Recognizing the urgent need for legislative intervention and law enforcement, they agitated for harvest restrictions and scientific management rooted in an understanding of animals and their habitats. And they lobbied for federal passage of the Lacey Game and Wild Birds Preservation and Disposition Act of 1900. The Lacey Act—which prohibited interstate traffic in game taken in violation of state law—is widely credited with turning the tide for the continent's plummeting wildlife populations.

For me, and for others who knew me, my taking up a rifle in pursuit of game would not be a simple act of predation, but a complicated shift, its meanings inevitably accented by the past.

Though the Puritans are long gone, the idea of people taking pleasure in killing still disturbs us deeply, perhaps more than killing itself. Though simplistic four-stage theories have been debunked, hunting still seems like a throwback to humanity's preagricultural past. Though American identity is no longer being thrashed out along an unstable geographic frontier, hunters are still vivid figures in our culture wars. Hunters still inhabit a metaphorical borderland. And we still debate what that borderland inspires: self-reliant virtue or bloodthirsty vice.

7

Double Vision

I never could stomach the straight-faced reveling in primi-
tivism, the barely concealed bloodlust, the whole macho
conceit that the most authentic encounter with nature is
the one that comes through the sight of a gun and ends
with a large mammal dead on the ground—a killing that
we are given to believe constitutes a gesture of respect.
—Michael Pollan, *The Omnivore's Dilemma*

The walls of the fish and game club were festooned with dead
animals. Near the main entrance hung the taxidermied head
of a whitetail buck with formidable antlers. Next to it, a plaque
displayed the fanned tail of a wild turkey. High on one wall was
a huge rainbow trout, petrified in midleap. Across the big, low
room were more bucks, caribou from Quebec, and a massive
moose head, its broad, palmate antlers spanning several feet.
On the adjoining wall hung a more exotic collection: deer and
gazelles killed in Africa.

As I sat down at one of the long folding tables, lined up classroom style with an aisle down the middle, I knew one thing

for certain: I was way out of my element. Partly, it was the rows of trophy heads, their artificial eyes staring down at me by the dozens. Partly, it was the people.

I was too old. At thirty-two, I had twenty years on most of the students with whom I would be spending a few late-summer evenings over the coming weeks, completing the state hunter-education course required to get a license. Most of the other adults in the room appeared to be fathers or uncles—and, in one or two cases, mothers or aunts—accompanying members of the younger generation.

My hair was too long. I had started to let it grow in college and it now hung down to the middle of my back, bound in a single braid to keep the flyaway strands out of trouble. If you're guessing that this marked some kind of nonconformist attitude—some affiliation with the counterculture that has taken root in Vermont over the past several decades—you're right. No other man in the room had hair much past his ears, let alone his shoulders.

And my clothes were too crunchy. Where some guys' chests were emblazoned with NRA-style slogans like "Give 'Em Both Barrels, It's Your Right!," I wore a T-shirt that depicted Mother Earth and her diverse inhabitants, from mice and crustaceans to moose and whales. I thought it safe to assume there was only one ex-vegan in the room.

When class started, the lead instructor—a small, wiry, white-haired man—cut to the chase. His main reason for volunteering to teach hunter education was to make hunting safer. When he was growing up, hunting-related shootings had been all too common: about thirty injuries and deaths per year in Vermont alone. Though the New York legislature mandated hunter safety training in 1949, Vermont didn't pass a similar law until 1974. He told us about his first morning of deer hunting as a kid. He sat at the base of a tree, terrified, listening to shots going off in every direction. He had been told that bullets travel faster than sound.

"I sat there," he said, "and each time I heard a shot, I thought, 'That one didn't hit me.'"

He followed that opening salvo by describing injuries and fatalities of every kind. Though things had gotten a lot safer in recent decades, the tragedies hadn't stopped entirely. In the most common incidents, hunters hurt and killed themselves or each other, usually members of their own hunting party. Typical causes included handling firearms carelessly, failing to be sure of the target and what lay beyond it, or swinging to shoot at moving game and forgetting that a companion might be in the line of fire. In this last category, the instructor described how one Vermont hunter saw a deer, shouldered his rifle, followed the animal for a moment, and fired. The top of his cousin's head was a few feet away, directly in front of the muzzle.

Leading us to a table in one corner of the room, the instructor showed us how easily such a thing could happen. On the table was a rifle, its stock and barrel cradled by a portable shooting rest, the bolt action open to show that it was unloaded. A foot in front of the muzzle stood a coffee can, the top of it clearly in the line of fire. When my turn came, I leaned over to look through the scope, its line of sight an inch and a half above the center of the barrel. I saw nothing but the wall ten feet away.

Far less common, but even more disturbing, were the cases where nonhunters were injured or killed. Less than a year earlier, just a few miles from where we now sat, a man—sitting in his living room watching the New York Giants play the Tennessee Titans—had been struck by a bullet. The hunter, shooting at a deer, had been more than half a mile away. The bullet missed the animal, flew thousands of feet, tore into the man's mobile home, and hit him in the head as he sat in front of the television. He died a few days later. Some had considered it a freak accident. But our instructor was clear: It should never have happened. A hunter has to be absolutely certain there is a solid backstop before firing a rifle.

Our instructor also talked about the 1988 shooting of Karen Wood in Maine. Fifteen years after the fact, he was still outraged, both by her death and by the 1990 acquittal of the deer hunter who squeezed the trigger. At the time, some had tried to blame Wood, who was killed less than fifty yards from her back door. She should have been wearing blaze orange, they said, and she shouldn't have been wearing cream-colored mittens that a hunter might mistake for deer tails. Our instructor was having none of it. In his view, it hadn't been a mere accident. It had been criminal negligence.

The first and longest chapter of the course manual was aimed at preventing such injuries and deaths. Reading those pages, we learned how various rifle and shotgun mechanisms worked, and how to handle, operate, and transport them safely. In class, we paraded around the room, demonstrating different ways of carrying a firearm, always with the emphasis on muzzle control: keeping the gun pointed away from humans. We read about establishing directional "zones of fire" when hunting with others, to keep from shooting each other. We reviewed the critical importance of identifying animals from head to tail, never shooting at a flash of movement, a sound, or a shape. And we talked about rifle ballistics—a bullet can travel for miles—and the imperative to never shoot at an animal "skylined" in an open field or on the crest of a hill above you.

Again and again, the instructor hammered the message home: "You have to be absolutely certain. Once you fire, you can never call that bullet back." The thought was sobering.

On the one hand, the course manual pointed out that hunting was safe. Statistics bear out the claim: Eight reported injuries per year per hundred thousand hunters. Hundreds—even thousands—of injuries per year per hundred thousand people who skateboard, ride bicycles, or play sports like baseball, soccer, and football. Annual firearm-related fatalities among hunters are less than one in a hundred thousand; more hunters die from car accidents driving to and from their hunting locations and from heart attacks in the field. And the more precautions hunters take—handling firearms with strict discipline, wearing blaze-orange clothing, and so on—the safer their pursuit becomes. The chance of a nonhunter's life ending at the hands of a hunter is less than one in a million; it's at least fifteen times more common to be killed by lightning, at least fifty times more common to be killed by hitting a deer with your car, and thousands of times more common to be killed by a careless driver.

On the other hand, hunting was optional. I might have to drive to work or to the grocery store, but I did not have to carry a lethal weapon in the woods. That was a choice. Weighing the heavy responsibility that came with it, I was only half sure it was one I wanted to make. Safety statistics couldn't dispel the images from my imagination: two cousins standing near one another moments before a deer appeared, a man watching Sunday football in his living room, a young mother stepping out her back door in Maine. Did I really want to hunt? More precisely, did I really want to mess with guns?

I knew some people who saw guns as sinister, alien objects. In their eyes, firearms were instruments of death and destruction. Looking at a rifle or pistol, they saw extreme danger, perhaps even a manifestation of evil. They would no sooner pick up a shotgun than a live cobra. Weren't guns the primary implements used by the powerful to oppress the powerless? Didn't they make conflict and warfare immeasurably more lethal? Historically, wasn't it guns that enabled European domination of American Indians and of so many other peoples around the globe? Today, wasn't it guns that made crime so violent?

I knew other people who saw guns as reassuring and familiar. In their eyes, firearms were instruments of self-defense, self-reliance, and sustenance. Looking at a gun, they saw a powerful weapon that ought to be respected and handled with care. They would no sooner give up their Second Amendment right "to keep and bear arms" than their right to "life, liberty, and the pursuit of happiness." Weren't guns the only implements with which the powerless could resist the powerful? Didn't they secure American liberty in the first place? Historically, wasn't it guns that allowed frontier hunters and settlers to provide for their families? Today, wasn't a gun in hand the only defense one truly had against violent crime?

I didn't stand in either camp. Though my father hadn't really been into guns, he had owned a few: a scoped .222 rifle, an old bolt-action .410 shotgun, and the six-shot .22 revolver he used to dispatch the occasional hen-killing raccoon. He didn't encourage me to be interested in firearms, but he did want me to be at ease with them—careful and unafraid, respecting them for their explosive power, seeing them simply as a kind of tool. As a boy, I enjoyed hours of innocent fun, plinking cans. In middle school, I built a simple pine gun rack in shop class, hung it on the wall beside the bunk bed Willie had made, set my father's long guns and my .22 rifle into the three felt-lined holders, and slept easily.

Yet as a boy I had also watched a family friend and Vietnam Special Forces veteran close his trembling lips around the blued steel end of a rifle barrel. When he sat down on the rock and asked me to hand him his .22, I had no idea what was coming. I don't remember anything he said. I just remember him putting the muzzle in his mouth and sliding one hand down toward the trigger. I stood there, transfixed, taking what reassurance I could from what I knew: He wasn't going to die if he squeezed the trigger. I had been carrying the gun and was certain there was no cartridge in the chamber. A long minute later, he withdrew the barrel, his hands and face trembling. He pointed the rifle at an old tree stump nearby and squeezed. At the click, he laughed: a small, choking sound.

In college, shortly before getting rid of my .22 and my father's few firearms, I had volunteered for a nonprofit that advocated peace and nonviolence, and had worn the organization's emblem pinned to my jacket: a tiny rifle, broken in half.

More recently, reconsidering guns, I had talked with Willie. He told me how he occasionally walked from his apartment just outside Boston to a local indoor shooting range, his fold-up .22 rifle in a briefcase. The shooting centered him, demanding that he focus. When he was off center, it gave him clear feedback. "The target doesn't lie to me," he said. Another friend—an engineer who had been a competitive shooter and occasional hunter in his youth—expressed a similar view: "I've never had any experience more meditative." I recalled my boyhood shooting and that focused, still-minded zone I had come to know, the one that kept my bullets consistently in the center of the target or kept the plinked can spinning, struck again before it could come to rest.

Just a few months before the hunter-education course, I had purchased a used bolt-action .22, nearly identical to the one I'd had as a teenager. It was disorienting to own a firearm again, after more than a decade away from them. Yet it was also familiar. Taking time to adjust the rifle's sights and get to know it well, memories were triggered: the smooth feel of a hardwood stock, the image of a front sight just below the target's center, the sharp smell of gunpowder. Though Cath had no fondness for guns, she did not object, provided I put safety first.

As far as I could tell, my fellow hunter-education students shared none of my ambivalence. Once, an instructor led us outside to where he had set up two targets depicting silhouettes of a wild turkey's head. With the class safely behind him, most of us covering our ears, he fired an old-style 12-gauge. The standard-length shell gave an emphatic blast, spraying the target with pellets. The kids smiled. Then the man fired a second, more modern gun. The magnum shell roared with pyrotechnic power and the target rocked as if struck by a baseball bat. The kids oohed and ahhed, laughing and nodding their approval.

Only dimly, in the recesses of memory, could I recall a time when I might have shared their wholehearted zeal. Now, I found it too easy to imagine the consequences of such a blast, should a human be mistaken for a game bird. We had been warned that turkey hunters—sitting on the ground, imitating turkey sounds, and wearing full camo to elude detection by the birds' sharp, color-sensitive eyes—had to be extracareful not to shoot each other.

Another chapter in the course manual addressed the topic of "hunter responsibility." This encompassed legal responsibility, of course: the cut-and-dried business of understanding and obeying hunting regulations. But it also encompassed the broader—and, in my view, more engaging—arena of ethics.

Hunters, the manual stated, must "think and care about wildlife, landowners, other hunters, and themselves." The guidelines for thinking and caring about myself included the obvious: Handle firearms carefully and don't hunt with folks who treat them like toys. The guidelines for caring about other people were straightforward as well: Respect others' ways of hunting, ask permission before hunting on private land, respect people's property and privacy, don't litter, and, again, handle firearms safely.

But what about that first proposed object of thought and care—wildlife?

As both a longtime vegetarian and a would-be hunter, animals were at the forefront of my mind. Yet the chapter on responsibility and ethics offered just one guideline for thinking and caring about them while they were alive—make a "clean kill"—and one for thinking and caring about them once they were dead—remove the entrails promptly to cool the body and keep the meat from spoiling.

I don't suppose I had expected much more. Like most U.S. hunter-education courses, Vermont's only totaled about thirteen hours and focused on preventing the accidental shooting of humans. Unlike some European courses, this one would not involve extensive study of wildlife biology. Yet it struck me as odd that the manual had so little to say about the living beings to be hunted.

Even the manual's discussion of making a swift, "humane" kill was marked by clinical detachment. It was important, the manual said, to kill with a single shot that minimized destruction of meat. It was a way of showing respect for the animal. Making such a kill required that the hunter know the anatomy of his or her prey, as well as his or her own limitations. The hunter must shoot only when the animal was close enough to insure a direct hit to vital organs, and only when nothing obstructed the flight path of bullet or arrow.

During one class, students had the opportunity to shoot laser guns at animals on a video screen—part of a training package intended to help new hunters learn when to shoot and where to aim. Watching the kids happily squeezing the triggers, I thought of my own boyhood enjoyment of arcade games. And I wondered: Were these youngsters getting the point of the exercise, or was it suggesting to them that hunting was as harmless as a video game?

Other than a vague reference or two to the risk of "crippling" an animal, the manual said nothing about the consequences of failing to make a clean kill. There was not one statement about how animals might suffer, not one mention of compassion. The word "humane" was the only tacit acknowledgment of philosopher Jeremy Bentham's centuries-old point—that animals *can* suffer. In studying firearm safety, we had watched a video reenactment of a shooting accident in which a boy killed his best friend. In studying the importance of making a clean kill, might not video footage of a few injured animals help drive the point home?

To their credit, the instructors did talk with us further, encouraging a sincere ethic of care. But I wasn't convinced that every student took their words seriously. Each time ethics were mentioned, one father would roll his eyes and lean over to whisper in his young son's ear. The boy would laugh.

One evening, I stayed after class to chat with the lead instructor. I asked him about the ethics issues we had been discussing in class, particularly concerning animals. He said he thought most hunters took them seriously. Most took care to make clean kills and ate the meat. But he told me about a moose that had been shot illegally and left to rot in Groton State Forest, just a few miles from where I live. It had been deer season and the hunter just wanted to kill something.

"I know some of these families," the instructor said. "As soon as some of these kids leave the classroom, I know they're being told, 'Don't listen to any of that stuff.'" There was a frustrated edge to his voice. "Their dads and uncles will tell them, 'If you see a deer on posted property, just shoot it in the gut and it'll run a long way to somewhere where you can get it.'" Thirteen hours of formal hunter education would not, I thought, put much of a dent in thirteen years of informal family training.

One section in the chapter on responsibility and ethics was titled "Positive Public Image." As part of being a responsible hunter, it said, "there are certain things one must do to project a positive image of hunting to the public." The items in the checklist below—obeying laws, being safe, respecting other people, picking up litter, eating the animals you kill, not abusing alcohol or drugs, and so on—were, I agreed, vital to hunter responsibility and ethics.

What did it mean, though, to couch them in terms of "public image"? As the hunter I was becoming, I certainly intended to abide by this code of conduct and wanted my fellow hunters to do the same. And I knew, having long been a member of the non-hunting public, that hunting had an image problem.

But the phrase "project a positive image of hunting" raised my hackles. It smacked of PR. What I wanted to see change was reality, not representation. I had no interest in helping to craft an image that in any way obscured the ugliness of a moose killed senselessly or a deer dying slowly of a shot to the gut.

Hunters, I realized, face a problem shared by many minorities: identity in the eyes of the majority. No single set of behaviors can be ascribed to them all, yet nonhunters often identify them as a singular group. If hunting was more common—like driving, say—we would make more sophisticated distinctions. Just as we can encounter bad drivers without drawing conclusions about all drivers, we would be able to encounter bad hunters without drawing conclusions about all hunters. Just as we can criticize drunk driving and road rage without condemning all driving, we would be able criticize poaching and cruelty without condemning all hunting.

Later in the manual, another section title jumped out at me: "Would it Survive Without Hunting?" I did a double take. I knew that "it" meant animals. In my years as a vegan and anti-hunter, such a question would have struck me as more than a little bizarre. And it still did. Now, though, I genuinely wanted to understand this brave new world of hunter-speak.

The question was posed in the context of a brief lesson in the history of North America's wildlife conservation model. The chapter noted how sport hunters rallied against nineteenth-century market hunting, championed wildlife conservation, and helped bring about the Lacey Act of 1900.

It highlighted how hunters, including Aldo Leopold and Theodore Roosevelt, advocated scientific wildlife management, and also how hunters have funded that management. In 1937, the Federal Aid in Wildlife Restoration Act—commonly known as the Pittman-Robertson Act—instituted an excise tax on firearms and other hunting equipment. Since then, revenues have provided states with over $4 billion for wildlife research, habitat protection, and hunter education. (A parallel excise tax on fishing equipment, initiated in 1950, has similarly funded fisheries research and restoration.) And hunting and fishing license fees have long been the core funding source for state fish and wildlife agencies. Additionally, hunters support a host of non-profit conservation organizations. Ducks Unlimited, for instance, has conserved over twelve million acres of North American waterfowl habitat since its inception in 1937.

The intended take-home messages were clear. First, hunting can benefit wildlife. Regulated hunting does not threaten or endanger wildlife populations. Rather, it serves as an effective wildlife management tool and makes huge contributions to successful conservation programs. Second, the North American model is a democratic system that makes hunting widely accessible to citizens. With the instruments of law and science, wildlife populations are managed as a sustainable public resource. It was, I thought, a good reminder of the oft-forgotten roles played by hunters in the past century of this continent's faunal history.

The word "resource" bothered me, though. When I started logging a few years earlier, I had felt uncomfortable thinking about living trees as mere volumes of material. I felt even more uncomfortable thinking about animals that way.

In the hunter-education manual, one diagram depicted wildlife as liquid overflowing a vat. Since habitat (the vat) can sustainably support just so many animals, there is an annual "surplus" in animal "production." This surplus of extra animals is drained off through various leaks and spigots: starvation, disease, car accidents, animal predation, and hunting. Considering the image,

I wondered what implications such an economic and scientific framework might have for us, for our fellow creatures, and for our understanding of them. I didn't know what it would be like to kill and eat a wild animal, but I was sure it would feel nothing like opening a spigot. (Nor, reflecting on the manual's euphemistic references to "harvesting," did I think it would feel much like picking a zucchini.)

And I had other questions, too. Was hunter-driven conservation the only way to go, or even the best? Did such an approach encourage us to think in terms of whole ecological systems? I was skeptical of humanity's ability to understand the complexities of nature with enough precision to "manage" it predictably. And I was more skeptical yet of a management system primarily motivated by hunters' desires and funded by their wallets.

Prominent game species, the hunter-education manual reported, have thrived under modern wildlife management. In 1907, for instance, only about 41,000 elk survived in the United States. By 2000, their population had rebounded to 1.2 million. In the same century, wild turkey numbers soared from an estimated 100,000 to 5.6 million.

Less popular game animals have not fared as well. The inauspiciously named Lesser Prairie Chicken of the southern Great Plains, for example, has received little conservation attention from hunters. Its numbers have declined by more than 90 percent in the past hundred years, mainly due to habitat loss, and it is now a candidate for protection under the Endangered Species Act.

The question that had struck me as so odd—"Would it Survive Without Hunting?"—began to make a strange kind of sense. Non-game and unpopular game species might benefit as a side effect of habitat protection intended to support popular game animals, but it was nothing like being in the spotlight. If animals understood the mechanics of hunter-driven conservation, I could imagine a bizarre contest ensuing, each species jumping up and down and shouting, "Hunt us! Hunt us!"

In some ways, the system's bias toward game species resembles what native peoples were doing long before Europeans set foot on this continent. Recall, for instance, that their periodic burning of the forest understory in what is now Massachusetts appears to have been aimed at increasing populations of deer and elk and making them easier to hunt. The contexts are different, however. Very few present-day New Englanders subsist on wild meat, and our obligations to the flora and fauna around us have become more and more complex, as we impose threats that would have been unimaginable five centuries ago. The Massachusetts Audubon Society estimates that in 1986, at the peak of the housing boom, more than eighty acres of open land—most of them forested—were lost to construction every day. By the early 2000s, that rate had dropped to twenty-two acres per day, but that still adds up to more than twelve square miles each year.

Whatever the ecological merits or failings of the hunter-and-angler-funded conservation model, its most pressing fault today is financial. The percentage of Americans who hunt has been waning for decades. Resulting revenue declines have impaired wildlife agencies' conservation, research, education, and law-enforcement efforts and have left states without the matching funds necessary to claim much-needed federal money. At the end of fiscal year 2006, for instance, Vermont left $2.9 million in federal funds on the table.

A few states have taken bold steps to spread the burden of conservation funding beyond hunters and anglers. In 1969, for example, Aldo Leopold's son A. Starker and two other consultants conducted a study of the Missouri Department of Conservation. They concluded that the state's conservation programs lacked the money necessary to safeguard the outdoors against development and to provide recreation opportunities for residents. Seven years later, the citizens of Missouri did the unthinkable: They voted to tax themselves. In a public referendum, they approved an amendment to the state constitution, increasing the sales tax by one-eighth of a cent and dedicating the resulting funds to conservation programs. In 1996, Arkansas followed suit, passing a nearly identical measure.

In 2002, both states published progress reports. In twenty-five years, Missouri had accomplished a great deal. Conservation education facilities had been constructed near all of the state's major population centers, access to 530 new lakes and 290 new sections of rivers and streams had been established, nearly 1,000 hunter-education classes were being offered annually, dozens of long-term habitat research projects were under way, free forest-management education and assistance were being provided across the state, and the list goes on. In just five years, Arkansas had purchased over 20,000 acres of new public-use land, completed the first of four planned nature centers, added thirty officers to its warden force, and more. A little public funding—in these cases, a mere eighth-of-a-cent sales tax—goes a long way.

What struck me most about the chapter on conservation, though, had nothing to do with ecology or economics. Reading those pages, I felt as if I had entered an alternate reality. After more than three decades of living in a world where hunting was said to be not good for much, I had stepped into a world where hunting was said to be good for everything.

Regulated hunting, the manual stated, was a crucial force for conservation and had brought about the resurgence of an entire continent's wildlife. When such resurgence was too successful—as in the case of white-tailed deer, which are now heavily overpopulated along the Eastern Seaboard—regulated hunting served as a crucial management tool, helping to keep animals wild and to bring populations back into balance with habitat and with human use of the landscape. (There was no mention of how humans ended up being the only predators available to keep deer populations in check, no mention of our systematic extermination of wolves and cougars, starting here in New England and working our way west.) The chapter even noted that hunting helped foster the American pioneer spirit.

True as that all might be, I couldn't help thinking of philosopher Abraham Kaplan's oft-quoted law of the instrument: "Give a small boy a hammer, and he will find that everything he encounters needs pounding."

And something else caught my attention, too. Behind the explicit claims about the positive roles played by regulated hunting, I sensed two other suggestions.

The first was obvious. If the Lesser Prairie Chicken might not survive without hunting, or if white-tailed deer might become too numerous, then hunting must be necessary. As a society, we *have* to hunt. Considering what I knew about the number of whitetails killed each year to keep North American agriculture viable, I realized there was some truth to this.

A second suggestion seemed to follow, however: Individual hunters hunt because they must. The manual never actually stated that hunters were motivated by a sense of duty to conserve or manage wildlife, but the notion seemed implicit. I balked. Hunters might genuinely love and appreciate the natural world in all its splendor and diversity, but it seemed terribly unlikely to me that many hunters took to fields, woods, and marshes to save animals from extinction, or to prevent damage to farm crops or flower gardens.

In a 1990 paper, Cornell University researchers Daniel J. Decker and Nancy A. Connelly argued that hunters needed to know more about deer overpopulation and be more effective in alleviating it. They noted that few hunters identified wildlife management as a reason for hunting when it was presented in a list with other reasons. "Although hunters commonly use the notion of 'hunting as a management tool' to justify hunting," the authors observed, "they generally do not seem committed to this purpose."

Was the hunter-education manual intended, in part, to arm hunters against criticism, to help them justify and explain their hunting? No, let me amend that: Was it intended to help *me* justify and explain *my* hunting, to arm the hunter I was becoming against the antihunter I had been?

Thinking about it, I realized that the hunter-education course didn't mention motive at all. The topic wasn't addressed in the manual. Nor did it come up in class discussions.

Not that this silence surprised me—any such talk would involve difficult tracking through the complex terrain of the human heart. But there was an irony to it, given that public opinions on hunting depend heavily on perceptions of why people do it. According to a 2006 survey by the natural resources research firm Responsive Management, 85 percent of Americans approve of hunting for meat. In contrast, only 53 percent approve of hunting for sport and only 28 percent approve of hunting for trophies.

Looking around at the taxidermied heads on the fish and game club walls, I wondered how the hunters who had done the killing saw those mounts. Did they see them as proof of their capacity for domination? Did they see them as ways of honoring the animal they had killed, or as ways of preserving the memories of those days, those moments? It would be easy to assume that these hunters were what social ecologist and Yale University Professor Stephen R. Kellert—in a classic 1978 study of American attitudes toward wildlife and hunting—termed "dominionistic" hunters: people who hunted primarily to compete with and master animals. But perhaps some were what he called "utilitarian" hunters: people who hunted primarily to obtain food. Perhaps others were "nature hunters": people who hunted mainly to experience close contact with nature. It was impossible to know.

Looking around at the boys—and the few girls—in the class, I had no idea what motivated them either. Would they, most of them following in their fathers' or uncles' footsteps, hunt primarily for the challenge of it? Would they hunt for a sense of connection to food and land? Would they hunt for camaraderie, for the pleasure of sharing an outdoor tradition with friends and family? Or would they hunt for all these reasons and more?

Kellert's threefold typology of hunters—"dominionistic," "utilitarian," and "nature"—was a useful analytic tool, allowing him to make comparisons among various groups. He observed, for instance, that dominionistic hunters and antihunters shared an intriguing characteristic: Both scored quite low on questions measuring their knowledge of animals. But, as Kellert noted, these three "ideal" types were artifacts of sociology. Each described only some of the attitudes and motives of any single hunter.

I knew there must be motivational differences among hunters. I could not imagine that the hunger felt by those hunters who, in at least a few corners of the world, still truly depended on wild animals for subsistence resembled the hunger that drove trophy hunters aiming to get their names in record books. Nor did I think that Uncle Mark was drawn to the woods by the same forces that motivated the father and son who guffawed at the instructors' discussions of ethics.

Yet I also knew that even my own motives could not be neatly divided and compartmentalized. I would be hunting to confront the death of fellow vertebrates, yes. And I would be hunting to learn about myself and the place I inhabited, to be nourished by the land and participate in its rhythms, and to answer a call for which I had no name. I could not separate these things. Together, my reasons formed a complex web. Why should other hunters' motives be any different, any simpler? Perhaps their reasons, too, like the interdependent organisms of the forest—hare and bobcat, maple and deer, ant and woodpecker—were deeply intertwined, impossible to understand in isolation.

On a Saturday morning in mid-September, we gathered for the final class. Following a multiple-choice exam, we headed out to the shooting range. There, under the close supervision of an instructor, who handed us live cartridges one at a time, we each fired five shots with a .22, aiming at a paper target twenty-five yards away. Keeping the rifle pointed downrange was required. Operating the bolt, safety, and trigger mechanisms without mishap was also required. Hitting the mark was not. Though most of the group's shooting was good—bullet holes clustering in and around the bull's-eyes—at least one target survived without a single blemish.

Passing the course was, I reflected, no proof of preparedness to hunt. The real education of American hunters still depends on the traditional transmission of knowledge and skills from one generation to the next. I hoped that the kids who had completed the course alongside me would have good guidance—in safety and in ethics—when they spent their first eager days afield.

At the conclusion of the live-fire exercise, the head instructor handed us each a blaze-orange Hunter Firearms Safety card, the document required to purchase a hunting license. One man looked down at his young son and asked, "Do you think we could possibly get to the store and buy that license fast enough?" The round-faced boy grinned widely and shook his head: No, not even sixty miles an hour would be fast enough.

I wasn't in that kind of hurry. Though Vermont's most popular hunting season—the two weeks of rifle hunting for deer—was still two months off, I had no plans to hunt that autumn. I wasn't equipped for it yet, in all kinds of ways.

8

A Hunter's Prayer

No culture has yet solved the dilemma each has faced with the growth of a conscious mind: how to live a moral and compassionate existence when one is fully aware of the blood, the horror inherent in all life, when one finds darkness not only in one's own culture but within oneself.

—Barry Lopez, *Arctic Dreams*

That fall I hunted through Uncle Mark's eyes.

In mid-October, he sent an e-mail about his first outing in archery season on Cape Cod, recounting the quiet pleasure he took in watching the woods come to life at dawn. Chickadees landed on branches within arm's reach, calling *dee-dee-dee*. A gray squirrel scolded as a big hawk swooped low. Shafts of early sunlight pierced the woods, illuminating a nearby patch of yellow ferns. After a day of rain, the fragrances of pine needles and oak leaves were strong.

In November, he sent pictures from his annual pilgrimage to Virginia, where his longtime buddy Jay has a cabin in the Blue

Ridge Mountains. One photo showed their old-fashioned caplock muzzleloaders, crafted from do-it-yourself kits years earlier: the reddish stock of Mark's nearly as dark as mahogany with a crescent brass butt plate, the wood of Jay's nearly blond, its butt plate carved of moose antler.

Another photo was of a vulture. The first morning of the hunt, Mark had let two deer pass, neither close enough for him to feel certain of a clean kill. The second morning, another had appeared in thick cover nearby. It had taken ten minutes for the young buck to wander into a tiny clearing where Mark could finally take a twig-free shot, enough time for his heartbeat to double and his hands to start trembling. "There was also plenty of time," he wrote, "to say the hunter's prayer about a dozen times: 'Lord, let me kill clean . . . and if I can't kill clean, let me miss clean.'" The buck had gone down on the spot. In the photo, the vulture stood by the bones and scraps that Mark returned to the woods. Mark had jotted a caption on the back: "Nature's recycling."

Back on Cape Cod, Mark sent an e-mail describing the last morning of archery season. Over the previous six weeks, he had hunted his favorite spot ten times without seeing a single deer. That last morning, though, after several hours of waiting, he heard a whitetail coming. The four-point buck strolled within twenty feet, so close that Mark could see his eyelashes and whiskers as he pawed the ground, then lifted his head to lick an overhanging branch. The buck paused in a shaft of morning sunlight, his coat shimmering with golden highlights. Then he took a few steps and stood broadside to Mark, his entire head behind a tree. It was a bowhunter's dream shot—the angle perfect, the deer unable to see the archer raise his bow. "I never did draw an arrow," Mark wrote. "It was just wonderful to be so close to such an incredible animal."

That, I thought, was how I wanted to hunt. Appreciating everything I saw, heard, and smelled. Admiring my fellow creatures and enjoying their presence. Not caring too much whether deer came my way. Often letting animals pass by. Choosing my shots carefully. Killing swiftly.

I was not my uncle, though. He had been hunting for nearly forty years, having started in his teens. In my teens, I had been on the brink of veganism. Hearing Mark's experiences and insights was helpful as I thought more seriously about becoming a hunter. But I had my own sorting out to do before I took to the woods, bow or gun in hand.

How would the compassion and respect I had for animals inform my hunting? Having grown up without a hunting tradition of any kind—in a broader culture that saw nature and wildlife as little more than scenery—what meanings would frame my experiences afield?

Inside the front cover of the hunter-education manual, I had come across a quote from one José Ortega y Gasset. As the manual's one oblique reference to hunters' motives, it annoyed me from the start: "To the sportsman the death of the game is not what interests him; that is not his purpose."

I soon discovered that the Spaniard was a luminary of hunting philosophy. His little volume *Meditations on Hunting*—originally published in 1942 as a long-winded prologue to another man's book—is quoted so often in the literature of hunting that it has taken on near-scriptural status. Reading it, I decided I was a heretic. Here and there, I wanted to underline a sentence, noting my emphatic agreement. Mostly, I wanted to cram the margins with question marks, exclamation points, and words of protest. (Unable to mark up a pristine hardcover the way I would a paperback, I did neither.)

Working my way through Ortega's flowery prose and convoluted logic, I could see why Edward Abbey referred to him as "that sly sophist." Ortega celebrates the "exemplary moral spirit of the sporting hunter" who hunts for diversion, but looks down on the "utilitarian" hunter, who, like "Paleolithic man . . . the poacher of any epoch," hunts for food.

> A sport is the effort which is carried out for the pleasure that it gives in itself and not for the transitory result that the effort brings forth. . . . In utilitarian hunting the true purpose of the hunter, what he seeks and values, is the death of the animal. Everything else that he does before that is merely a means for achieving that end, which is its formal purpose.

Ortega misses a crucial point. What the utilitarian hunter seeks and values is not death. It is life: food. But Ortega goes on.

> In hunting as a sport this order of means to end is reversed. To the sportsman the death of the game is not what interests him; that is not his purpose. What interests him is everything that he had to do to achieve that death—that is, the hunt. Therefore what was before only a means to an end is now an end in itself.

Setting aside the fact that some sport hunters do seem quite interested in "the death of the game," I agreed with Ortega, if only in part. There would, I imagined, be far more to hunting than the death of the animal. From personal experience, I knew that fishing could be compelling in and of itself. Part of the point was to be on the water in an old, battered rowboat, to learn the habits of the fish I sought and to master techniques that would fool them, to watch the complex, cross-patterning of riffles as the breeze changed direction, to stand on a bridge with an old friend at sunset. The process of the hunt could, I imagined, be equally compelling.

But, here again, Ortega misses something, for utilitarian hunters also find enjoyment in the hunt itself. As anthropologist Richard Nelson wrote in reflecting on a year he spent living in the Alaskan coastal village of Wainwright, "Inupiaq men lived to hunt as much as they hunted to live." In his attempt to establish a simplistic binary model of hunters and their motives, Ortega divorces means and ends, obscuring complexity and truth. Inupiaq men enjoyed hunting, and they also aimed to bring home an animal—a seal, perhaps—and to eat it. I enjoyed fishing, and I also intended to bring home fish, make use of my fillet knife, and take down one of our cast-iron skillets from where they hung beside the kitchen window.

Ortega's celebrated sportsman might live to hunt, but he does not hunt to live. And that makes the killing—and Ortega's explanation of it—more tenuous.

> Death is essential because without it there is no authentic hunting: the killing of the animal is the natural end of the hunt and that goal of hunting itself, not of the hunter. The hunter seeks this death because it is no less than the sign of reality for the whole hunting process. To sum up, one does not hunt in order to kill; on the contrary, one kills in order to have hunted.

That last bizarre line—enough to make one wonder about the accuracy of the translation from Spanish to English—may be Ortega's most frequently quoted phrase. On first reading it, printed there inside the front cover of the hunter-education manual, I had no words for the feelings of irritation and offense that welled up within. If I could have articulated a reply in the moment, it would have been far less civil than Edward Abbey's: "Not good enough."

Ortega's ideal sportsman kills not to eat, but to fulfill some kind of symbolic necessity. The animal's death is a "sign" that the hunt is "authentic" and "real." To my ear, such insistence on authenticity suggested one thing clearly: The philosopher's hunter was out of touch with reality. Why else would he need a sign of it? Would the Inupiaq kill seals or other creatures merely to assure themselves that they were really hunting? What kind of deranged angler would I be if I beheaded trout so I could think, *Ah, now I have authentically fished?*

The philosopher's sportsman, moreover, seems to be above mere killing. Killing is "the natural end of the hunt and that goal of hunting itself, not of the hunter." What are we to make of this hunt that apparently hurtles toward a natural end of its own accord, without a hunter who really wants—let alone needs—to kill? What are we to make of this sportsman who does not hunt to eat, who—immune to such contamination—has risen above the base realities of life and death?

Ortega's case for the superiority of sport hunting over utilitarian hunting stems from a fundamental cultural arrogance. Tribes who depend on hunting for survival, he writes, "represent the most primitive human species that exists." Ignorant as these primitive brutes are—lacking "the slightest hint of government, of legislation, of authority"—their hunting and their philosophical understanding of it must, naturally, be inferior to those of civilized Europe. But it is his own ignorance—of tribal cultures such as the Inupiaq of the Arctic and the San of the Kalahari, and of their enormously complex "utilitarian" hunting traditions—that Ortega demonstrates.

I was thankful to find a kindred skeptic in Robert Kimber. His book *Living Wild and Domestic* helped clarify why Ortega's attitude toward utilitarian hunters and "primitive" tribes bothered me so intensely. "It is the utilitarian hunter dependent on the hunt for sustenance," Kimber writes, "who will have the greatest knowledge of, and respect for, his wild brethren and whose culture will make that knowledge and respect manifest in its arts, rituals, myths, and day-to-day behavior."

The sport hunter, Ortega admits, is never as skilled as the true subsistence hunter: "Today's best-trained hunter cannot begin to compare his form to that of the sylvan actions of the present-day pygmy or his remote counterpart Paleolithic man." He even allows that the modern European subsistence hunter is more skilled than the sport hunter. But, for Ortega, that modern subsistence hunter is an uncivilized brute: "the poacher," an "eternal troglodyte" who "always smells a little like a beast."

Call me a troglodyte then. Unlike the Inupiaq, I did not need to hunt to survive. But it was for food—not for a sign that my hunting was real—that I would take aim at a whitetail's heart.

Prowling through a local used bookstore one day, I paused in front of the small shelf devoted to hunting and fishing. My eyes fastened on a beige-and-yellow spine bearing the title *A Hunter's Heart*. As soon as I opened the book, I knew I was in good company.

In the introduction, I learned that Richard Nelson—whose account of the vast numbers of deer killed to protect agricultural crops had brought me up short in my latter days as a vegan—had grown up opposed to hunting. As a boy he had believed that "hunting was entirely evil—no matter who did it, how they did it, or why." Yet, living among native peoples in Alaska, he had learned to hunt. Now, in middle age, he found hunting for food to be a vitally important part of his life, an activity that served to remind him that he was not separate from his fellow creatures but "twisted together with them in one great braidwork of life."

In the essays that followed, I encountered dozens of hunters—
and a few nonhunters—willing to ask hard questions, to write
honestly about animals and killing and eating. In one essay, philosopher Ann Causey tackled a deceptively simple question—"Is
hunting ethical?"—and contended that there is no simple answer.
In another, outdoor writer Mike Gaddis rejected the premise "that
life other than human is devoid of feeling and is, individually, of
small consequence." In yet another, farmer and professor George
Wallace—having shot an animal badly—stated bluntly, "If elk
would scream, the woods would have fewer hunters."

For me, the book opened up a whole landscape of recent
hunting literature. One essay, for instance—about hunting during
a brutally cold winter on the northern Great Plains when deer
died of malnourishment and froze solid—had been penned by
women's studies professor Mary Zeiss Stange. The essay led me
to Stange's intriguingly titled book, *Woman the Hunter*.

As a college student in Manhattan, I had studied feminism.
During that period, I read only one article about hunting. In it,
the author contended that hunting (violence against animals) and
environmental destruction (violence against nature) were both
akin to violence against women. All three were, in essence, rape.
The parallels made sense to me.

If I had come across other feminist critiques of hunting in those
years, I would almost certainly have agreed with them as well. I
would have been especially taken with activist Marti Kheel's essay
"License to Kill," in which she argues that all attempts to justify
hunting, and to link it to environmental ethics, serve a sinister
purpose: "to camouflage and to legitimate violence and biocide."
Kheel gives special attention to what she calls the "holy hunter,"
who uses the language of spirituality to mask his psychosexual
urge to dominate and kill.

Ten years later, I still cared deeply about animals. And I still
embraced the values summed up by the button I kept pinned to

my backpack in college: "Feminism: The Radical Notion That Women Are People." But now I was reading Stange alongside Kheel.

Kheel emphasizes that hunting has always been a predominantly male pursuit. Stange points out that one in ten American hunters is female and that hunting is becoming increasingly popular among women. Kheel contends that hunting is, in essence, a "quest to establish masculine identity in opposition to the natural world." Stange argues that such a simplistic understanding fails to account not only for women's hunting, but for men's hunting as well. Kheel, disturbed by the apparent similarities between the (presumably evil) ideology of the "holy hunt" and the (presumably good) ideology of ecofeminism, seeks to demonstrate that the two are diametrically opposed. Stange embraces these similarities, arguing that a meaningful understanding of women and men—indeed of all human existence in the greater natural world—must be rooted in a more complex moral framework.

Stange acknowledges that hunting—framed by the cultural myth of Man the Hunter—has long served as a metaphor for men's relationships with other humans, nonhuman animals, and the world in general. In short, men have been associated with aggression, domination, and the violent subjugation of other beings and of nature as a whole. Women, in contrast, have been associated with passivity, victimization, and the violently subjugated natural world.

This metaphor and its associations have, of course, been useful to defenders of the male-dominated status quo. If men—as hunters—are naturally aggressive, and women—as men's gathering and cooking helpmates—are naturally passive, then longstanding inequities can be explained and even justified. As Stange points out, however, ecofeminist critics like Kheel are retelling the same story. In valorizing women as nature-loving nurturers, ecofeminism romanticizes the natural world and perpetuates stereotypes about women's moral purity. Simultaneously, it perpetuates stereotypes about men as nature-hating killers; that is, as hunters.

In my college years, I would have resisted the idea that women can, and perhaps should, act just as violently as men. Now, though, I understood that Stange was making a far more complex point. The figure of Woman the Hunter has the potential to disturb both the male-dominated status quo and its ecofeminist critics. She can, and perhaps should, force us to rethink our cultural assumptions about women, men, and the human place in nature.

Considering the case Stange made, I realized that a female hunter had, in fact, helped open my eyes to what hunting could be. Cath and I met wildlife conservationist Susan Morse shortly after moving to Vermont and were immediately impressed. I had never heard anyone speak so passionately about the importance of habitat protection, particularly the danger of habitat fragmentation and the crucial need to protect the travel corridors that keep wildlife populations interconnected and genetically viable. Her love for wild animals was palpable.

"These are our neighbors," she said.

The next year, while Cath and I were taking part in a series of training sessions with Sue, learning how to collect field data on wildlife habitat, I discovered that she was a deer hunter. It did not compute. How could she spend the vast majority of her life working to understand and protect her wild "neighbors," and then turn around and kill one of them? Only years later, as the possibility of hunting began to bubble up into my own consciousness, did it begin to make sense.

In her early forties, Sue had recognized a basic disconnect: what she calls her "schizophrenia" about predation. Carnivores were the focus of most of her research. When she came across signs of a mammalian predator's successful hunt—perhaps a place where she could track a bobcat's stealthy movements in the snow and read the story's end in scattered turkey feathers—she celebrated, knowing the animal had survived another day. A meat eater, Sue had been raising lambs for years. She detested the cruelties and ecological impacts of the meat industry, and valued having a personal connection with the flesh foods she consumed. Yet she wasn't participating in the forest life cycles she studied.

By the time we met Sue, she was an avid hunter and hunter-education instructor who spoke candidly of her discomfort with the popular portrayal of hunting in television shows and videos. She saw far too much emphasis on competition and success in bagging game, far too little room left over for cherishing and respecting animals, for pausing to reflect on the meaning of hunting and killing. Even more vocally, she challenged hunters to become more active conservationists, to give back more to the land, to work at building people's awareness of the preciousness of all life, from invertebrates to wolves.

Sue pointed out that good hunting—like good birding, good hiking, and good berry picking—begins with good habitat. "Such habitat," she said, "includes the air that's breathed, clean waters, and productive soils, which grow the abundance and diversity of foods needed by deer and countless other species." And our vision of good habitat, she said, should also include people, with "our uniquely human capacity to partake of nature's harvest while steadfastly guarding its future." She contended that hunters, of all people, should understand "the relationship between a healthy natural environment and what makes us whole."

Echoing many of Sue's sentiments, another essay in *A Hunter's Heart* took hunters to task. It is high time, argued writer Ted Kerasote, to stop pretending that American hunting is always the conscientious, respectful activity it claims to be. Rather than denying the careless and gratuitously brutal attitudes and behaviors that characterize some hunters—ones that lodge themselves in the memories of nonhunters—Kerasote acknowledged that many of the charges leveled against hunting are well founded.

But he pointed out that disrespect of nature and animals is not unique to thoughtless hunters. As a whole, our society operates with little regard for its impacts. From rapacious development and logging to ecologically devastating agricultural practices and the application of toxic herbicides to suburban lawns, we inflict enormous damage—most of which we never see. A careless hunter's behavior may be visible and upsetting, but it is merely one facet of larger cultural patterns.

In his essay, Kerasote offered several ideas for reforming American hunting. He suggested, for instance, that hunter-education programs should be made more rigorous, with far more attention given to ethics, ecological knowledge, and shooting skills. (In his book *Bloodties*, Kerasote specifically suggests that U.S. hunter education should emulate the central European model, in which students must develop expert marksmanship and must also devote up to one hundred hours to studying wildlife biology and forestry.) Such a change, he acknowledged, would be hard to make. Many American hunters would protest, noting that participation is already declining, and arguing that another barrier is the last thing we need. State wildlife agencies would need to increase license fees or find alternative funding sources. And objections from the hunting-equipment industry would need to be overcome.

Having once become a vegetarian in an attempt to "outwit" the pain caused by his own eating, Kerasote also suggested that hunters publicize a more accurate accounting of the ecological and animal costs incurred by American diets and lifestyles. He suggested that women's participation in hunting be welcomed and encouraged. He suggested that the pursuit of record-book trophies be de-emphasized, and that killing competitions be condemned.

And he suggested that hunters reconsider the ways they talk and think about hunting, moving away from words like "sport" and "recreation." The concept of hunting as "sport" goes back to the ancient Greeks and the nobility of the Middle Ages, in whose agrarian societies hunting was no longer a matter of survival and had started to become a ritualized, rule-bound game. The term itself is an abbreviation of "disport," which goes back to the Old French word *desporter*, meaning to amuse or divert oneself—literally, to "carry" the mind "away" from serious matters. In the history of the idea and the word, Kerasote sees antecedents of the modern connotations of "sport," invoking everything from frivolous, individual amusement to the National Football League. Even in antiquity, hunting had been stripped of its original and most serious meaning: food.

But Kerasote's recommendations went deeper than specific fixes. He argued that the reformation of American hunting depends on recreating it as "the disciplined, mindful, sacred activity it once was for our species." Likewise, he suggested that the redemption of our culture as a whole depends on bringing greater compassion and restraint to our relationships with animals and nature, on returning to an attitude of reverence, humility, and mutual regard. And he contended that such a cultural reformation can only be accomplished if more of us participate in "the world that feeds us"—whether by hunting, fishing, gardening, or growing a bit of lettuce or basil in a pot by a window.

I concurred with Kerasote on many points, including his suggestion that hunting should be rooted in reverence. In taking an animal's life, I should be mindful not only of that creature's physical form—and its bodily capacity for suffering—but also of its spiritual essence. Matters of spirit, however, led me onto tricky ground.

Growing up, I'd had three allergies. In order of increasing severity: cat dander, dust mites, and organized religion. The first two might have been passed down genetically. The third might as well have been. My mother, raised Catholic, had rejected the church in her youth. My father, raised Protestant, had become a devout atheist. In his world, everything could be explained by science.

Before I was old enough to think about such things, some sense of mystery must have inhabited me. As I sit here writing, I pick up a small black-and-white photo from my desk. About four years old, I stand under the eaves of my father's house. A thin mantle of snow covers the ground. In the background, pines and white birches. I'm dressed in boots, pants, and hooded jacket. Pinned to the back of the jacket is a bird outfit made of white fabric, forked tail extending below my knees, wingtips reaching out beyond my hands. You can see that I've been decorating my regalia with a magic marker. On the left wing, the jumbled scrawlings include three mammalian figures. Behind the right shoulder is an oval with angular, finlike wedges radiating from one end; it might be a glyph for "fish." Affixed to the jacket's hood, a gauzy white mask envelops my face. Eyeholes are cut above the great beak. I'm looking up at a birdfeeder and the winged creatures that flit there. My hands are raised over my head, as if in supplication.

Now, examining the photo thirty-some years later, turning it to the light, I'm not sure what I was doing. Disguised as a bird, maybe I was simply hoping for the delicate, thrilling pinpricks of a chickadee alighting on my hand. Or maybe, never taught to pray at any other altar, I was appealing to the visible powers about me, seeking communion.

As an older boy and teenager, I adopted my father's atheistic views. I respected the moral teachings common to all religions, but had no patience for superstitious window dressing, let alone institutions that condemned other systems of belief, proselytized aggressively, exerted control over the faithful, preached peace while sanctifying brutality, and proclaimed themselves to be necessary intermediaries between people and their deities.

Once, in high school, my U.S. history teacher divided the class into two teams, each assigned to one side of the historical debate we were studying: slavery. It disturbed me to be assigned to the proslavery faction, arguing that white folks like me had the prerogative to enslave black folks like Willie. Nonetheless, I set about helping my team build its bigoted case. Like nineteenth-century slave owners, we turned to the Bible, and had no trouble finding precedent and justification for the ownership of fellow human beings. The ease with which we won the debate reminds me of the bumper sticker "Jesus called. He wants his religion back." (I'm sure the Prince of Peace isn't the only one. Mohammed has almost certainly left a similar message at Theology Central.)

Religion could, I knew, be separated from spirituality. Cath had parted ways with the Roman Catholic Church early in life, yet had kept her sense of the mystical alive. Willie had done the same. During our long talks in Boston that weekend when he returned my fillet knife, he told me that he had still been a boy when he recognized the hypocrisy of the church—the conceit that only Catholics went to heaven, the rolling out of the red funeral carpet for a New York Mafia boss while Willie's mother, a divorcee, was refused Communion. As an adult, he rarely set foot in church, but every night he got down on his knees to pray.

In my twenties, years after my father's death, I had begun to reconsider the question of spirit, of mystery. I realized I was not an atheist, but an agnostic. The concept of the "supernatural" still made no sense to me: Why banish the inexplicable upward, beyond the realm of nature? But I began to suspect that "nature" ran far deeper than the visible surface of the world, that webs of unseen force and meaning might connect all things. And I began to have experiences for which I had no language but that of spirit.

Once, walking along a woods trail near Bird Cottage, Cath and I found a tuft of downy feathers. *Turkey,* I thought, *or grouse.* A few yards farther on, we found another tuft. Then another. Wondering what happened there—what story those clumps of down told—I thought of Chickasaw poet and environmentalist Linda Hogan's essay "The Feathers." For years, Hogan had prayed for a feather from a living eagle. One morning she woke from a dream, saw a golden eagle flying toward her window, and ran outside. There, at the edge of the dirt road, lay a feather.

For no reason I can recall, Cath and I turned off the trail at a small brook. Upstream a short distance, we found another downy tuft and I thought of what Hogan had written about the mysterious forces at work in nature, what she called "simple powers, strange and real." If I ever emerged from the uncertain landscape of agnosticism, it would be as an animist: a movement not out of wilderness, but into it. How, Hogan asked, did the feather arrive just there, at the edge of the road by her house, just before she awoke from dream time?

I looked up, again for no reason I can think of. There, a few feet above my head, cradled by the branch of an evergreen, rested a single feather, russet with a black band and narrow strip of white at the tip. Red-tailed hawk. With a stick, I jostled the feather free and caught it in midair.

To account for such occurrences—even to grapple with the simple fact of being a conscious creature, alive in a world of simultaneous beauty and horror, where death feeds life in a constant, complex flow of calories and nutrients—I needed something more than logic, something more than emotion. Despite my allergy to it, was "religion" such a bad word for that something?

The word's ancient meanings are debated. Some contend that it comes from *religare*—meaning to rebind or reconnect—"lig" stemming from the same root as "ligament." Others suggest that it comes from *relegio* (reread), *relegere* (reconsider carefully), or *reslegere* (gather). In these times of alienation, of forgotten connections with nature, what could be more healing than a rebinding with the larger-than-human world, a rereading and reconsideration of our place within it? "For too long we have been away somewhere," the late Thomas Berry reminded us, "entranced with our industrial world of wires and wheels, concrete and steel, and our unending highways, where we race back and forth in continual frenzy."

If engaging with the sources of our bodily sustenance helped return our attention to the earth, why should not hunting be part of our rebinding and reconsideration? For some hunters, I knew that the hunt was a kind of Sabbath. In one e-mail, Uncle Mark had described it as "a time to listen to my senses and really *look* at what is there and slow down from our frenzied way of life." Time spent hunting, like time spent in the garden, was never wasted. And wild meat, like freshly plucked tomatoes and basil, was a kind of sacrament. Again, Uncle Mark: "I look at a deer as a great gift from the Higher Power and always give thanks when I manage to kill a whitetail."

In the back of my mind, a critical voice remained wary of the hunt as a path to communion. Some hunters might indeed resemble Kheel's "holy hunter"—reveling in the power to inflict pain and death, disguising it by speaking of earth and animals in soulful terms. Yet I wasn't at all certain that such clever sadists were found any more frequently among hunters than among the general population.

Listening to Sue Morse talk, or reading Uncle Mark's e-mails, I could not imagine that their words concealed a secret bloodlust. Their honest attempts to say why they hunted might be unintelligible to people who only ate food from Stop-n-Shop, prepackaged and prekilled, but their respect for nature was no mask.

Their compassion for animals and their concern for the health of the planet were undeniable. They, and others like them, chose hunting as a way of living in accord with the earth. They took to woods and fields, as Stange writes, "for the same inner reasons they always have: for food, of course, but also for connection, and for knowledge about what it means to be human in our complex and increasingly fragile world."

One week in late October when Cath was out of town, I thawed a hunk of moose steak, a gift from a local hunter. My first attempt at cooking and eating a chunk of wild meat seemed like an oddly private thing. If I was serious about going after meat on the hoof, I had to consider not only philosophical questions, but a practical one as well: How would it feel to cook and eat the flesh of a wild mammal?

After years of veganism, chicken and fish had seemed strange enough. Handling their flesh, I was intensely aware of their origins as living beings. Some of the chickens were ones I had seen pecking away in a friend's grassy yard. Some of the fish were ones I had caught and killed. Once they had been reduced to food, though, I didn't dwell on them as individual creatures.

Moose was different. Under my hand, the cool, firm muscle felt odd as I sliced. I sautéed it in a cast-iron skillet and made a creamy sauce with onions and mushrooms. The first bite felt strange, the flavor only distantly familiar. And there was more to it than just the texture and taste of red meat. With a piece of moose between my teeth, the huge, dark animal stood there, vivid in my imagination. Perhaps my awareness of the individual creature stemmed from his sheer size. Perhaps it stemmed from my categorization of moose as part of the local landscape, but—unlike cows or pigs—not part of the modern American diet. With the moose in mind, I took his body into mine uneasily, aware that I was in a nutritional relationship not just with mammals in general, but with this one in particular.

A night or two later, I sat down to the leftovers and found that the strangeness was gone. The flesh went down easily, tasting rich and good.

The next week, when I thawed another package the hunter had given me and prepared a venison scaloppine, Cath nodded her approval as well.

By late that fall, two months after completing the hunter-education course, I was seeing the land with new eyes. I noticed game trails with keener interest. When I crossed bobcat tracks—an early-season snow showing a round paw and the feline's telltale leading toe, much like my own middle finger—I was just a curious conservationist, hopeful for the cat's future in the region. But when I found sign of deer or hare, I became hungrily attentive to details and patterns. Mark had been sending me articles on tracking whitetails and when I came across fresh scrapes— patches where a recent dusting of snow had been disturbed and the leaves beneath pawed up—I looked to see where the buck was headed.

I dug around in a bottom drawer and came up with the well-worn belt Mark had made for me twenty-five years earlier, the leather band encircled by arrows. When he first gave it to me, I had to punch extra holes to snug it around my small hips. Now it was too short. I mentioned it to Mark and asked him for suggestions on how to make a new one for the big brass buckle.

A couple days before Christmas, a cardboard box arrived in the mail. Inside were a deer call and a new belt, decorated with arrows like the old one, but narrower and with its own buckle of polished deer antler bearing the scrimshawed image of a flint arrowhead Mark had scratched there years before. The belt went around my waist right away.

Also in the box was an old hunting knife Mark had found amidst his basement's bewildering array of tackle and gear. It was secured in a heavy-duty sheath he had crafted for me, a red buck on its front, black deer tracks hidden by the haft. I felt certain the knife would bring me luck.

A week into the new year, I went looking for hare tracks. An inch of fresh powder had fallen overnight, with an extra dusting in the morning. In the woods a quarter mile from home, I found fresh squirrel sign, what might have been old coyote prints, and some old deer tracks, now partially filled holes in the deep snow. I saw one spot where a grouse had roosted: a branch almost devoid of snow and, below it, curved brown droppings the thickness of a pencil. Still hopeful, I headed for a big fallen aspen where, a few weeks before, I had found several snowshoe-hare trails converging. The hares had, it seemed, been taking shelter in a gap under the trunk, safe from the predatory eyes of owls. Today, though, no tracks.

I headed home and, on a whim, checked the woods just to the other side of the house. There I found a set of hare prints, big rear feet set down ahead of the smaller front feet. Even under a thick canopy of spruce and balsam, the tracks were covered with a dusting of snow and could have been many hours old. But I decided to follow anyway. Maybe I would find another spot where hares were taking shelter.

In one stretch, the hare had meandered slowly, making little hops of a foot or so, stopping, changing directions. In the next stretch, it had covered ground rapidly, two and three yards between tracks. Rounding a small knoll, I noted where the animal had paused and stood to nibble the bud of a maple seedling, the toes of each rear foot clearly outlined.

The tracks led into a thick patch of softwood saplings and then, still on the same few acres, started heading roughly back the way I had come. When the tracks intersected and passed close by that same nibbled maple seedling, it occurred to me: I would have noticed this set of prints when I came through here five minutes ago. I leaned over to look more closely. Yes, the edges of the tracks were sharp. The trail was hot.

Not that I had any illusions about my chances of catching up to the creature whose delicate signs I followed. I was no coyote or bobcat. I was no tireless Kalahari tracker or stealthy latter-day Hawkeye. I was slow and loud, my clumsy booted feet propelling my gangly hundred-and-fifty-pound body along, my boots cracking the icy crust and, at every fifth or sixth step, breaking through with a startling crunch. No wild creature could fail to hear me coming, least of all a lagomorph with big, hypersensitive ears.

I slowed, stopped for a minute to survey the woods ahead, galumphed onward, and stopped to look again. I was staring straight ahead into the brushy, dead tangle of a fallen balsam top. And there crouched the hare, its dark eye staring back at me from fewer than ten yards away, confident in its wintry white-coated camouflage. We had come round to within a few dozen yards of where our paths first crossed. The .22 came up, the safety eased off, the sights steadied behind the hare's eye.

Part of me took the shot and gutted the animal. Part of me watched, digesting the idea.

Seeing this living being transformed into meat, the stain of blood on snow, grief welled up inside. The feeling was stronger than anything I had ever felt in the act of catching or beheading fish. It wasn't, I thought, just that I had numbed myself through repetition, through killing hundreds of fish over the years. Nor was my mind crowded with images of Thumper; I had, thankfully, been raised on a low-Disney diet. If anything, I would have thought of the rabbits of *Watership Down*. But Hazel, Fiver, and Bigwig weren't haunting me either. No, there was something more basic at work here, some primal mammalian sympathy. Clumsily, I murmured a prayer of thanks and apology.

Hunting, I had felt compelled by the chase. But why had I killed? I had wanted to succeed in my first hunt, yes. But, having done so, did I need the meat from this particular warm, limp form? Clearly not. My body did not depend on this one for survival. What I did need was the honest confrontation, the reminder of what it means to eat. This one creature's heart had stopped beating, but its flesh was far from lifeless. It would go on, not as bobcat or coyote or owl, but as human.

Cath had been out that afternoon. By the time she came in the front door, the meat was simmering on the stove top, a recipe Mark said he used for gray squirrel. Curious, Cath sniffed the air.

"What's for dinner?"

9
Healing Ground

I go to Nature to be soothed and healed, and to have
my senses put in tune once more.
                   —John Burroughs, "The Gospel of Nature"

Willie said the doctors had caught his cancer early. There
were no symptoms. It had just shown up during a routine
exam and was still highly treatable. The surgery would be no
problem. He told me he wasn't worried.

In September, a couple weeks after his operation, Cath and I
headed to the coast of southern Maine for a weekend getaway.
Willie was tired, still regaining his strength, but said he felt up to
seeing us. We picked him and Beth up, and drove over to one of
their favorite restaurants in Portsmouth, crossing the Piscataqua
not far from where it flows into the open Atlantic. Though tired—
his affect softer than usual—Willie was in his usual "good humor
and good spirits."

At the restaurant, he ordered a pitcher of sangria for the table.
I don't remember what we ate. The food was good, but mattered
little. What mattered was the warmth and laughter. Thinking back

to that evening, I remember how it felt to sit there beside Willie, and a line of Longfellow's comes to mind: "Ah, how good it feels! The hand of an old friend."

I remember, too, the look in Willie's eyes when he realized I had put one over on him. Toward the end of the meal, I had excused myself to go find the restroom. Walking past the waitress, I passed her my credit card without breaking stride. Later, when she brought the bill already charged, the master poker player looked at me sharply, the surprise on his face mixed with appreciation, not so much for the meal as for the move.

"That was smoothly done," he said, laughing his high-pitched, full-chested chuckle.

We lingered over the meal until Willie's eyes started losing focus, his heart still in the conversation but his body demanding rest.

"We'd better get you home," I said, putting a hand on his shoulder.

Back at their place, we sat in the living room visiting a bit longer. Cath and Beth compared knitting and quilting projects. Willie sat on the couch, I on the floor. I had never thought of him as someone who needed to be taken care of. He was a joyful force of nature, a great rock and the river running round it. That deep strength remained, but now, in his fatigue, there was room for tenderness. Sitting on the carpet in front of the couch, I took off his socks and rubbed his tired feet.

"Any luck with the stripers at the bridge?" I asked.

Willie shook his head. He hadn't been out recently. Earlier in the summer, when he had, nothing had taken the bait.

We spoke of future outings. It had been two years since we fished from the bridge over Spruce Creek. In that time, we had talked about fishing together again, but never got around to breaking out rods and reels. He and I had both been busy with work and family. And weddings.

Twelve months after Cath and I tied the knot, Willie and Beth had done the same. I was delighted for them, and astonished, too. At nearly fifty-nine, Willie had never married and I hadn't imagined he ever would.

The wedding itself had been a small church service in Manhattan, bringing together Beth's family from Jersey and Willie's from the Bronx. The serious party—and food—came a few weeks later, in Maine. With a front yard big enough to accommodate a large tent, they hired a local outfit to put on a full-fledged clambake with all the fixings: fresh-caught lobster, roasted corn, steamed mussels, and the best seafood chowder we had ever tasted. Willie relished his role as host, greeting friends and dispensing bear hugs. When he finally sat, he tucked a big lobster bib into the front of his shirt and settled down for a feed. Watching him dig in, I recalled a line from one of his favorite books, *The Problem of Pain* by C. S. Lewis: "I think we all sin by needlessly disobeying the apostolic injunction to 'rejoice' as much as by anything else." It was not an offense that Willie was at any risk of committing.

Later that evening, after most folks had left the reception, Willie and I sat down at a picnic table with another old friend of his to shuck the leftover lobsters. We sat in the dark, with only faint light from an outdoor bulb some yards away, cracking shells one by one, pulling out the tender flesh and setting it aside for future meals, our hands drenched with sweet, salty juice.

Now, a year later, Willie's schedule and mine were both looking more spacious: friendlier to fishing. Soon he would be fully recovered from surgery and we would start making plans for spring or summer. We would go for stripers. Or we would head to a nearby river mouth where a friend of his said we might find big trout: sea-run browns.

Beth's call came the next Sunday. That morning, Willie had suddenly felt uncomfortable. They rushed to the Portsmouth hospital, but it was too late. A blood clot had struck Willie in the lungs. The clot might have come from the surgery; more likely, it was caused by the cancer, which had been more advanced than anyone guessed. It hardly mattered now. He was gone.

I felt like I'd been kicked in the chest. Yes, I told Beth, of course we would be there for the funeral. Yes, I would be honored to be one of the pallbearers.

Cath and I held each other, mourning our loss, and Beth's, unimaginably greater.

Back in Maine a few days later, we stopped at the house. We gave Beth long hugs and met a few of her friends and Willie's, along with members of both their families.

In the dining room, I admired the exquisite black cherry table. Willie had, I thought, been like the furniture he built. His life and character were not happy accidents of inborn personality, the way the grain of his being just happened to lie. They had been carefully crafted. "We are responsible," he once told me, "for the refinement of our own souls."

Atop one of the matching side cabinets, I noticed a big wooden bowl. Resting in it was the cherry cooking spoon I had carved as a wedding gift. On the back of the handle, using my woodburner's finest tip, I had etched a tiny, leaping trout.

That night, in our motel room, Cath and I made an altar. In the center, a candle and a single red flower. In front, my fillet knife in a half circle of seashells. To one side, the little notebook I was using as a fishing log, three trout on the front. To the other side, an old copy of Henry van Dyke's *Fisherman's Luck*, and a photo from our wedding—Willie and me walking toward the altar, shoulder to shoulder, our heads inclined slightly toward one another, laughing.

At dawn we walked the beach. Gentle swells rolled in as the sun eased up out of the sea. Here and there we bent to pick up shells.

Later that morning, we gathered for the funeral at the local Catholic church. Willie had almost never joined Beth in attending Saturday evening Mass, but I didn't think he would have objected to the venue. What had bothered him about the church was its double standards, not its basic teachings. He needed guidance as much as the next person. Though he didn't normally seek that guidance within the four walls of a house of worship, he wasn't picky about where it came from. On one of his rare visits to the building where his funeral was now being performed, he was standing just inside the door when a priest approached.

"Can I help you?" the priest asked.

"Father," replied Willie, "I need all the help I can get."

In a nearby cemetery, we carried the heavy, dark casket from hearse to fresh-dug grave. Two young navy sailors folded a flag and presented it to Willie's mother.

Then we gave Willie back to the earth.

A low jumble of dark rocks pointed toward the open ocean. Uncle Mark, his son Adam, and I had paddled across to this spit in the dim light of an overcast dawn and anchored the old aluminum canoe in a few inches of water. Now the three of us stood among the rocks, rods in hand. To our right lay the deep channel we had just crossed. With the tide beginning to fall, Cape Cod's East Bay was giving its waters back to the sea. With those waters came baitfish, streaming out through the channel. Drawn by the small fish came larger ones, the hunters we hunted.

I had only fished with Mark once or twice as a boy and never since. But a few days after Willie was buried, Mark had written. He had noticed that the tide charts indicated favorable conditions for striped bass and bluefish the following weekend. Knowing how important Willie had been to me and how central fishing had been to our friendship, Mark wondered if I wanted to come down to the Cape and wet a line. Did I ever.

Standing there, our feet wedged among the rocks, cold saltwater swirling around our ankles, Mark, Adam, and I heard an occasional splash as fish broke the surface nearby. If we happened to be looking in the right direction, we would see a silver flash or two before the turmoil subsided, leaving the flow of the tide unmarred. Minutes later, the surface might erupt again just a few yards away.

In that violent slapping and swirling of tails, I felt a hint of the wild, open ocean. I thought of a photograph Beth had told me about: Willie standing atop a great rock at the surf's edge, his feet set, his fishing rod doubled over, the vast, raw power of the water making the big man look tiny. I thought, too, of the photograph in the back pocket of my jeans, the laminated card from the funeral home, bearing Willie's broad smile.

This flinging of lures and bait into the salty, wind-driven swells was nothing like the fishing I had done with Willie when I was a boy: standing under the granite cliffs or sitting in my father's battered old rowboat, watching our lines straighten on the breeze-riffled surface, praying for the gentle tug of a brookie. But it was, I thought, very much like the fishing we would have done if he had lived longer.

There, casting a line into the churning sea, I could begin to say goodbye.

Other goodbyes had been like this, too. After my father died, I went to a spot where he and I often swam together when I was a boy, the same spot where Willie had nabbed the huge brookie with a salmon egg. Back then, I would stand on that small granite shelf just a foot above the water, my back to the quarry wall. I would look high over my left shoulder and glimpse my father taking that last casual step toward the late-day summer sun, testicles cupped in one hand: He swam naked and the human body picks up momentum in twenty-three feet of free fall.

He would hurtle past and hit with a great splash, spraying me and the stone around me. When the froth settled, I would dive straight into the long column of air he had left, hundreds of tiny bubbles tickling skin as my small body shot through. Back on the surface, we would exchange a few playful splashes before hoisting ourselves out to towel off. Later, over a game of backgammon, we would hear the big yellow-throated bullfrogs begin their nightly chorus among the cattails.

Returning to that spot after his death, and diving in again, the simple fact struck me: I would never again feel that bubbly plume rise up around me. In that moment—and later, in walking that land with my sister, scattering his ashes on earth and water—my heart opened to loss.

Cath also turned to nature at such times. Years before we met, when her father called to tell her about the results of her mother's first biopsy—*Yes, it's cancer*—she went to the backyard and set hundreds of daffodil and tulip bulbs into the soil, tears running down her cheeks as she dug each hole and planted each tightly packed bundle of beauty-to-be. Nine months later, when her father was struck by his final heart attack, she dug a new rose bed, a circle, an opening in the ground where she could pour her grief.

In our first two years together, when her mother's cancer returned to lay its final siege, Cath helped her at home and took her to chemotherapy appointments. Every time they walked into the chemo room, it took Cath's breath away. The rows of big recliner chairs. The people, with or without hair, their faces ashen. Some sat up, alert, maybe reading. Others just lay there, often alone. Once, a mother sat with her sick teenage son.

After each session, Cath came home drained. We talked. She wrote in her journal. She sat by the brook, needing to hear the rhythm of the water. And she gardened, needing to feel soil against skin, to coax loveliness and sustenance from the earth.

My fishing, like Cath's gardening, was not a simple matter of procuring food. Nor would my hunting be. As Canadian wildlife biologist Valerius Geist once phrased it, I would "no more hunt to kill deer than I garden to kill cabbages."

A solid tug on the line spurred my hands into motion. The fish was close. In the swirling water, I caught the broadside flash of a silvery flank marked by dark lines: a little striper. I brought the bass to hand and eased the hook from the corner of its mouth. One powerful flick of the tail and the fish was gone. From the massive swirls we had seen and heard, we knew there were bigger fish nearby. But they would not strike. Mark and Adam, like me, caught only small bass, nowhere near the twenty-eight-inch legal minimum for stripers.

Bluefish came, though, in a toothy swarm, chattering at the ends of our lines. We landed three of them, each a foot or more long, and—there being no size restrictions—killed them.

By late morning, we were back at the house where Mark lived with his wife, daughter, and son. On the back deck, Mark filleted the blues deftly, using a knife that must have cleaned thousands of fish, its handle weathered, its blade narrowed by constant re-sharpening. By lunchtime, the rich, oily flesh was on our plates, broiled—the so-recently-living, so-recently-surging-through-the-sea feeding the so-far-still-living, so-far-still-wandering-the-earth.

That afternoon, Mark and I went to the woods across the street to walk his dog, Hunter, a burly Australian Cattle Dog he had trained to tree squirrels. As we walked, I watched Mark move.

Several inches shorter than I, he had the strength of a much larger man, arms tightly muscled, shoulders sloping powerfully. Despite his physique, however, there was nothing aggressive or even assertive about how he carried himself. On the contrary, I was struck by the lengths to which he went not to take up too much room. As we approached each narrowing of the trail, Mark slowed, his pauses longer than politeness required, insisting that I pass through first. Later, running errands, he did the same at the grocery-store door. And, in his interaction with the checkout clerk, he seemed intensely self-conscious, almost apologetic, as though concerned that he might offend someone.

As we ate dinner that evening, I glanced around the small dining room. The shell of a horseshoe crab hung on one wall, photographs of sandpiper chicks and wood duck drakes on another. Two shed antlers—dropped by whitetail bucks in winter and later found by Mark and Adam—were suspended from a curtain rod.

Earlier in the day, I had taken a good look around the house. Wild things inhabited every space, indoors and out. At the street, the mailbox was painted as a striped bass, seven dark lateral lines running along its sides, with wooden head, tail, and dorsal fins attached. At the corner of an outdoor railing perched a carved wooden owl. Three fish swam below, two carved out of wood, one cleverly fashioned of metal odds and ends welded together.

In the bathroom hung a small painted relief carving of a blue whale Mark had made in his twenties, and two *gyotaku* fish prints he had made more recently: one showing four yellow perch, the other a pair of sea robins, their wedge-shaped bodies and broad, winglike pectoral fins realistically inked in brown and orange. In the living room, books on fishing, hunting, canoeing, and tree identification shared the shelves with painted duck decoys, rabbit sculptures, and stacks of scallop shells. Aldo

Leopold's *A Sand County Almanac* stood beside Gerald J. Grantz's *Home Book of Taxidermy and Tanning*. Small sculptures of a loon and two sandpipers rested on the mantel above the wood-pellet stove, alongside another owl Mark had carved.

And there were the big buck heads, two of them now. The one I remembered from years ago, an eight pointer with slender, elegantly curved antlers, hung above the stairwell beside a longbow. In the living room was a larger nine pointer, its rack heavy and craggy.

As a vegetarian and antihunter, I had dismissed stuffed trophy heads as grotesque displays of prowess and machismo. Now, I considered these two more closely. The taxidermists' craftsmanship was impressive. Technically speaking, these were not "stuffed heads" at all. Though it was impossible to tell by looking, the antlers were attached to quite small sections of skull, which were in turn attached to foam forms manufactured in the shape of a whitetail's head and neck. What looked like a deer was, in fact, an expertly tanned hide with glass eyes.

I could tell Mark admired these two deer, yet I didn't think he was exactly "proud" of them. I knew he didn't hunt for trophies. When I first expressed interest in hunting, he told me that he had learned long ago not to rate deer by their weight or antlers. As far as he was concerned, every whitetail he took—big buck or small doe or anything in between—was a gift. If he didn't appreciate it, then he didn't deserve it.

When I asked, Mark told me that both of these bucks had simply come his way. He had killed the eight pointer many years ago, there on the Cape. The buck had come within a few yards of where Mark waited with his longbow. The larger nine pointer had been taken just five or six years ago, during a trip he and Jay made to New Hampshire. Mark had killed the animal with a single-shot black-powder pistol at close to forty yards. At the check-in station, people congratulated him again and again, oohing and ahhing over the deer. Mark was mortified: "They treated me like I'd sired the animal."

Mark valued the buck mounts, I thought, not as proof of his hunting prowess, but as reminders of particular hunts and as symbols of the relationships he cherished—with deer in general, with the specific animals whose paths crossed his, with the land they shared. He must value them aesthetically, too. I wasn't sure I would ever hang a deer mount in my own house—I thought of a line penned by hunter and author C. L. Rawlins, "those ranks of trophy heads on walls stare down at me like the jury in a capital case"—but I had to admit: Mark's deer were beautiful.

All these things—the deer, the striped-bass mailbox, the photos and carvings of wildlife, the sculptures and paintings of fish—struck me as altarpieces. Mark had grown up Catholic, but rarely spoke of religion. To the degree that he followed one, I thought it must be rooted in a pantheon of wild creatures and wild places, symbolized by these objects: things he had found, things he had crafted by hand. Perhaps his path was akin to totemism, which French sociologist Émile Durkheim contended was religion's most elemental form. What creatures might watch over Mark, I couldn't be sure. But I would willingly hazard guesses at several species of fish, the owls he frequently carved, and the deer he stalked each fall.

When Mark had a loss to grieve, I imagined that he, too, must turn to water and woods. He had understood what a weekend of fishing would do for me, so soon after burying Willie.

That evening, we descended to the basement. The long, low, cave-like room—cluttered with outdoor paraphernalia—reminded me of the first time I walked into Mark's room as a boy. Fishing rods were racked up on the walls alongside longbows, recurves, quivers, and arrows. Camo and blaze-orange clothing peeked out of boxes stacked up against coolers and tackle bags. On top of one box lay a leather satchel Mark took to the woods whenever he hunted with his muzzleloader. Tucked inside were lead roundballs, patches for seating the balls against a powder charge, a waterproof tin of firing caps, and a gorgeous powder horn, the tip plugged with a threaded stopper made of horn, the back end capped with a cross section of deer antler. Tethered to the powder horn was another piece of whitetail antler, one end hollowed out so that it held the exact measure of powder Mark used when hunting.

The workbench proffered tools, assorted hardware, rust pre-ventative and lubricant sprays, spinning reels in various stages of repair, and lengths of wire leader for foiling the line-shearing teeth of bluefish. Above the bench hung a tool rack and above that, at the very top of the wall, hung the small skull plates and antlers of three whitetails Mark had killed there on Cape Cod: a spikehorn, a four point, and a five.

As we tinkered with fishing gear, we talked about deer. My first autumn of hunting whitetails was about to begin. I would hunt in Vermont first. Then, the week after Thanksgiving, when Ver-mont's rifle season was over and Mark was back from his annual hunt with Jay in the Blue Ridge Mountains, I would return to the Cape. The first few days of Massachusetts firearm season, Mark and I would finally hunt together.

At dawn, Mark and I were back at the water's edge. It being a Sunday, I recalled a story Beth had told me the day before Willie's funeral. Four years earlier, Father Bernard, a friend of Beth's from Mount Angel Abbey in Oregon, had come east to officiate at a friend's wedding in Boston. After the Saturday wedding Mass, Willie and Beth brought the Benedictine monk to their place in southern Maine. On Sunday morning, Beth dropped off the two men at the bridge over Spruce Creek. When she returned an hour later, they were surrounded by a dozen or more anglers.

The men—accustomed to Willie's friendly ways and the six-pack of root beer he typically brought along to share—had been curious about the unfamiliar octogenarian with the cane, the lawn chair, and the wraparound sunglasses. Hearing that he was a priest, they might have backpedaled, or started thinking up quick excuses for why they weren't in church on Sunday. But Father Bernard told them all that they were just where God wanted them to be. They did not have to go to Mass. They were enjoying exactly what God would want for them that day.

By midmorning, Mark and I were both shivering under our windbreakers. A cold October wind had begun to blow, buffeting us where we stood among the rocks and along the adjoining bayside beach. The stripers had vanished entirely. Though Mark reeled in a fluke—a spotted, oblong pancake of a fish, also called summer flounder—and then a big bluefish, sleek and silvery and as long as my arm, I had no luck at all. Yet, thinking of Willie, I knew there was no other way I would have wanted to spend those hours.

10

Into the Woods

When we see land as a community to which we belong,
we may begin to use it with love and respect.
                    —Aldo Leopold, *A Sand County Almanac*

In theory, I was ready to hunt deer. Thanks to Uncle Mark, who
patiently answered the barrage of questions I sent his way, I had
the basic gear. I had a pair of warm camouflage pants and a warm
camouflage jacket, to break up the visual outline of my body and
prevent that body from freezing solid during long hours in the
woods. I had a blaze-orange vest and hat to make me glow like a
neon sign during firearms seasons—deer, fortunately, do not see
the color the way we do.

I had a fanny pack ready to go. With guidance from the hunter-
education manual and from articles I'd read, I had stuffed its
pockets with odds and ends that might come in handy: a tiny
flashlight to help me navigate the woods in the predawn and
postdusk dark; a compass in case I got turned around out there; a
miniature first-aid kit for minor incidents; an emergency whistle,
space blanket, and fire-starting materials for major ones; a flexible

wire saw and lengths of cord for various situations; a folding multitool; a rifle-cleaning rod that broke down into eight-inch sections; a sharpening stone for knife and broadheads; and a small bundle of toilet paper, in case nature called. My hunting and fishing license was tucked into a ziploc bag with one of the laminated cards from the funeral home—Willie's face smiled up at me broadly. In the largest pocket was the hunting knife Mark had given me, plus instructions on how to gut a deer. (On a shelf in the basement, I even had a boning knife—a flexible blade not unlike a fillet knife—for removing meat from bones, and a hand-crank grinder that I could clamp to the kitchen counter.)

I had a simple bow—an old recurve generously sent to me that summer by Jay, Mark's longtime hunting buddy from Virginia—and a quiver full of arrows.

I had an old-fashioned caplock muzzleloader, much like the one Mark used for most of his deer hunting. He had helped me find it, secondhand and in excellent condition. He had also offered technical advice as I went about transforming a cow horn Jay had given me into my own powder horn: its cherry plug wood-burned to show a buck and doe in silhouette, its variegated brown-and-blond surface roughly scrimshawed to suggest Cold Brook, the rocky little waterway that tumbles through the woods behind our house, along whose banks I might look for tracks.

And I had a modern rifle. Fortunately, I did not go straight from the hunter-education class to the nearest gun shop. If I had blundered in and started asking questions, it wouldn't have been pretty.

Me: "Hi, I want to buy a deer rifle."

Gun guy: "What are you looking for?"

Me: "Uh, a *deer* rifle?" At this point, ignorance would still have been bliss. I knew only that I needed a centerfire rifle, so called because the firing pin strikes an explosive, impact-sensitive primer located in the center of the cartridge case's back end.

(Rimfire cartridges like the ubiquitous .22, which have a primer encircling the rear of the case, lack the power needed for deer hunting, and are better suited for smaller game like rabbit, hare, or gray squirrel.)

Gun guy: "Okay. Do you have a brand in mind? Remington, maybe? Or Browning? Or Winchester?"

Me: "Uh, not really." Here, I would have had a first, faint inkling of what I was getting into.

Gun guy: "Okay. What kind of action do you want: bolt, lever, pump, semiauto?"

Me, relieved: "Bolt." This was one thing I did know. In hunter education, I had learned how different types of rifles and shotguns functioned. Any of them would work just fine, but I felt safest and most confident with the simplest design, and the most familiar. My first .22 and my father's few long guns had all been bolt-actions.

Gun guy: "Do you have a caliber in mind? Are you thinking a two-seventy, a thirty-aught-six, a three-oh-eight, a two-forty-three, an old thirty-thirty?"

Me: "Uh." This is where it would have begun to dawn on me that I was in deep.

As I say, though, I did not flaunt my ignorance in such a spectacularly public manner. Instead, I did it privately, throwing myself on Uncle Mark's mercy. He was kind. When I asked him about the vast array of available calibers, he explained: The main differences were power and effective range. Though caliber designations indicated the bullet's diameter—in hundredths of an inch for American cartridges, and in millimeters for European cartridges—the size of each cartridge case and the amount of powder inside were entirely different matters. A .30-06 and a .30-30, for instance, both fired a bullet about three-tenths of an inch wide. The former, however, was far more powerful.

Scouring the Internet for relevant articles, I came to the realization that hunters and shooters and industry professionals had
written roughly a gazillion words of advice on rifles and rifle
cartridges, and on how to choose the right one. There were pages
and pages of history, parts of which helped me decipher common
caliber notations: The "aught-six" in .30-06, for example, refers
to the cartridge's introduction in 1906, while the second "thirty"
in .30-30 refers to the cartridge's standard load of thirty grains
of smokeless powder. There were ballistics tables, showing the
trajectories of various cartridges with various powder loads
shooting bullets of various weights and shapes, and the kinetic
force each would deliver at various distances. There were even
charts detailing the "sectional density" of any given bullet: a
mathematically precise way of telling me whether the projectile
was shaped more like a spear or more like a rock.

After a brief descent into endless rabbit holes of facts and data,
I emerged, shook my head, and looked back at one of Mark's first
e-mails. He had summed up what I needed to know. Given the
distances at which I would likely be shooting, any one of a long
list of centerfire cartridges would provide sufficient power to
kill a deer instantly and a flat enough trajectory for me to hit my
target. For hunters in Northeastern forests, the average shot at a
deer is well under fifty yards.

Mark also confirmed one pertinent fact that my baffled
brain had begun to deduce: Firepower mattered far less than
being able to hit what I was aiming at. The best rifle would be
one that—in my inexperienced hands—would deliver a bullet
to a deer's vital organs every time. And the main factor apt to
interfere with such accuracy was recoil, a direct correlate of
firepower.

Not that recoil makes a rifle itself inaccurate. The bullet is long
gone by the time a firearm bucks from the explosion that just
occurred within its chamber. But it can easily make the shooter

inaccurate. Having fired only small-caliber guns as a kid, I had no idea how a big-game rifle would kick or how serenely I would absorb it. If I ended up with an over-powered gun that kicked too hard, I ran the risk of developing a flinch. If I started flinching in anticipation of the recoil—just before the cartridge detonated—then my marksmanship would deteriorate in a hurry.

Online, I found several articles that offered maximum-recoil suggestions for first-time owners of deer rifles, and explained the mechanics. In short, I needed to pay attention to Newton's Third Law of Motion: For every action there is an equal and opposite reaction. The lighter the rifle, the greater the powder charge, the heavier the bullet, and the faster that bullet flew, the more force my shoulder would be asked to absorb.

Other articles emphasized the "knockdown power" of various types of large-bore, supercharged ammo. But I was not going to be hunting Cape buffalo in Africa or brown bears in Alaska. I was going to be hunting white-tailed deer in New England. I did not need some kind of armor-piercing, antitank ordnance. Nor did I particularly want to contract even a mild case of magnumitis: the irrational desire to possess a firearm capable of stopping a freight train.

In the end, the choice was easy. A few articles suggested that the American-made .260 cartridge—and its older Scandinavian equivalent, the Swedish 6.5x55—offered a good balance of power and low recoil, especially for a first-time shooter. A local hunter offered to let me touch off a round or two with a pair of his rifles, one of them a .260.

I was sold. The rifle was lightweight, but still didn't kick that hard.

Walking around a shop's impressive arsenal, I eliminated every rifle that was out of my price range. Then I eliminated every rifle that didn't feel right in my hands. That narrowed the field to two or three. I kept coming back to a modestly priced gun made by Tikka, a high-quality Finnish manufacturer that Willie had suggested I consider. The pattern of the checkering carved into the stock was a bit modern for my taste, but the gun felt well balanced, the smooth walnut fore end and grip fit my hands, and the butt and comb settled comfortably against my shoulder and cheek. I ordered one, chambered for 6.5x55.

In preparation for that first autumn of deer hunting, I practiced with the recurve Jay had sent. It felt good to have a bow back in my hands after so many years, feeling string across gloved fingers and fingertips against jaw, looking down the shaft and visualizing the path the arrow would take toward my target: a fifty-pound birdseed sack stuffed with lightweight tarps I'd collected on a carpentry job, the kind used for shipping lumber. I felt confident out to twenty yards.

I practiced with my firearms as well. Mostly, I shot my .22— each round cost only a few cents. Less frequently, I practiced with my 6.5x55—cartridges were a dollar apiece. And I familiarized myself with the more involved procedure of pouring black powder into my caplock's .54-caliber maw, ramming in a bullet or patched roundball, placing a percussion cap under the cocked hammer, and sending the projectile through a paper plate. Whether looking through the low-power scope on my Tikka or through the peep sight on my muzzleloader, I knew I could hit a deer's vital organs at fifty yards or more. Rudimentary shooting skills, however, wouldn't do any good unless I could first succeed in deer hunting's most basic task: finding deer.

I began my quest close to home. Cath and I didn't see white-tails there often—every few weeks we might catch a glimpse of a doe or two standing under the apple trees or crossing the driveway, and once in our six years there I had seen an antlered buck within fifty yards of our front porch, near the forest's edge. But we often saw their tracks, and evidence of their passage through our unfenced flower gardens: Hosta leaves were a favored delicacy, as were daylily buds, particularly when they were just about to bloom. Their visits to our yard were mostly nocturnal. By day, they disappeared into the hundreds of acres of privately owned timberland stretching out behind our house toward Groton State Forest. That, I thought, would be the place to hunt. There were no houses back there, or even any hunting camps.

Poring over the town tax map, I determined whose properties I hoped to hunt and contacted the owners for permission. Landowners who had grown up elsewhere thanked me for asking, and said yes. Landowners who had grown up here were baffled by my question. Their land wasn't posted. Didn't I know that meant I could hunt it? I did. The Vermont Constitution of 1777 guarantees residents the "liberty in seasonable times, to hunt and fowl on the lands they hold, and on other lands not inclosed." (Vermont was the first state to provide constitutional protection for hunting. The second, Alabama, didn't follow suit until 1996. By 2010, eleven more states had done the same.) But asking was still good manners.

It would also be good manners, I decided, to reconsider how we marked our own property. When Cath and I moved here to the eastern side of the Winooski Valley, we wanted to keep hunters off our few acres. Anywhere you stood—or fired a rifle—you were within a few hundred yards of our house. In most spots, you were a lot closer than that. Our driveway is part of an old railroad bed, long used as a trail by hunters, hikers, bicyclists, cross-country skiers, and snowmobilers. Decades ago, after part of the rail-bed embankment washed out and disappeared downstream, a trail detour was put in around our house and driveway. That detour winds through our woods just seventy yards from the back porch.

So I did what most safety-conscious, non- and antihunting newcomers do. I bought a roll of those ubiquitous bright-yellow signs: "Posted. Private Property." Several went alongside the trail detour: not blocking it, but telling folks to stick to it.

Now, though, I was becoming a hunter. I had been granted the privilege of hunting on other people's private property. It didn't feel right to continue sending the "Posted" signs' message: Stay the hell off our land. Yet I didn't want to tempt fate by removing them entirely. I still thought about the local man killed while watching football in his living room two years earlier. Hunters still needed to know that our few acres were not a place for shooting. So I took down the yellow signs and replaced them with black-and-white ones provided by the Vermont Fish and Wildlife Department: "Safety Zone. No Hunting Allowed. Shooting Prohibited." In other words, you can't see it, but you're really close to our house.

With permission to hunt hundreds of acres, I started my scouting in summer. I took a compass, a pencil, and a paper map I'd printed from my computer, topographic lines overlaying a black-and-white aerial photograph. A quarter-inch on the map was, I estimated, just over fifty paces on the ground. Hike after hike, I explored the woods, slapping black flies as I went. I learned where beavers were actively tending dams a half mile up Cold Brook. I saw where several clearcut acres had been taken over by wild raspberries. I found where old stone walls—from the merino sheep's heyday, I guessed—intersected along the western flank of a long ridge known as Lord's Hill. (On its far side stands Devil's Hill and nearby lie the remains of a long-abandoned settlement called Jerusalem, a trinity that makes me curious about the intertwining of theology and geography in local history.) On my map, I marked a spot along one stone wall where I had found artist's conk and turkey tail: wild mushrooms Cath used in medicinal recipes.

Here and there, I also noted old wooden platforms perched in trees. The makeshift tree stands did not appear to have been used in recent years, but at one time some hunter must have thought each of these spots a likely one for seeing deer. That was my task now: to decide where, in all these hundreds of acres, I might actually see whitetails in daylight. Like an angler sizing up a river, I needed to pay attention not just to the broad sweep of the landscape—the slopes and saddles and ridges that might shape deer's movements—but to the details.

Where might deer bed down in thick cover? To what spot might they go to bask in the sun's warmth? Where might they habitually feed? Fifty miles to the south, stands of oak might provide acorns, one of the whitetail's favorite autumn foods. Here, though, oaks are rare. I would need to look elsewhere, perhaps to late apples or to stands of beech trees in years when beechnuts were plentiful. What trails did the deer use to travel between bedding areas and feeding areas? And how would all these patterns change come fall, as the season turned and mating began?

Walking the woods, I watched for deer tracks and droppings. I kept an eye out for old rubs—places where, in some previous year, a buck had rubbed and hooked his antlers against small trees, stripping bark and leaving telltale scars. I looked, too, for spots where I might lie in ambush.

From Mark's e-mails and magazine articles he had clipped out and sent, I gathered that the various hunting strategies available to me boiled down to two: going to deer, or waiting for deer to come to me. I wasn't too sure about the former.

I knew that some hunters could track a single deer for miles and eventually get close enough for a shot. I just wasn't one of them. Not yet, at any rate. The approach intrigued me, though, and in fresh snow I would happily give it a try.

Another variation on going to deer intrigued me as well. "Still-hunting," despite its moniker, means hunting while moving, albeit very, very slowly. Mindful of wind direction, still hunters do their best to blend in to the woods. They take a slow, quiet step, then pause for a minute or more, sharply attentive to any movement or sound that might indicate the presence of an animal nearby, before taking another step. It can take them an hour to go a hundred, or even fifty, yards. With soft snow or damp, quiet leaves underfoot, I'd willingly give this a try, too. But I had no experience at it.

The better bet—the tactic a greenhorn like me was less apt to bungle—was to wait for deer to come to me. Once I picked a spot, my task would be simple: not to move. In the woods near active deer trails and old rubs, I looked for potential "ground stands"— places to sit or stand with both my feet on terra firma.

A good spot would give me a dual advantage in the visual landscape, simultaneously providing trees, bushes, or branches to break up the visible outline of my predatory form, and giving me a clear view of locations where whitetails might appear. "Clear view" was, of course, a relative notion. In these woods, hunting wasn't visual in the way I gathered it often was out west, where trees are sparse and binoculars can help you spot an animal half a mile away. But I wanted to avoid sitting in such thick cover that dozens of deer might pass within twenty yards, unseen.

The olfactory landscape was harder to predict. I knew that an ideal spot would be downwind of where I expected to see deer. Yet, as I started paying attention to them, I realized that air movements changed not only from day to day, but from hour to hour and even from minute to minute. The light breeze I felt in my face now might, in a moment, swirl around to push my scent out in front of me. In general, a west wind might prevail, but I couldn't plan on it.

Near the same deer trails, I also kept an eye out for well-positioned trees to which I might strap a metal tree stand. Perching twelve or fifteen or more feet off the ground would, in theory, make deer less likely to see me, especially if I could arrange to have trees—not open sky—above and behind me. Deer should also be less likely to smell me, as my scent would be wafting along on the breeze several yards above their noses. My chances of having a deer get very close would be better: a vital factor if I was using a bow. Though I felt more confident about making a clean kill with rifle, scope, and cartridge, bow and arrow were appealing in their simplicity.

By mid-September, when Willie passed away so suddenly, I had a few spots picked out. Whether they were good ones, I did not know. But no matter. I wasn't in any hurry to kill a deer. Just seeing one during hunting season would be a success, and I felt I had a fair shot at that.

Judging by the tracks I had been noting, there were definitely deer in these hills. The historical record, however, makes it easy to imagine a Vermont, a New England, indeed an entire continent, without white-tailed deer.

Prior to European settlement, whitetails (*Odocoileus virginianus*) may have numbered twenty-five million or more across what is now the United States and southern Canada, where they were hunted by wolves, cougars, and bears, as well as humans armed with atlatls, bows and arrows, spears, snares, pitfalls, fences, corrals, and fire. Here in the densely wooded, mountainous regions of Vermont, there might have been only two or three deer per square mile. Further south, in what is now Massachusetts, where habitat was enhanced by American Indian clearings and periodic burnings of forest undergrowth, whitetail densities may have been closer to ten or fifteen per square mile.

By the seventeenth century, though, with intensive farming by Massachusetts settlers leaving little cover for large mammals, whitetail numbers were dropping fast. In 1698, with deer nearly extirpated in eastern parts of the Bay Colony, hunting was prohibited between January 15 and July 15. But continued habitat loss and hunting—in both the open and unenforced closed seasons—further depleted the population. In 1718, the colony enacted a three-year moratorium on all deer hunting. Finally, in 1739, Massachusetts hired its first game wardens or "deer reeves." It was too little too late.

At the peak of New England agricultural activity and deforestation in the early- and mid-nineteenth century, when even steep terrain had been cleared as sheep pasture, only a quarter of Vermont, and even less of Massachusetts, was wooded. Though some wildlife species, including grassland birds like the bobolink and meadowlark, thrived in this human-crafted habitat, elk and wolves had disappeared from the region. And whitetails were almost gone, too. Yet remnant deer populations persisted wherever the land seemed too poor or too remote to be worth domesticating—in the sandy-soiled pine and oak woodlands at the base of Cape Cod, in the still-forested parts of the Berkshires, along the spine of the Green Mountains, and in the least settled sections of Vermont's Northeast Kingdom.

To the west, the depletion of whitetails was slower. By the early 1800s, massive trade hunting—much of it done by Indians in response to economic and political pressures—had reduced the North American whitetail population by half or more. Deer hides were used for everything from clothes and wall coverings to saddles and book bindings. In the Midwest during the 1830s, settlers could buy venison for three cents a pound, or they could buy a whole deer for one dollar—leading, some suggest, to the phrase "a buck." On the continent as a whole, however, whitetails were still numerous and habitat changes remained relatively insignificant. It was in the second half of the nineteenth century that the slaughter began in earnest.

As for the passenger pigeon, the bison, and so many other species, the rapid expansion of the U.S. railway system—from just over 9,000 miles of track in 1850 to over 160,000 miles in 1900—was a decisive factor for deer. Market hunters, armed with the newly invented lever-action repeating rifle, headed west and shipped millions of pounds of deer hides and meat back east. In a single year, 1860, a father and son team in Minnesota killed some 6,000 whitetails. In a single month, December 1882, six tons of venison were shipped from Litchfield, Minnesota, to Boston, using the newly invented refrigerated railcar. By the turn of the twentieth century, the nationwide population of whitetails had plummeted by 97 percent in just forty years. With only a few hundred thousand animals left, the species was nearly extinct.

In part, white-tailed deer were saved by the Lacey Act of 1900, the nation's emerging conservation ethic, and the advent of scientific wildlife management, all vocally promoted by recreational hunters. In part, they were saved by their own scarcity. Deer were so few that they no longer warranted attention. As wildlife researchers Richard and Thomas McCabe sum it up, "The whitetail rarely was hunted, even for the table, because it was rarely seen."

At the peak of western market hunting, though, remnant deer populations were already starting to recover in the Northeast. As the railroads took farmers westward and sheep pastures were abandoned, forest habitat began to return to New England, especially on the higher terrain. In some cases, deer were reintroduced. In 1878, for instance, seventeen whitetails were imported from New York and released near Rutland, Vermont.

During the twentieth century, with game laws actively enforced and very few large four-footed predators remaining in the lower forty-eight, deer numbers rebounded with astounding rapidity. As early as 1910, with only five thousand deer in the state, Massachusetts farmers were already complaining of crop losses, helping prompt the opening of regulated hunting seasons. By 1991 there were fifteen hundred deer living within the Philadelphia city limits, more than existed in all of Pennsylvania in 1900.

Today, just over a hundred years after near extinction, the nationwide deer population stands at thirty million or more, at least as many as were here before Europeans arrived. In some places, they number fifty or more per square mile. Most hunters and wildlife watchers are pleased by this cervid resurrection; as a friend once said to me, "Some people just can't imagine such a thing as too many deer." But the recovery of the whitetail has its complications.

For one thing, the United States is also now home to over three hundred million people. Whitetails and humans are living in closer proximity than ever before, resulting in all manner of conflicts. Deer on highways. Deer on airport runways. Deer landing in homes and businesses, having crashed through plate-glass windows. Deer carrying ticks that serve as vectors for the spirochete that causes Lyme disease, especially in the Northeast and upper Midwest. And, everywhere, deer eating.

Collectively, America's deer ingest about ninety billion pounds of vegetation a year: an average of three thousand pounds per animal. In agricultural areas, whitetails' voracious appetites take a heavy toll on crops. In places like eastern Massachusetts— where rural and suburban housing development has broken up farms and forests, creating the kind of edge habitat on which deer thrive—they take a toll on backyard vegetable gardens and front-yard ornamental plantings. And deer take a toll on forests, too, threatening both the economic viability and the biological diversity of our woodlands.

As Richard Nelson explains in *Heart and Blood*, deer evolved under heavy predation and their reproduction is not self-limiting. In good habitat without severe winters, deer populations can increase by 40 percent per year despite mortality from vehicle collisions, moderate animal predation, and the hunting of bucks. When completely protected, they can reproduce even faster, as demonstrated by studies at the 1,146-acre George Reserve in southern Michigan. With no predation and contained by an 11½-foot fence, 10 deer multiplied to 212 in just six years.

At high densities, deer quickly overbrowse their food sources. Constant overbrowsing destroys the understory, killing tree seedlings and wiping out smaller plants, including rare and endangered species. This alters the composition of forest regeneration, subjects some areas to erosion, and eliminates niches for many other wildlife species. Studies in Virginia and Pennsylvania have shown that many smaller mammals and songbirds dependent on close-to-the-ground vegetation become extremely scarce when deer become too numerous. Many reptiles, amphibians, and insects also suffer significant losses when deer remove the understory. Eventually, the deer themselves become malnourished and starve, setting up a boom-and-bust cycle that never allows deer, other species, or habitat to recover fully.

"Just as a deer herd lives in mortal fear of its wolves," wrote Aldo Leopold in *A Sand County Almanac*, "so does a mountain live in mortal fear of its deer. And perhaps with better cause, for while a buck pulled down by wolves can be replaced in two or three years, a range pulled down by too many deer may fail of replacement in as many decades."

In much of Vermont, the mountains are partly protected by climate. When deep snows limit access to food sources and temperatures drop well below zero for extended periods, deer can easily die of malnutrition. Among the hills I would be hunting, whitetails might only number ten or so per square mile. But they were far and away the most common big-game mammal in the area. If any animal was going to stock our freezer with free-range meat, it would be a deer.

My first hours in the October woods were peaceful. I sat on a rock near an old logging road, watching. The recurve that Jay had sent lay across my lap. A red squirrel, apparently unaware of me, scampered by within a few feet.

Another day, I perched in my tree stand not far from where I had recently seen a pair of deer. It was a gray dawn, damp and misty. Chickadees alit close by. A chipmunk bounded through leaves and ferns. I felt no need to do anything but listen and watch, bow in hand. No need even to think. As Zen teachers say, *Just sit*.

In moments of delusion, I found myself assuming that a deer would soon appear, and thinking through the steps I would take to properly care for the meat. In other moments, I realized how unlikely that was—as a novice, I had only just begun to learn— and felt relief. I wasn't sure how it would feel to kill a deer. Nor was I sure I was ready to find out. Killing the hare nine months earlier had been unsettling, and I imagined that taking a deer would hit me harder.

It might be better to focus on more modest goals that autumn. Just get out in the woods. Spend some time with Uncle Mark. Settle into the idea. Start getting a sense of what it would mean to be a hunter.

Partly, it would mean quiet reverie, watchfulness, and learning to navigate the woods. Partly, it would mean learning to navigate more complicated, human terrain.

Hiking home one Saturday afternoon, I detoured to check for deer sign along the back edge of an overgrown beaver meadow. When I got to the spot—the trees sparse, the long grasses bent over by the repeated passage of whitetails headed down to the water's edge—I found a tree stand set up near illegal bait: two blocks of salt. And the hunter had gone further.

While it's common enough for hunters to nip off a few small branches here and there to allow a clear shot, this one had carried in a chain saw and felled a six-inch-diameter balsam fir, leaving a wide-open shooting lane between tree stand and salt. The landowners, I imagined, might object to that much disturbance. I hoped the deer would, too, steering clear of the bait and denying the hunter any ill-won gains.

I left a phone message for the local game warden. Even if the hunter wasn't caught in the act of hunting over salt, he would get a warning letter in the mail. Finding him would be easy enough, for he had obeyed the law in one respect, by prominently displaying his name on the tree stand.

Headed home the next morning after two more quiet hours in the woods, I saw a neighbor coming down the rail-bed trail, out for a walk with his young golden retriever. I winced. I felt certain that he, like most of my friends and acquaintances, wasn't keen on hunting. Given my own longtime opposition to the killing of animals for food, let alone for sport, I could hardly blame him. In his eyes, I would be one of *them*.

As he drew near, I could see surprise on his face.

"It *is* you!" he said, taking in my camouflage clothing and bow. "I thought, 'It's some redneck out hunting and I need to watch my back.' But no, it's you out hunting and I need to watch my back."

We had a polite if awkward chat, and parted ways.

Walking home, I considered the encounter. Though I knew I posed no danger to my neighbor or his dog, it didn't surprise me to hear his safety concerns. Nor did his phrase "some redneck out hunting" shock me. He was merely articulating the stereotype of the hunter as an ignorant backwoods rube—a common view rooted in the kind of tree-felling, law-breaking

behavior I had come across the day before, and also in centuries of history.

Recall that when early English colonists arrived in the New World,
they came with the notion that hunting was an elite avocation.
Whatever they thought of hunting—and the Puritans despised
it—they associated it with European nobility, for whom the
chase had been reserved both as a privilege and as a method of
developing martial prowess in young gentry. Colonists came,
however, to a continent already inhabited by millions of other
hunters: Indians. In the native peoples of North America, and
in their hunting, colonists saw humanity at its most animalistic,
primitive, and brutal.

When European colonists hunted, they trod a cultural no-man's-
land between these two extremes: nobility and savagery. As Daniel
Herman argues in *Hunting and the American Imagination*, common
folk who hunted were, in one sense, claiming an element of genteel
identity. But they were also bringing the hunt down to the commoner's level, especially by ignoring the "sporting codes" of elite
hunting and instead killing game as efficiently as possible. Just
below the hunting commoner lurked the savage, always threatening
to undermine the foundations of agrarian civilization.

Recall, too, that when tales of Daniel Boone became popular
in the first half of the nineteenth century, the backwoods hunter
was elevated from bloodthirsty brute to noble adventurer. This
new American was at home in the wilderness yet lived according to
middle- and upper-class values. And it was middle- and upper-class
men who swelled the sporting ranks of the day and who—when
populations of deer and other animals plummeted in the late
1800s—led the call to conserve wildlife for future generations.

A legal cornerstone for such conservation had been set in 1842,
when the case of *Martin v. Waddell* came before the U.S. Supreme

Court. At stake were oysters, and a New Jersey property owner's claim that he held title to the land that lay beneath the water of the Raritan River and to the mudflats below the high-tide mark of Raritan Bay. In a ruling based in part on an interpretation of the Magna Carta of 1215, the court declared that the oyster fishery was a public commons. This set the foundation for what came to be called the Public Trust Doctrine: the principle that fish and wildlife cannot be owned by individuals, and are to be held in trust by the government. This doctrine has been a key part of the North American model of wildlife conservation ever since.

The ideals of a public commons and the praiseworthy achievements of early American conservation, however, were not without their dark sides. As white sport hunters asserted their vision of wildlife as a national commons, generations-old conflicts with American Indians took on an added dimension and their hunting rights came under increased fire, both figuratively and literally. As historian Louis S. Warren recounts in *The Hunter's Game*, in 1895 a white posse arrested and then massacred a group of Bannock Indians in northwestern Wyoming for violating state game laws, despite the fact that the Bannocks' right to hunt elk on public land was guaranteed by treaty. The next year, that treaty right was abrogated by the U.S. Supreme Court. In 1903, wildlife officials again opened fire on Indian hunters in Wyoming. In 1905, government authorities encouraged New Mexico ranchers to kill Indian hunters. In 1908, officials opened fire in Montana.

The flames of old conflicts among whites were fanned as well. For decades, elite urban hunters had been clashing with poor rural hunters. Herman documents, for instance, how, in the 1820s, gentlemen of the Unadilla Hunting Club in Otsego County, New York, hired thugs to catch and beat local men who—hunting legally—tried to shoot deer being pursued by members of the club.

In advocating game conservation, middle- and upper-class sport hunters spoke out not only against market hunting, but also against subsistence hunting: hunting for "the pot." The "pot hunter," wrote Philadelphia author Elisha Jarrett Lewis, would "lay waste all animated nature . . . without regard to etiquette, humanity, law, or even the common decencies of life." (Arguably, my own objection to the two salt licks and the felled tree were rooted in some version of this same revulsion at lawlessness and indecency.) The shots taken by such hunters were, according to Lewis and his brethren, easy, cheap, careless, and opportunistic, not at all in keeping with the rules of sport—hence our modern use of the word "potshot."

The rhetoric of urban sport hunters promoted particular ideas about who should hunt and how, including culturally specific ideals of masculinity that echoed the sporting traditions of England. Like the subsistence-hunting "troglodyte" Ortega y Gasset later berated, backwoods hunters did not belong on hunting's pedestal of nobility, for the pursuit of game should be a chivalrous enterprise, conducted within the bounds of a highly refined code of conduct. It should not be a crass matter of bagging meat to provide for one's family or community. It should not, in short, be savagery. (The parallels with dietary rhetoric of the same era are striking: Idealized sport hunters sound much like the gentlemanly, vegetarian University of Chicago football team of 1907; backwoods pot hunters sound much like the team's savage, leg-breaking, beef-eating opponents.)

In the early 1900s, sport hunters were at the top of their game. Their recreational interests had triumphed over subsistence traditions, as rural, lower-class white folks who had been hunting local hills and valleys for generations were suddenly faced with enforcement of state and federal laws that defined their hunting as poaching. In those early years of the twentieth century, upper- and middle-class hunters also enjoyed widespread public approval, as most nonhunting Americans associated the hunt with chivalrous men the likes of President Theodore Roosevelt. Ironically, though, the very popularity of hunting soon tarnished its public image.

Herman notes that as cheap firearms, cheap automobiles, and labor laws mandating more time off for workers made hunting and hunting grounds more accessible, more people took up the pursuit. Between 1910 and 1920, sales of hunting licenses doubled. By 1945, a quarter of American men were hunting. Many of these men were working class. No longer associated primarily with noble urban citizens, hunting lost its respectable sheen. It came to be associated, once again, with the rural recklessness and savagery that haunted the colonial imagination. It became, as my neighbor succinctly phrased it, the kind of thing that "some redneck" would do.

By the end of the fourth and final weekend of Vermont's archery season, I had seen exactly zero deer from my tree stand. From the ground, though, I had seen white-tailed does three times. And I had also encountered creatures I was not hunting, each unanticipated meeting a gift.

One day, I came across a flock of sixty or more wild turkeys, little ones and big ones, clucking, pecking, scratching, walking, hopping, and flapping through the woods. Another day, I caught a glimpse of two bears and—along the edge of a cornfield cut to stubble—found signs of their passage: scat, black hairs snagged on barbed wire, and corn stalks dragged into the woods for secluded nibbling. And, once, as I approached Cold Brook just below a beaver pond, a great blue heron burst up suddenly from among the alders in front of me, huge wings lifting the hunter's sinuous body into the sky.

11
Kinds of Killing

I will never know if animals and plants have spirits,
if the tree I stand beside is aware of my presence, if
respectful gestures bring hunting luck and protect my
well-being. But I am absolutely certain it is wise and
responsible to behave *as if* these things were true.
                        —Richard Nelson, *Heart and Blood*

A shot cracked the frosty quiet of sunrise. I flinched, my body
reacting before I could process the sound and think, *Rifle.*
My hunter-education instructor's words echoed in my mind:
"That one didn't hit me."

The shot had been close, maybe two hundred yards from
where I waited behind the jagged remains of a fallen fir,
watching the deer trail that traversed the slope below. Bright
patches on a pair of young maple stems told me that a buck had
been there, rubbing antlers against trees, stripping bark.

A minute later, a second shot rang out. *Finishing the animal
off,* I thought, *or taking a long shot.* I hadn't seen any other

hunters scouting these woods in recent weeks and was surprised by the close company.

I thought of Cath. I wasn't far from home. She would have heard those shots, too. When I left the house with my rifle slung over my shoulder, I could tell she was uneasy. She knew that I would be careful and that I was wearing a blaze-orange hat and vest. Until now, though, I had only been out during bow season, when few hunters were in the woods and when neither of us imagined there was even the slightest risk of getting shot. I had never set foot in the woods to pursue deer with a firearm, let alone gone out in the predawn darkness of that most popular Saturday in mid-November, the first day of Vermont's two-week rifle season. Safety statistics would not quell Cath's instinctive reaction to those sharp reports. By midmorning, concerned for her and feeling crowded by the nearby shots, I headed home.

A few days later, curious whether the hunter had, in fact, taken a buck in those early hours, I went looking. Tufts of white and brown hair snagged on fallen branches told me that a deer had been dragged along a narrow game path. A hundred yards farther, the drag signs stopped. The body must have been pulled up to the path from the right-hand side, across a slope covered with rocks and wild raspberries.

Avoiding that tangle, I kept to the path and circled around to the hemlock-cloaked shoulder of a ridge where the hunter might have fired those shots. I could have missed the spot in the brush below but for the blaze-orange trash. Someone had indeed field dressed a whitetail there, leaving behind a pair of giant bright-plastic gloves, complete with the wrapper advising, "Don't Litter."

The trash seemed a potent expression of disrespect: for the land, its owners, and the graceful animal whose life had been forfeit. In the scheme of things, I knew this was a minor infraction. It paled in comparison with the more flagrant crimes I had read and heard of: the gut shooting of deer my hunter-education instructor had described, for instance, or the moose pointlessly shot and left to rot. I e-mailed Uncle Mark about it and his reply resonated: "Leaving a kill site trashed is inexcusable." For both of us, those gloves beside the deer's entrails touched a nerve.

It wasn't just the littering. Every spring, Cath and I work with neighbors to clean up our several-mile-long dirt road. I don't like the garbage we find—soda bottles, beer cans, fast-food containers, the occasional tire or two—but it doesn't sicken me.

The hunter's trash was different. Walking home with those gloves dangling from my hand, my revulsion was visceral. I could get no distance from it. I felt lonelier than if I had been in deep forest, miles from the nearest human being. Days later, an emptiness lingered. The word that came to mind was *desecration*.

What was it that made the deer's death feel sacred, and thus vulnerable to defilement? What sanctified the place where the animal fell? It wasn't simply death. When I see road-killed animals, I feel sad. But that spot on the highway doesn't seem sacred to me. Tragic, yes, but not sacred. I'm not especially horrified by the presence of nearby litter.

It was the killing. Somewhere along that hemlock-covered ridge, a hunter had squeezed a trigger, deliberately ending a life. In the brush below, a hunter had slit open the belly of a deer's still-warm body. That act of intentional killing demanded reverence. It should have pushed the event and place into the realm of the sacred. The trash declared that it had not.

Many traditional hunting cultures say that the land is watchful, that the animal's spirit objects to disrespectful behavior. Whether that was true I had no idea, but it made more sense to me than the common Christian claim that animals have no souls. The very word "animal" derives from the Latin word *anima*, meaning "life," "breath," "spirit," and "soul." If we want to deny the spiritual essence of animals, we will need to come up with a different name for them. "Resources," perhaps. Or "livestock."

During my militant vegan years, any attempt to link killing with the sacred would have struck me—much as it did Marti Kheel in her critique of the "holy hunter"—as an especially deceptive sort of deviance, a ploy intended to sanctify brutality. Now, though, what struck me as bizarre was the attempt to segregate the two. In the history of human cultures around the world, such compartmentalized thinking seemed a radical aberration.

Joseph Campbell once said that the "essence of life is that it lives by killing and eating." That, he contended, is "the great mystery that myths have to deal with." We have managed to forget this. We have distanced ourselves from the killing, fashioning a system in which few modern meat eaters ever make a pilgrimage to woods or farmyard to deal directly with that mystery and look those other lives in the eye. We have relegated killing to the profanity of industrial processing, pigs and cattle whacked dead along the disassembly line with the same soulless regularity as widgets being put together. And we have sanitized and fluffed up our notions of the sacred, elevating the saccharine sweetness of the beatific and the heavenly, glossing over the deeper, darker aspects of life.

In the days after finding the hunter's trash, I returned to the scene in memory. I returned, too, to the blocks of salt I had found under the tree stand by the beaver meadow during bow season the month before. I thought of the bowhunter who told me he had fatally wounded a young buck but failed to find it; he paid only brief lip service to regret. And I thought of the newspaper story from opening weekend of rifle season: Two local men, drunk, had been caught jacking deer, poaching them in a field at night with spotlight and rifle.

Hunting brings us into close contact with land and animals. Approached with humility, such contact can help us recall our place in the natural world, reminding us to celebrate all those lives intertwined with ours. Approached with arrogance, it only alienates us further.

The following weekend, I could have hunted, but I left my rifle locked away. Soon I would be hunting with Uncle Mark.

Along the edge of a small plateau, in thick oak woods a few miles from Mark's house, two deer trails intersected. Earlier in autumn, Mark had propped a few fallen branches against a tree, forming a backdrop of intersecting shapes and lines. More recently, he had cleared a place for me to sit or stand, removing the loud, crunchy oak leaves from underfoot. Nearby, he had used a stick to make a few mock scrapes, hoping to arouse whitetails' curiosity by imitating the pawed-up patches often left by bucks. In the faint predawn light, we saw fresh tracks in the exposed soil.

Mark wished me luck and disappeared back the way we had come. He would circle around the plateau and end up a quarter mile from me, at the base of another tree. I sat down to wait, muzzleloader across my lap.

It was opening day of the Massachusetts shotgun season, so hunters would be in the woods with all kinds of firearms. They might be hunting with guns they believed to be especially practical and effective, or with ones that had sentimental value, perhaps having been handed down by grandfathers, or simply with the only deer guns they owned. Some would be carrying recent-model 12-gauge slug guns. Others would be toting older shotguns. Still others would be armed with modern in-line muzzleloaders. And a few oddballs—like Mark and me—would have old-fashioned caplocks in hand.

In that last oddball category, some would have made the choice based on pure aesthetics: a preference for walnut stocks over black composites, blued steel over stainless, perhaps coupled with a nostalgic affection for buckskin and Boone. Others might have something like Aldo Leopold's thoughts in mind: "Our tools for the pursuit of wildlife improve faster than we do, and sportsmanship is a voluntary limitation in the use of these armaments. It is aimed to augment the role of skill and shrink the role of gadgetry in the pursuit of wild things." Though Leopold tempered his criticism of gadgetry by noting that he did not "pretend to know what is moderation, or where the line is between legitimate and illegitimate gadgets," some hunters would go further, arguing that choosing a firearm was a question of "fair chase."

Such questions, which go back to ancient Greek, European, and Euro-American definitions of sportsmanship, boil down to these: How much skill should be required of the hunter? How challenging should it be to find and kill an animal? What chances should the prey have of evading the hunter?

Technology could, I thought, raise important ethical questions. In one of the essays in *A Hunter's Heart*, for instance, writer and ex-Marine David Stalling—who hunts elk with both a compound bow and a scoped rifle—asked how far technology should go: Should hunters employ advanced military weaponry in pursuit of game, shooting elk from a half mile off, using .50-caliber rifles mounted on off-road vehicles? Should they use airplanes to locate animals? Should they use infrared heat-sensing technology, night-vision goggles, and electronic calls? I thought not. But where to draw the line?

In my search for a muzzleloader, I had talked with one shop owner who made no secret of his opinion: Vermont's muzzleloader season should only be for traditional side-lock guns, so-called because the ignition mechanism involves a hammer on the side of the rifle. In his view, modern in-line guns—so-called because the ignition mechanism is inside the rifle, in line with the powder charge and projectile—were too much like centerfire rifles. They had no place in a "primitive arms" season. I thought

I knew where he was coming from. And yet, despite my aesthetic affection for simplicity and my admiration for the skill required to hunt with more basic weapons, I always wondered where arguments for lower-tech hunting would stop.

If the shop owner objected to in-lines, why not object to caplocks, which use nineteenth-century percussion cap technology? Why not insist on flintlocks, the seventeenth-century technology in which ignition is triggered by a piece of flint striking steel? If a hunter argued against hunting with compound bows, why not argue against bows altogether? Why not insist that hunters only use spears or atlatl darts? Why not go all the way back, insisting that we only use rocks or that we return to persistence hunting, running animals to exhaustion and throttling them with our bare hands?

For me, sportsmanship and aesthetic preferences would be tempered by practical considerations. I wouldn't seek every possible advantage, loading my pack and pockets with every hunting gadget I could find. On the other hand, I wasn't auditioning for a part in a frontier flick. I was hunting for food. In Vermont rifle season, I would use my scoped Tikka. In Vermont muzzleloader season—and here in Massachusetts, where centerfire rifles were prohibited due to safety concerns over longer-range projectiles—I would use the caplock that rested across my knees.

I sat, watching the morning sky brighten. I heard a rustling of oak leaves, peered among the trees for a hundred-pound deer, and found myself staring at a one-pound squirrel instead. I wondered: Would my first whitetail come to me here, during my first hunt with Mark?

Not if success hinged on knowledge and skill. By hunting in a spot Mark had selected, I could borrow from his familiarity with prey and landscape. But I still knew little about deer, and I knew nothing of this particular place, nothing of when and where deer fed and bedded, what trails they habitually used, how their movement patterns changed with the seasons. And I lacked the skills of an experienced hunter. Though I could sit fairly still and shoot fairly straight, I came up short in every other department: moving silently, unraveling the stories told by tracks and other signs, responding decisively to shifts in the breeze or to the movements of deer.

If success hinged more on luck, though, I might stand a chance. A deer might simply appear. A shift in the wind might carry my scent away just before it reached the animal's nose. A deer might see me, but hesitate for one fatal moment.

And what if other factors were at play in the woods? What if other forces, unseen and mysterious, helped shape the movements of deer and hunter alike, determining whether their paths would cross, and how? I thought of the red-tailed hawk feather I had found cradled in tree branches just above my head.

In many traditional cultures, hunters are taught to approach the hunt with humility and prayer, taking care not to speak discourteously—or even directly—of the animals to be hunted. In such traditions, knowledge and skill are vital, of course. Yet it is understood that disrespect guarantees failure. Thinking of the blaze-orange trash I had found, it was hard to place much faith in the idea that animals had the ability to avoid arrogant, ill-mannered slobs. Yet my attitude might still be a factor. My thoughts might be woven into the web of influences that would either bring deer or keep them away.

Sitting there at the base of the tree Mark had picked out, I spoke silently to the unseen deer. I praised their beauty, agility, and speed. I praised their ability to become nearly invisible, standing still, blending into the forest. And I asked them to appear. Even if success was not framed by some moral universe, it felt as though the hunt—this seeking to kill an animal whose body would yield sustenance for mine—demanded this kind of attention. The practice, however, felt strange. I was praying. To animals.

I had grown up in a culture where people spoke and listened to only one unseen power. Though I wasn't taught to pray to God, I heard talk about it all around me, so I had a grasp of how one went about doing it and what it meant. Praying to animals, on the other hand, was foreign. I did not come from a lineage of people who spoke or listened to wild things. I came from people—Italian, German, French, English, Welsh, Scottish, and Irish, all now thoroughly Americanized—whose animistic traditions were uprooted centuries ago. The inclination to talk to wild animals, even to send entreaties their way and attend to their voices, might have been in me as a boy, but that inclination had not been cultivated. Now, in trying to shape a hunting prayer, I found myself unsure how to address the larger-than-human world.

It was not just that I lacked a repertoire, a range of particular words and phrases to draw from. It was that I lacked a way of thinking in which prayerful interaction with animals was coherent. Consciousness of this kind has been central to human existence for the vast majority of our hundreds-of-millennia-long tenure on the planet, but I had not learned it. Intellectually, it might make sense to me, but it was not ingrained in my patterns of thought and speech and listening. This was the kind of disconnection Thomas Berry had in mind when he spoke of our spiritual autism: "We have broken the great conversation."

Trying anyway—clumsily piecing together silent prayers—I felt like a klutz. I also felt like a thief.

Even as words surfaced—*singing, rain, lightning*—and were cobbled together in my dim mental recesses, I knew they had been lifted from things I had read: perhaps from Claus Chee Sonny's account of a Navajo ceremony known as the Deerhunting Way, or from prayers attributed to the Oglala holy man Black Elk by John G. Neihardt, the white poet and amateur ethnographer who wrote the famous book *Black Elk Speaks*.

It made me uneasy. My ancestors had sought to exterminate American Indian peoples, robbing them of their lives, their land, and the freedom to practice their own religions and speak their own languages. At the same time, my people adopted Indianness when and how it suited them, from the Boston Tea Party to the Daniel Boone stories, from the Boy Scouts to New Age shamanism. As historian Philip J. Deloria argues in *Playing Indian*, the two are linked. The co-opting of Indian identity has long gone "hand in hand with the dispossession and conquest of actual Indian people." And here I was, sitting in woods long hunted by the Wampanoag, with a frontier-style musket across my lap, stitching together borrowed verbal fragments into some clumsy parody of a native deer-hunting prayer. Did my superficial need for language justify the cultural rip-off? As much as I respected the indigenous cultures of the Americas, wasn't it high time my Euro-American psyche stopped feeding off them?

Even if I knew a traditional native hunting prayer in its entirety and could, somehow, borrow it respectfully, what meaning or power would it really have? The transplanted words would have no roots. For me, such mimicry made no more sense—and was fraught with more troubling subtext—than mouthing the words of a Catholic High Mass. Even with an intellectual understanding of what such a prayer was supposed to mean, I would still be "playing Indian."

For that matter, even if I knew the details of an ancient European hunting ceremony like putting vegetation into the mouth of the fallen animal, giving it a "last meal," what meaning would that have for me? That, too, was anthropology. That, too, was history, not a living tradition in which I was raised. I would just be "playing ancient European." The act would not have emerged organically from my lived experience.

Prayers or no prayers, squirrels were all I saw those first two days.

The third morning, though, a blast came at sunrise, sudden and final. Soon, I saw Mark walking toward me through the woods, the blaze orange of his hat and vest startling in the drizzly, shrouded light.

Returning to the fallen deer, we stood together in the mist. I didn't know what prayer, if any, Mark might have said before he came looking for me, what small ritual he might have performed to honor the life he had taken. Now, there was simply silence, our thoughts and feelings unspoken.

The lead slug had taken the doe in the chest, dropping her on the spot. Though she was small, it didn't surprise me that Mark had squeezed the trigger. During his recent trip to Virginia, he had had no luck. Now, in early December, with the annual end of Massachusetts deer hunting only a few weeks away, his chances for venison were waning. Any whitetail was a blessing.

Quietly, Mark began the field dressing, slitting the skin and abdominal wall, and easing the stomach, intestines, and liver out onto the forest floor. (Years earlier, Mark would have saved the liver and eaten it, but health advisories had since deterred him: Deer liver can contain high levels of cadmium.) Then he cut the diaphragm free and removed the heart and lungs. I recalled Cath describing how she had watched her brother dress out rabbits when she was a kid. She hadn't been horrified. Rather, she had been fascinated by the anatomy lesson, the shiny muscles and complex organs unveiled. As I watched Mark work, I found myself relieved that he had done the killing, not I—that his hands, not mine, were pulling out this animal's innards.

Once the entrails were removed, Mark covered the pile with leaves. We were on public land, near a trail where people sometimes hiked, and a passerby might be offended by the sight. The area was also frequented by other hunters, one of whom might take the viscera as a clue and start hunting this edge of the small plateau. Over the years, Mark's luck had been good here and he had grown fond of the spot. He didn't want to show up on opening day a year from now and find another hunter sitting under the tree he had used as a backrest this morning. In any case, coyotes would soon find the entrails. This patch of earth would be licked clean in a matter of days.

When Mark was done, he said he would hike out to the car, drop off his gun and pack, and come back with his deer sled, a sheet of rugged plastic that eased the dragging of a deer across bare ground and kept the carcass clean. He suggested that I stay put, gun loaded. Unlikely as it seemed, he said he had seen whitetails, perhaps drawn by curiosity, walk right up to where another deer had just been gutted.

So I sat a few yards away and waited, meditating on dripping forest and freshly killed mammal. Five years earlier, as a vegan, I could not possibly have imagined the scene: me watching over a cooling carcass, scanning the woods for a second deer. Even now, I felt ambivalent.

When Mark returned some forty minutes later, we lashed the sled around the doe like a black cocoon, then dragged her to the road. It was easy going—the sled smooth, the terrain gentle. In the back of his old station wagon, Mark had spread a doubled-over tarp. We hoisted the animal in.

As Mark drove, I nestled into the passenger seat and watched the light rain bead up on the windshield between wiper strokes. I savored the moment, being there with my uncle, knowing we had accomplished what we had set out to do. And I felt something shifting. Cruising down the road with our dead mammalian cargo, I was crossing another threshold into the unfamiliar.

After checking in the deer at a sporting-goods shop, we headed back to the house. On the way, Mark asked if I wanted to get back to the woods that afternoon. Though the day was already warming into the fifties, he could get the doe quartered and iced down in coolers so we could head out again. The rest of the butchering could wait. I told him I saw no reason why it should. I was there to learn. Cutting up a deer was as much a part of the hunt as tracking or stalking. And we still had tomorrow, the last day of our hunt.

Under the back deck, Mark hung the doe upside down from a gambrel, a simple device resembling a large, rugged coat hanger. At each end, a steel hook passed through the gap between tendon and bone, just behind the anatomical equivalent of the human ankle. Mark made a slit up the inside of each rear leg and cut the skin free just below the gambrel. Then, with something to get hold of, he pulled downward, peeling off the doe's hide, only using his knife when necessary.

The skinning startled me. Though Mark worked without haste, the metamorphosis seemed abrupt. As the hide peeled away from hind legs and back, the inside of the doe's skin was revealed, white tissue overlapped by fine layers of subcutaneous muscle. When Mark was finished, the whitetail—an animal whose identity had, in my eyes, been defined by her grayish-brown coat, white belly, elegant head, and great ears—was gone. In her place hung an unrecognizable, headless carcass: muscle, fat, and bone. Mark was one of the most sensitive and softhearted people I knew. Yet he had just turned a graceful, living being into a hunk of meat.

The remainder of that gray, damp day passed quietly. We cleared the small kitchen island of its usual homey clutter and worked opposite each other. First, the hind quarters, then the front, and finally the ribs, back, and neck. I was slow and tentative with the boning knife, mimicking Mark's sure, practiced motions. Tendons and silver skin were carefully trimmed from backstrap and steak. Smaller pieces were set aside for stew meat. The rest went through a hand-crank grinder clamped to the countertop. By night, the doe was in the basement freezer.

The last day of our hunt, Mark and I found fresh tracks in the moist earth. Neither of us saw deer. Toward dusk, a dark gray coyote trotted by on the slope below me. Perhaps the four-footed hunter would soon feast on the entrails of the doe we had butchered.

The next morning, Mark insisted that I leave with half his venison, as generous with me as the land had been with him.

I thought about the meat in the cooler behind me as I drove north. Cath and I still got the bulk of our calories and nutrition—fruits, vegetables, grains, chickens, and more—from farming done by others. From our own gardening, we got a smaller portion of our food—greens, peas, beans, carrots, squash, and the like—plus an invaluable sense of involvement and connection. From wild food, we got something else.

Whether unsought and unforeseen like a bagful of wild blue-berries spontaneously picked on a sunny hillside, or hunted and hoped for like chanterelles sought in summer woods or like this deer that Mark had killed, wild food was not something grown or owned, bought or sold. It was something given and taken.

In *Living Wild and Domestic*, Robert Kimber clarifies the differ-ence. Unlike the hunted animal, he writes, "The animal raised and slaughtered is not a gift. We have earned that food in a dif-ferent way, and when we eat that animal, we are not accepting a gift as much as we are exercising our property rights." If Cath and I were raising chickens, we would know when those birds would go from yard to freezer. Buying them from local farmers, we could make an appointment. Buying them from the local food co-op, we could simply walk to the cooler. The food would be there.

As much as we depended on such relentless certainty, something in me craved the unpredictable. I thought once again of Willie, of poker and fishing, of Henry van Dyke's "enchantment of uncertainty." In hunting, the outcome would always be mysterious. Entering the woods, I would never know whether an animal would appear. Perhaps hunting would feed soul as much as body, reminding me of our oldest, humblest way of eating. To fallen deer, as to blueberry bush, I would not be master, standing over that which was rightfully mine, but supplicant, on my knees, hand outstretched.

12

Fickle Predators

There is the difference between the animal and humankind. The animal has no alternatives. We make choices.
  —William A. Caldwell, "Hawk and Hare Are One"

A year later, in the growing light of a late October dawn, a crew of chickadees darted around me in fearless curiosity. I could not imagine killing one of these birds, the way I once had as a boy. As the air warmed to just above freezing, birch leaves began to fall, round and golden, as if all that held stem to twig had been a tiny speck of ice.

Coming into my second autumn of deer hunting, I still didn't know the land well. But I had scouted hard that summer, exploring the woods behind our house. The deer trails marked on my home-made map formed an increasingly complex web, quilting the land-scape with movement as large herbivores threaded their way among pines, maples, and balsam firs, across brooks and around ponds, along old logging roads and through breaches in old stone walls. I was beginning to see how whitetails lived, here, in this place.

So far this fall, I hadn't hunted much. The first weekend of archery season, the mercury had hovered around eighty. I could not imagine killing a whitetail in that heat: The chance of meat spoilage seemed too high. My first go at the entire process—field dressing a deer, dragging the animal out of the woods, driving it to a local check-in station, getting it home, skinning it, and breaking the carcass down into parts that would fit into coolers where they could be iced down—would, I suspected, be anything but swift.

The second weekend had brought rain. That was weather I might have hunted in with high hopes during rifle season. Mark had told me that deer often seemed less wary in a light rain and it had, in fact, been a misty day when he shot that doe on the Cape. But even with a perfectly placed arrow, straight through the heart or both lungs, I knew that a deer could run fifty or a hundred yards in the few seconds before it collapsed, and I wasn't keen on following a faint blood trail as it washed away by the minute. The thought of shooting a deer and failing to find it made my stomach turn.

The third weekend, Mother Nature—apparently bored with just hell or high water—had concocted an unsavory mix of warm temperatures, rain, and winds that whipped through the forest, stripping the maples of their orange and red glory.

Now, though, with just three days left in bow season, the sky was clear and the air cool. Getting an unexpected Friday off from work, I had hiked into the woods under a fat quarter moon. In the dark, I had climbed into my tree stand and now sat here, perched a dozen feet up a large maple, waiting. I watched the chickadees and warblers around me. I listened to the Canada geese honking overhead, winging south. I savored the quiet, knowing that now, in archery season, the forest would not be rocked by a rifle's sudden blast. For over an hour, I contemplated the steady fall of birch leaves, each yellow oval letting go silently and coming to rest on the forest floor with a faint rustle.

The flicker of movement came as a shock. Then another flicker. Deer legs moving through the brush straight ahead. The soft crunch of leaves under each hoof. I had an impression of one deer, then two. My heart began to thud. Cautiously I stood, bow in hand.

The whitetails came slowly, through thick cover. Then they stepped into view just fifteen yards away: a doe and a fawn, no longer spotted but noticeably smaller than its mother. The two deer turned directly toward me, coming down the narrow game trail over which I perched. The doe was in the lead. Ten yards away. Then five. I had never been so close to a living deer. I could see muscles and shoulder blades gliding under her grayish-brown coat.

As she passed below, her back only nine feet from my boots, she spooked and leapt forward, then stopped. She did not look up, so she had not seen me. She did not bolt, so she had not scented me. And I didn't think she had heard me. But she had sensed something.

The feeling must have passed, though, for she relaxed, twitched her tail from side to side, and nibbled at a maple seedling. Here they were: two whitetails, ten yards away. If I was careful, moving only when their eyes were averted, I might get a shot before they stepped back into cover.

I wouldn't, though. As soon as I saw them clearly, I had known I would not draw an arrow.

My decision wasn't rooted in reluctance to kill a doe, or even a fawn. I had heard that venison from a doe killed in October tasted better than venison from a buck killed during the November rut, when testosterone was coursing through his system. And though very young deer didn't yield much meat, their venison was best of all—a kind of free-range veal. If doe or fawn had appeared alone, the one apparently childless, or the other apparently orphaned, I might have drawn string to jaw and sighted down the shaft, looking for that clear path to heart and lungs.

But they had appeared together. Though I knew that the doe would survive without her fawn and that the weaned five-month-old would stand a fair chance without its mother, I could not bring myself to kill either of them. I knew they had each other. That bond was stronger than any claim I could stake.

In writing of relationships among animals, of course, I invite the charge of anthropomorphism: the suggestion that I am projecting human emotions on to other species. That may be so. I don't know what it is to be an animal. I have no access to the interiority of a deer. But I would rather err in that direction than make the conceited assumption that we are the only species capable of feeling, that our brand of awareness and connection is something so special. In his essay "A Killing at Dawn," writer and hunter Ted Kerasote recounts seeing an elk calf torn apart by wolves. After the wolves have made off with the remains, the mother elk returns to the spot where her calf was killed and begins to "grunt mournfully, her sides contracting and her muzzle elongating into the shape of a trumpet." Fifteen hours later, at sunset, she still stands there, her head hanging low. What can we call that but grief?

Glad to have a reason not to kill, I stood silently, my heart quiet, admiring doe and fawn as they browsed together, nibbling at small trees and shrubs. I took quiet pleasure in observing their movements: a twitch of the ear or tail, a sudden lift of the head. Half an hour later, they vanished into the woods.

A subsistence hunter whose family depended on wild meat would, I supposed, have shot the doe. So would a hunter who based such decisions on strictly ecological grounds. In this part of Vermont, the deer population is not extraordinarily dense, but their numbers do need to be controlled to allow for diverse forest regeneration, to protect species that depend on a healthy forest understory, and to prevent overbrowsing of the sheltered "deer yards" where whitetails congregate when the snow is deep. Because bucks breed with multiple does, the hunting of male whitetails has little effect on a population's reproductive potential. If population growth is left unchecked, deer can literally eat themselves out of a home.

But I figured that most Vermont hunters would not have taken a shot. Some, like me, would have been swayed by the mother-child relationship. Others would simply have been waiting for a buck. Though I had no particular interest in inedible head gear, I knew that plenty of hunters wanted more than meat for the freezer. They also wanted antlers for display and the prestige of having taken a buck: Male deer are scarcer than females and are seen as more challenging prey, especially as they get older, warier, and wiser to the ways of hunters. Some hunters would even have chipped in a few dollars for one of the "deer pool" bets run at local check-in stations and would be hoping for biggest-buck prize money.

And then there were those who would have let doe and fawn pass by for the simple reason that they opposed antlerless hunting outright. Though in the minority, these Vermont hunters vocally maintain that doe killing imperils the state's deer herd. Their distrust of wildlife biologists has deep roots, in a local history both political and ecological.

Back in the late 1800s, when the state's deer population was first starting to recover, farmers began complaining of crop losses and pressured the legislature to take action. Legislators responded by establishing a monthlong bucks-only season. In October of 1897, Vermont's first deer season in three decades, 103 bucks were legally taken in the state. Predictably, whitetail numbers continued to grow. A decade later, in response to continued outcry from farmers, the legislature went further, allowing five either-sex seasons between 1909 and 1920. Two years after each season in which does were taken, buck kill numbers dropped substantially.

By the 1920s, though, hunting was becoming popular and the political tide had begun to turn. Vermont settled into a bucks-only hunting model, protecting does and allowing deer numbers to rise. In 1940, the annual buck kill was up to thirty-four hundred. In 1950, it exceeded six thousand. By this point, as anthropologist Marc Boglioli discusses in his book *A Matter of Life and Death: Hunting in Contemporary Vermont*, wildlife biologists were already warning of imminent danger. In a 1947 booklet entitled *The Time Is Now!—A Pictorial Story of Vermont's Deer Herd*, they argued that whitetails were becoming overpopulated. Vermont's forests—which had recovered dramatically in the century since the collapse of the sheep industry and the widespread abandonment of farms as residents headed west—could support just so many deer. If antlerless seasons were not implemented, biologists warned, deer would overbrowse their winter habitat. Before long, they would not have enough food to survive a harsh winter and their numbers would crash.

Vermont, however, was gaining a reputation as a deer-hunting destination. Hunters' political clout was growing and they, unlike farmers, liked what they were seeing: more and more whitetails. They did not want to see a reprise of the heavy toll taken by the either-sex seasons of 1909 to 1920. Though state biologists reassured the public that doe hunting would be more controlled this time, the legislature was reluctant. Antlerless hunting was allowed for a single day in 1961 and a single day in 1962, to little effect. By 1966—with the state's deer population peaking around 250,000—the buck kill exceeded 17,000.

In the late 1960s, antlerless seasons were expanded slightly, but were still limited to a small fraction of the buck kill. Unfortunately, those marginally effective seasons coincided with the brutal winters of 1969–70 and 1970–71. Deer are resistant to winter: In preparation for it, they put on a thick layer of fat and shed the short, solid hairs that make up their summer coat, replacing it with a highly insulated, double-layer winter coat of long hollow hairs over fine, woolly fur. But they are not impervious, especially when malnourished. In those two winters, with limited food available, the snow deep, and the air frigid, tens of thousands of Vermont deer died. In the fall of 1971, the buck kill dropped below eight thousand for the first time in two decades.

As Boglioli notes, this was precisely the kind of collapse biologists had predicted. Many hunters, however, refused to believe that overpopulation and resulting habitat decline were at the root of the problem. Instead, they pointed to the killing of does, which they had opposed all along. For the next twenty years, antlerless seasons were closed and reopened. The buck kill ticked up and down, but never rebounded to anything like the glory days of earlier decades. In 1991, rifle hunting of does was prohibited altogether.

Over the years, opposition to antlerless seasons has declined, as younger generations of Vermont hunters accept the scientific evidence concerning the importance of habitat health. Most hunters support the current regulations: Antlerless deer can be taken during archery season. They can also be taken during the nine-day December muzzleloader season, by special permits issued in varying numbers around the state, depending on where biologists see a need.

Reflecting on the passionate intensity of these historical and ongoing debates, I wonder: Are the arguments and resulting regulations rooted only in hunters' and biologists' assessments of various approaches to deer management? Or are they also rooted further back, in the sporting codes of old? In the nineteenth century, reports historian Louis Warren, white middle- and upper-class American men's preoccupation with their own masculinity was frequently expressed in terms of hunting. As sport hunters lobbied for wildlife conservation, they also lobbied for hunting regulations that mirrored their particular codes for masculine behavior. In Warren's words, "How one hunted and what one killed came to define what kind of man one was." Hunting big, antlered bucks was manly. Hunting does and fawns was not.

Once, as I read down a roster of deer reported at a local check-in station during archery season—4-point buck, 135 pounds; doe, 108 pounds; 7-point buck, 172 pounds; doe, 94 pounds—I came to several entries without a field-dressed weight listed, each noted simply as "BB" or "FF." The first, I figured, stood for "button buck," meaning a male fawn with tiny "button" nubs instead of antlers. But the second? I asked the guy behind the counter.

"Fuzzy-faced fawn," he said. "Female."

Ah, yes, I thought, *the fuzziness factor: the undeniably cute, foreshortened features of young mammals. Button Bambi and Fuzzy Faline.*

He explained that they didn't bother to weigh fawns, male or female. Unlike the biologists who attended major check-in stations on opening weekend of rifle season, the staff members at this sporting-goods shop weren't gathering detailed data. So why embarrass the hunter?

What strange and fickle predators we modern humans are. If a hungry cougar had been in my place, perched in that maple as doe and fawn passed below, it would not have hesitated. The cat might have pounced on the larger, meatier doe. Or, like the wolves that killed the elk calf as Ted Kerasote watched, it might have gone for the easiest prey: the fawn.

Whichever animal the cougar pounced on, the cat would not have invoked some moral calculus, giving special consideration to the relationship between doe and fawn. Nor, I thought, would a cat have shared my impulse three months earlier, when another whitetail went down.

It had been a Saturday evening in mid-July. I was out for a walk, with the thick, drizzly remnants of a hurricane blowing overhead, bringing an early dusk and filling the woods with dripping, rustling noises. I paused on the trail, sensing something. What was that, standing there under the softwoods? Gradually, I made out the form of a doe, rusty brown in her sleek summer coat. A moment later, she leapt across the trail and disappeared.

Movement caught my eye, though, in the ferns below the trail. A fawn? I moved closer. The doe who had just leapt across in front of me now lay on the ground, thrashing. I had no idea what had just happened, but I felt certain that she was done for. If I'd had a gun with me, mercy might have trumped law.

I hurried the fifteen minutes back to the house, and an hour later, a game warden and I were driving down the rail-bed trail in his truck. He suspected that the doe might be long gone, having only pinched a nerve or temporarily subluxated a joint, but he thought it was worth looking.

We reached the spot at full dark. Our flashlights showed the place where she had been and the wide swath of matted ferns where she had dragged herself downhill. She had gone just thirty yards. The warden drew his pistol, covered his ears as well as he could with one hand and a hunched-up shoulder, and did the only humane thing. Then a second shot, just to be sure.

I watched her body twitch. When she was still, the warden pointed out that her legs looked fine. Then he felt along her back and found the spot where her spine had snapped. Leaning over, I felt it, too: under the smooth hair, a soft distortion in the regular rhythm of her vertebrae. The warden had heard of this happening, but had never seen it before. We wondered aloud: Did she land wrong, the force of impact traveling through her body just so? Or had she been thrown in midleap by a piece of the rusty, broken telegraph line that ran along that stretch of rail bed, sometimes hanging in trees, sometimes buried, sometimes looping up to catch unwary feet? And how long would she have lingered, before being finished off by coyotes or dying of thirst?

The warden asked me if I wanted the meat. Poachers, I had heard, swore there was no finer flesh than summer venison. "Side-hill salmon," some called it. This would be a remarkable way to get my first deer, the animal falling nearly at my feet. But it would take me a long while to drive out with the warden and back in again with my own truck, complete my first clumsy field dressing by flashlight, get the doe up to the trail and into the vehicle, get home, and get the body or quarters iced down for the night. Too long for this July heat, I thought. Besides, I knew that coyotes and other scavengers would make good use of the remains. The food might even spare the life of a fawn who would otherwise be hunted down. So I left her there.

I was a hunter now, yes. But when I found the doe flailing on the ground, I had not seen the prey I would be pursuing in October. I had seen a fellow creature suffering—exactly what I would have seen five or ten years earlier, in my days as a vegan.

The day after the doe died, I was driving, brooding over her fate, when I caught sight of another deer. She stood her ground in the middle of the dirt road, apparently unconcerned by the several thousand pounds of growling truck that rolled toward her. Finally, she broke for the woods. When I stopped to look for her, she was there among the leaves, whole and healthy, dark eyes and great ears turned in curiosity.

13
Blood Trails

We tracked the deer for three hours before losing the trail. Neither of us said much, just followed small, scattered dots of blood, vivid red against the snow.

—Susan Ewing, "To Each Her Own"

Saturday, the second-to-last day of bow season, dawned in an icy fog, a great ghostly halo around the quarter moon. Perched in the maple that morning, I saw only mice—or voles, perhaps—scurrying to and fro where doe and fawn had stood just twenty-four hours earlier.

My thoughts wandered to the chores I should be doing and I found myself longing for Uncle Mark's companionship. The previous December, on Cape Cod, just knowing he was nearby had helped me stay fully present to the woods and to the moment, banishing the nagging voice of productivity. This year, given the constraints of schedules and finances, Mark and I would not be hunting together.

After several hours of watching rodents, I hiked home.

Sunday, I did not plan to hunt. It was supposed to rain all day. But Cath and I awoke to a white world. With three inches of fresh snow, the tracking would be perfect. I had to go see what stories the ground might tell.

Not that I was fooling myself about the odds. Even with a rifle, I doubted whether I could pick up a deer's trail, follow however far it led, get within sight of the animal, and find the opportunity for a clean-killing shot. With a bow, my chances were pathetic. After all, I had never depended on hunted meat for survival. Nor had my father or mother. Nor had any of my grandparents. Far from being honed to sharp and deadly perfection, my predatory skills were dull. White-tailed deer, on the other hand, have been alert to pursuers, both four legged and two legged, for thousands of years. They have had no hiatus from the chase. Except for those animals lulled into semidomestication by life in the suburbs, they have never forgotten how to vanish.

Around my tree stand, I scanned the surface of the dense, moist snow. Nothing. No sign that even a squirrel had passed by. Slowly, I hiked farther into the woods. I walked under tall hemlocks, eased around boulders, and wove through thick undergrowth, looking for tracks.

Then I looked up and froze. A doe, bedded down in the shelter of small evergreens, stared straight at me, both ears up and funneled forward. I stared back, motionless.

There was a tree just two steps to my right, but even if I got behind it she would still know I was there. She might even get more suspicious. I thought back to an e-mail that Mark's buddy Jay had sent the year before: Walking through the woods near his cabin in the Blue Ridge Mountains, he had startled a doe. When he stopped and stood still, she got curious, moved toward him, then relaxed and began feeding. Might that work for me now?

I stood there, trying to keep every muscle still. She lay there, stiller yet.

Nearby, limbs and small treetops snapped under the heavy, wet snow. As the air temperature rose, clumps began falling from branches above, thudding down all around. When the first fist-sized clump struck my shoulder, I flinched. In response to my movement, I felt sure the doe would spring to her feet, snort in alarm, and disappear among the trees. But her eyes and ears didn't waver.

We were about thirty yards apart: too far for a shot. That summer, I had switched from Jay's recurve to a longbow that better suited my body. Though I stand just shy of six feet, my fingertip-to-fingertip wingspan turns out to be six foot three, which makes it hard to shoot a bow designed for someone with more reasonably proportioned arms. For months, I had been practicing with the longbow. Beyond twenty yards, though, I could not be sure of keeping my arrows in a five-inch circle.

The minutes slipped by. I glanced down at the length of teased dental floss dangling from my bow. When dry, it would tremble like dandelion down, lifting at the faintest breeze to show where my scent was drifting. Now, though, in the near-still air, it hung limp, clotted with wet snow.

Finally, an ear twitched. The doe turned her head slightly, then looked away completely. Had she forgotten about me? Had I, in my stillness, become a tall, oddly shaped stump for her?

I took a slow step to the side. As I eased my full weight over, the wet snow compressed with a sudden soft *shunk!* The doe did not look my way. One more careful step and I was in cover. I glanced at my watch. We had been motionless for a full half hour.

Now what? Looking around, I couldn't see any good approach. If I went to the left, I would be too visible as I moved from tree to tree. If I went to the right, I would have to navigate a tangle of saplings and fallen branches. Either way, I would lose sight of the doe—I would have no idea if she was alert to my presence. There was only one way to go. I slipped an arrow from my quiver, and set it to string and bow. Then I eased back into the open, headed straight for the doe.

For five minutes, or ten, I would stand still. Then the doe would look away and I would take a cautious step, the *shunk!* of compression masked by the thudding of snow clumps falling all around.

Once, facing me, she coughed up her cud and set to chewing it. Later, when low-flying Canada geese honked over with swishing wings, she looked skyward, perhaps in curiosity. When she tucked nose to tail, averting her eyes, I took five steps in fifteen minutes. It felt like a sprint.

Bits of snow clung, dripping, to bow and arrow. My fleece jacket and pants were soaked, struck everywhere by falling, wet clumps. I trembled—from the damp cold, from holding my muscles so still, and, yes, from a kind of excitement.

Marti Kheel and other feminist critics of hunting would, I knew, seize upon such a feeling. They would interpret it in sexual terms: me, a male predator, in a state of agitation as I closed in on my prey, in this case a female. In "License to Kill," Kheel argued that the various ethical codes espoused by hunters are all rooted in the need to restrain aggressive sexual energy and channel it appropriately. In building her argument, Kheel quoted suggestive passages from hunting literature: Paul Shepard's references, for instance, to "treating the woman-prey with love" and to killing as an "ecstatic consummation," and Ortega y Gasset's lurid commentary on the "unequaled orgiastic power" of blood. Like Kheel, I found such words disturbing.

The excitement I felt now had nothing to do with sex or blood, or even killing. What I felt was aliveness. My senses were intensely engaged. My whole being was focused, trembling with energy. Was this what a cougar felt as it prepared to pounce? In that moment, despite my longstanding unease with the idea of hunters enjoying the actual pursuit, I understood how compelling this part of the hunt could be, this kicking into sensory overdrive. And I wondered what moral value there could possibly be in not feeling this, in hunting as a Puritan might want me to—setting off into the woods like a somber executioner.

There was, I realized, a second deer. Not a fawn, but another full-grown doe, off to the side in thicker cover, facing away from me.

The first doe stood. Not in swift alarm, but casually. She shook herself and took a step. Then she stopped, broadside to me.

Should I shoot? How far apart were we? Maybe twenty yards? I still felt no particular urge to kill, but what better opportunity could I hope for? The whole scenario seemed impossibly lucky, from first seeing the doe nearly two hours ago to this moment. Slowly, I drew string to jaw and looked down the arrow. I still wasn't sure.

According to the anatomical chart I had pinned to the basement wall beside my workbench, the doe's heart and lungs were just behind her shoulder. With a firearm, the shot angle wouldn't matter as much—a bullet could break large bones, busting through sternum or shoulder from the front, striking vital organs or simply killing by dint of massive systemic shock. With a bow, it mattered far more. To kill quickly, my arrow would need to pass through the doe's most vital organs, stopping her heart or destroying her lungs. And an arrow could be deflected by major bones. Like most bowhunters, I would not shoot if a deer was facing me. The animal had to be angled away or standing perfectly broadside, as this doe was now.

I released the string.

Instantly, I knew it was a bad shot. Rather than flying toward that spot behind the doe's shoulder, the arrow went left—far left—and stuck, quivering, in the smooth bark of a maple that stood only halfway from me to her. I stared at the arrow.

The doe hadn't even noticed. Calmly, she took a few steps and disappeared behind a thick stand of balsam saplings. A minute later, catching wind of me, she circled back suddenly and both deer bounded off in great leaps, white flags aloft. The intensity of the stalk drained away.

I paced off the distance. Yes, it had been twenty yards. But I had established that range limit under the ideal conditions of practice, when I was steady and relaxed. It had been much too far when my muscles were shaking with tension and cold.

I turned to my arrow, embedded in the maple. There were so many other paths the shaft might have taken. If my aim had been a little better, the arrow would have struck the doe in the hind leg or belly. I had come that close to wounding her or, worse yet, killing her slowly. My stomach turned at the thought. What good were my romantic aspirations to communion with nature, or to respectful confrontation with death, if I couldn't adhere to the most basic hunting ethic—taking only the surest, cleanest shots?

I had begun the stalk not because I imagined I might actually get close enough for a shot, but because the attempt itself appealed, as a challenge and a chance to learn. Then I had botched it. Prying the broadhead from the tree, I knew I should have heeded the voice of doubt within. The doe and I had both been very lucky.

I shambled home and turned my attention to chores. But that afternoon Cath saw a solitary doe cross the clearing below the house. Though I couldn't imagine taking another shot that day, there were still two hours left in bow season. I could get out and learn something. Maybe I could even walk off some shame.

I followed the doe down into the woods. Before long, her hoofprints crossed those of another deer and I lost track of which was which. Oh, yes, still plenty to learn. Minutes later, I found two sets of boot tracks, one as large as mine, the other smaller. I imagined a father and son and envied them their companionship. The humans were tracking a deer. The hoofprints showed clear in the wet snow. Curious, I followed.

Then I found a small patch of blood. And another. The pattern was regular: blood staining the snow every fifty yards. After a quarter mile, I knew the shot had been a bad one.

The animal might die slowly, its intestines torn open. Or it might survive. The arrow might have passed clean through a leg muscle that would heal well, or the broadhead might stay lodged in spine or skull and never fully heal. In any case, the animal would suffer.

Most of a mile later, I had found no end to the story. No spot where the deer had been gutted. And, to the hunters' credit, no spot where they had abandoned the search. Boot prints still pursued hoofprints. The whitetail still ran across brooks, through thickets of softwood saplings, along the river, leaving blood here and there. In the gathering dusk, I turned for home, steps slow and uncertain.

With archery season over, I was glad to hang up my longbow. Aesthetically, I enjoyed the weapon: its simple grace, its lightness in hand. And I respected hunters who used such primitive technology successfully. But I wasn't sure I should aim it at anything with the capacity to suffer. I had taken up bowhunting because it gave me an extra four weekends to try for a whitetail, because it allowed me to take antlerless deer, and because I had enjoyed archery as a boy. Now, doubts were surfacing.

Bows, especially longbows and recurves shot "bare" (without sights), are praised by hunters and nonhunters alike for making the hunt more challenging, giving much of the advantage to one's prey. Most traditional barebow hunters have to get within twenty or twenty-five yards; most compound hunters using sights have to get within thirty or forty. Yet bows also draw criticism—again from both hunters and nonhunters—for being less dependably lethal than firearms.

Recent studies in Maryland and Connecticut suggest that 10 to 25 percent of arrows shot at deer miss the animal entirely. And even a practiced and disciplined archer, whose arrows almost always fly true, is launching a projectile that travels far slower than the speed of sound. Deer, their reactions lightning fast, can move at the snap of a bowstring—usually crouching in preparation for a leap, so that the arrow strikes higher than intended. Those same studies suggest that at least one in six deer hit by an arrow is not recovered by the hunter. An estimated two-thirds of these deer survive, while one-third die of their wounds.

Even when an arrow hits exactly as the hunter meant it to, bypassing major bones and slicing through heart or lungs, it rarely kills instantly. In the past, I—like other antihunters—would have argued that this makes bowhunting cruel. In recent years, though, I had read accounts of deer and elk flinching as a razor-sharp broadhead passed through them, calmly going back to feeding, then collapsing a few seconds later. Though I didn't care much for hunting videos, I had watched a few. I had seen how arrow-shot deer sometimes went only a few yards, walking slowly, before going down. In slow motion, I had seen how those that ran were already springing into motion before the arrow struck, apparently reacting to the sound of the bowstring, rather than the impact of the arrow. And I had read accounts of people being hit by broadheads and feeling no pain.

A well-placed arrow, I had decided, might not be a bad way to go. I would certainly prefer it to getting hit by a car—which is, of course, how lots of whitetails die. According to the National

Highway Traffic Safety Administration, more than a million auto-deer collisions occur on U.S. roadways each year.

Having come so close to wounding that doe, however, I was uneasy. Mark had told me about the few times he had hit and lost a deer, despite careful shooting and exhaustive tracking. Such experiences had brought him close to giving up hunting. If even longtime hunters could be sickened by such an incident, I had a good idea how this greenhorn would fare. If my first shooting of a deer resulted in an endless blood trail, it would be my last.

Three weeks later, I sat with my back to the base of a maple, awaiting first light. Overhead, spruce and fir wove a dense canopy. In the faint dawn, and into the full brightness of midmorning, I watched and listened. When a barred owl swooped in and perched, a nearby squirrel ceased its chattering.

Now and then a rifle popped softly in the distance. The desire for quiet was part of what brought me this far back into the woods—a half-hour hike from home, far enough from roads to deter most hunters. I did not want to repeat my first opening morning: shots close by, orange gloves discarded alongside entrails.

The place felt good, like the sweet spots I had chosen to fish each summer as a boy. Not far off, two saplings had been rubbed bare by a buck's antlers. I had a hunch I would see deer here.

Whether I would see a *legal* deer was another matter. Rifle-season regulations dictated that I could only shoot a buck. More-over, the rules had changed in the past year. Under pressure from hunters who wanted to start seeing more mature bucks, Vermont had instituted a spikehorn ban. ("Spikehorn," meaning a buck with only a single "spike" antler on each side, is technically a misnomer. True horns, such as bovines have, grow throughout an animal's life, while a cervid's antlers are shed and regrown annually.) Under the new regulations, a buck was only legal if it had a "fork" on at least one side: the main antler plus a second point at least an inch long.

The next morning, I was back in the same spot. The air was still. A few minutes before sunrise, I heard steps in the dry, frozen leaves. My heart started jackhammering. I caught a glimpse through the thick woods: a deer walking away, about forty yards off. I grabbed the grunt call that hung around my neck. It was a gift from Mark, a simple tube housing a plastic reed that vibrated when I blew through it, imitating the grunting sound often made by whitetail bucks during the autumn rut. Hearing the sound, a territorial buck would often investigate. The instant I blew, I heard the animal change direction, turning straight toward me.

It could be a doe, I told myself. I raised my rifle, bracing arms against knees. Or it could be a spikehorn. Whatever it was, the deer was coming, weaving among the close-grown softwood trunks.

Moments later, the animal stepped out from behind a spruce just fifteen yards away, stopped, and stared at me. I stared back.

It was twenty minutes into legal shooting time, but light was sparse under the evergreens. Even with the deer that close—even looking through a low-power scope—it was hard to make out details. Were those just ears, or was I seeing antlers, too? After a second, I made out tall spikes. Then I saw a small side prong at least an inch long. A legal buck. I lowered the rifle a fraction, crosshairs moving toward heart and lungs. In that instant, the whitetail wheeled back into the trees.

A moment later, through a narrow slot between tree trunks, I caught his silhouette as he paused to look back. Almost without thought, I put the crosshairs behind his shoulder and squeezed the trigger. The silhouette disappeared.

All was still. I hadn't really heard the shot, or even felt the rifle kick. That was how Mark had said it would be. During target practice, you feel the recoil and hear the cartridge detonate, even with ear protection on. When you fire on a deer, though, you hardly notice the gun going off. For several seconds, I just sat, stunned.

Get up, I thought. *Get up and walk down there. Your first deer is lying there on the moss and leaves.*

I worked the rifle's bolt, chambering a second round just in case, and flipped the safety back on. Then I stood and took a step. There was a flash of movement at fifty yards as a deer pranced into thick cover, tail held high. A second deer?

I walked to where the silhouette had stood. The buck was not there.

Damn.

Would there be a good blood trail? I could see where the earth had been gouged by hooves, as the animal leapt away. If there was plenty of blood, following would be easy. If there was only a little, I would do as Mark did: I would dig out the short strips of bright orange and blue survey tape I carried in my pack and mark each spot of blood as I went, tracking carefully.

Crouching, I examined the ground. Nothing. No blood. Not even a single bullet-clipped hair. I was baffled. Had I flinched, yanking the trigger and pulling the rifle off target? Had the buck wheeled again at that very moment? I didn't think so.

I went to where I had been sitting and set my blaze-orange cap on top of my backpack. Then I returned to where the deer had been standing, crouched down, and looked back at the cap, reconstructing the straight line between rifle and animal. The narrow slot between trunks was crisscrossed by dead branches.

You fool.

In the dim light, I hadn't seen the branches against the deer's dark silhouette. In these woods, though, I should have assumed they would be there.

Retracing the bullet's path, I found the branch, the torn wood on its underside showing where the small lead torpedo had struck as it screamed along at over twenty-five hundred feet per second. I looked closely. How dramatically had the branch altered the projectile's flight path? Did the bullet angle down into the moss and leaf duff? Did it shatter? Most critically, did any part of it hit the deer?

I checked the ground again: the spot where the deer stopped to look back, the hoof gouges in the forest floor. I worked my way along, following the buck's flight.

Inch by inch.

Foot by foot.

Yard by yard.

Still nothing. No trace of injury. Not a speck of red.

Two hours later, I finally shouldered my rifle and pack and trudged home, replaying the scene again and again in my mind, going over all my mistakes, all the if-onlys. The first arrow I loosed at a deer had struck a tree. Now, the first bullet I fired had struck a branch.

I had violated another basic hunting ethic—to take shots only when you're certain there are no obstructions—and I didn't even know why. Maybe it had been a mindless predatory reflex, an instinct untempered by reason, my shot triggered by the deer's flight. Maybe I was just overeager.

I thought of an oft-quoted passage from *A Sand County Almanac*:

> A peculiar virtue in wildlife ethics is that the hunter ordinarily has no gallery to applaud or disapprove of his conduct. Whatever his acts, they are dictated by his own conscience, rather than by a mob of onlookers. It is difficult to exaggerate the importance of this fact.

> Voluntary adherence to an ethical code elevates the self-respect of the sportsman, but it should not be forgotten that voluntary disregard of the code degenerates and depraves him.

Until this morning, I had agreed with Leopold. Now, I wondered: What if Uncle Mark had been beside me, the man whose disciplined practice of waiting for twig-free shots I aimed to emulate? Would I have squeezed the trigger? I thought not.

My highfalutin ethics did little good if I—in solitude—lacked the judgment necessary to implement them. A gut-shot deer, after all, wouldn't care whether its wound was inflicted by voluntary depravity or involuntary stupidity. Nor did my marksmanship do much good. So I could shoot far more accurately with rifle than with longbow. So what? If I didn't know my own limitations and couldn't accurately assess the circumstances, it hardly mattered.

Maybe I should give up hunting. Cath and I didn't need the venison. We were getting the nutrition we needed without eating chicken or fish every day, let alone red meat.

Two years earlier—after sending me the knife, belt, and grunt call—Mark had written me a note. He acknowledged that hunting, and especially killing, were not for everyone, and assured me that he would not be disappointed or critical if, somewhere down the road, I came to a place where it felt best *not* to pursue the hunt. Had I come to that place now?

I wanted to confront death, not maiming. I could deepen my connection to earth and food in other ways. Maybe I should stick to hiking and paddling, gardening and fishing. Maybe I should leave deer to other hunters, to farmers defending their crops, to the front ends of the cars and trucks I could hear whining along Route 2 in the valley below.

Back at the house, Cath mentioned that she had heard a shot around sunrise, off to the north.

"That was me," I said. "Taking another shot I shouldn't have." I stripped off my fleece pullover and hurled it at the wicker laundry hamper in the corner of the bathroom.

I returned to the woods two days later, subdued.

Once more in rifle season I saw a whitetail, strolling past some sixty yards from where I had taken my foolish shot. Within seconds the animal vanished, leaving me with the uncertain impression of tall spike antlers, and perhaps a small side prong on one or both sides. I prayed that this deer, apparently whole and healthy, was the same one I had fired on.

In December, I saw one last deer. On the final day of muzzleloader season, after half a mile of tracking in fresh snow, I caught a glimpse of the animal turning to look back and realized she was a doe. My caplock rested in my hands, the stock nowhere near my shoulder. Even if the deer had been a legal buck, there would have been no quick shooting among the trees.

14
Hunting with the Buddha

I can't untangle regret from celebration.
                    —Robert Kimber, *Living Wild and Domestic*

Aweek later, at a local general store called the Riverbend, I
noticed a list posted on the wall: the names of hunters who
had checked in deer during rifle and muzzleloader seasons. I
scanned the roster, paused halfway down, and did a double take.
Richard hunted?

I had met him six years earlier, through Paul, my forestry
mentor. Only once had I ever heard Richard talk about hunting,
and he had spoken in the past tense, explaining that his Buddhist
meditation practice had led him to become a vegetarian. Apparently his diet had changed again. According to this list, he had
dragged a buck out of the woods last month.

I wondered if Richard might make a good hunting partner.
That fall, hunting alone, I had been keenly aware of my lack of
companionship. When Mark e-mailed me about his annual trip
to Virginia, I wondered when he and I would get a chance to hunt
together again. When I crossed paths with a trio of hunters who

occasionally parked their truck along the rail-bed trail, I envied not their success—two of the three had taken bucks in rifle season—but their camaraderie. In January, I jotted Richard a note.

Nine months later, I drove the ten miles to Richard's place and parked at the bottom of the front field, beside his small red twenty-year-old pickup truck. Pieces of sheet metal were riveted over rusted-out holes in the side panels. A bumper sticker read, "The Best Things in Life Aren't Things." Taped inside the rear window of the cab was a paper sign: "Veterans for Peace."

I hiked the hundred yards up to the house. The small, rough structure stood in the shelter of tall pines, with fruit trees and a vegetable garden nearby. The few lights inside were powered by a single, diminutive solar panel. Richard, who had built the place three decades earlier, took pride in his small ecological footprint, living, as he put it, "low on the hog."

When I knocked, Richard met me at the door and invited me in through the cool, dim entryway, sweet with the scent of the apples he stored there. In his midsixties, Richard was agile and strong, with the sure, graceful movements of a man in his prime, the angular planes of his face lively, gray only beginning to salt his thick brown hair. His clothes—a long-sleeved shirt and pants, simple, worn, and rugged—suited the kinds of work he favored: gardening, cutting firewood, milling lumber with the portable sawmill he had purchased a few years earlier. And they suited the hike we were about to take. Richard was introducing me to his woodlot and hunting grounds, which he had dubbed the Hundred Acre Woods. We would make a circuit of the property's perimeter, checking and replacing the homemade signs: "Hunting and All Other Uses by Permission Only."

Up through his orchard we went, then into the forest, through a neighbor's sugarbush, up a steep, shale-studded pitch, and further up onto a north-south running ridge. As we went, we talked.

Richard, I learned, had grown up in Wisconsin, hunting grouse and rabbits with his brother and cousins. He hunted deer briefly as a young man, but never killed one. In his early thirties, after college and five years in the navy, he landed in Vermont and started hunting again, taking a shotgun for the occasional walk, looking for grouse.

A flash of movement and the thudding of hooves caught our attention. Two or three deer bounded off among the trees, startled by our approach. A good omen, I thought. I hadn't seen a whitetail in weeks. The previous weekend, Mark had come to Vermont to bowhunt, but despite my scouting efforts, we had seen little in the way of deer.

Several minutes later, Richard and I reached the boundary of his woodlot. He had purchased the property just a few years ago, but had been hunting deer there for almost two decades. The hunting started when the previous landowner offered to loan him her late husband's .300 Savage. It had taken Richard a few years to get to know the place, to learn how to hunt it, and to kill his first deer.

Not far beyond the property boundary, Richard paused atop a broad, wooded ridge and pointed to a spot where he often sat on the ground, waiting. He called it the Four Directions Stand. Four years in a row, he said, bucks had come to him there. He shot one to the north, one to the east, one to the south, and one to the west. He was not, I thought, prone to exaggeration. But given how few deer I had seen in my first two autumns afield, his track record in that spot—not to mention the tidy geometric symmetry of it—struck me as nearly unbelievable, like something out of mythology.

We turned north, hiking past a small pool cradled in the ridge top. Richard said it was inhabited by wood frogs, spotted salamanders, and a species of tiny mollusks known as fingernail clams.

It wasn't long after he started hunting deer that Richard became a student of Buddhist meditation. From the very beginning, he found it hard to embrace the tradition's first precept: to refrain from harming other sentient beings. He didn't want to do harm, but was it possible not to? Could anyone escape the natural cycle of things, the fact that the death of one being means life for another? Year-round, he practiced meditation, focusing on mindfulness and stillness, on the passage of thoughts and emotions, on his own breathing and the sounds around him. In November, he hunted deer, focusing on the same.

A decade into his meditation practice, about the time I met him, Richard had taken a hiatus from hunting. It started during one of the annual weeklong meditation retreats he had been attending, when he went to the front of the meditation hall and asked his teacher about that troublesome first precept. As they talked, it came out that Richard was a meat eater and a hunter. His teacher had been flabbergasted. By the end of the conversation, neither had convinced the other, but Richard had agreed to give his teacher's path a try. With a hundred fellow students as witnesses, he committed to a year as a vegetarian. One year stretched into two. He didn't eat meat, buy meat, or hunt. He paid even greater attention to his food, to where it came from, to what impact it had.

"It was a good practice," he told me. "I got sensitive to things. All critters are just trying to make a living."

As his awareness and compassion increased, Richard found that he couldn't take killing as lightly. If a housefly annoyed him with its buzzing, he didn't need to swat it. He began to notice things he hadn't before. When he planted his garden, wasn't he killing creatures with every shovelful of dirt he turned? When he live-trapped mice in his root cellar and then released them on the far side of the beaver dam across the road, wasn't he just feeding them to the mink that hunted there?

In the end, Richard had taken up the .300 Savage again. He didn't recall any moment of grand revelation, just the gradual realization that, for him, it felt hypocritical to pretend that he wasn't causing any harm. For him, the solution was to accept the harm, to refrain from causing it unnecessarily, to avoid wasting anything. Vegetarianism helped Richard see that, for him, hunting was part of the balance, part of the Buddha's Middle Way.

We were heading east, hiking down the side of a second ridge, when two or three deer again leapt off among the trees below us, white flags held high. "The deer nibble on my garden and I nibble on them," Richard said. "Everything is chewing on everything else, yet there's a harmony in it." Here in the forest, or in Richard's garden, it made sense to speak of harmony—a word I would never use to refer to eroding cropland, factory farms, or the clean, brightly lit aisles of a supermarket.

We turned away from the property's perimeter, walking deeper into the woodlot, and Richard stopped at a place where a deer trail cut down the side of a rocky shelf and descended toward a small wetland. Two years ago, he said, he had been sitting here when a four-point buck came along. The shot was a bad one. For the first time in all Richard's years of hunting, the whitetail did not drop. Instead, the buck ran, leaving a sparse blood trail. It had taken several hours and three shots at a running animal to finish the job. Imagining the scene—recalling my misses with both arrow and bullet the previous autumn, recalling the two pairs of boot prints following that blood trail in the snow—I grimaced. If I got a chance at a deer this fall, it would have to be a quick, clean kill or no shot at all.

If such a chance came, I thought it might happen here in the Hundred Acre Woods. Richard said the deer trails had been wider and more heavily worn ten years ago, but there were still signs of frequent hoofed traffic and we had already bumped into whitetails twice in one hour. Maybe deer were more numerous here than in the woods I had hunted near home. Maybe the terrain encouraged animals to move in more regular patterns, along and between the three parallel ridges, avoiding the steepest slopes, skirting the wetland, pausing to drink at the stream. Or maybe Richard just knew where to look.

I would continue hunting the timberland behind our house, out past Lord's Hill, but the deer sign there seemed spotty, and clear shots beyond thirty yards would be rare amidst the thick vegetation. Here, in Richard's woods, stretches of mature soft-woods and well-thinned young sugar maples provided an open view at ground level. I might get a shot at fifty yards, or even seventy-five.

Three weeks later, we were in the woods before first light, the morning frosty and clear. We hiked in most of the way together, Richard leading, me following, my flashlight pointed down so I wouldn't stumble on the unfamiliar ground. We walked on past the Four Directions Stand—movement patterns had changed, Richard said, and it had been some years since he had seen any deer there.

Then our paths diverged. He turned south, toward the lower end of a small valley where a well-worn trail snaked through a break in a ridge's rocky spine. I continued east a few hundred yards and sat down on the earth with my back to a tree. There, I watched the gradual dawning of the day. When enough light filtered in among the trees, I could see what Richard and I had spotted during our first hike: fresh, bright patches on a nearby alder stem where a buck's antlers had stripped the bark.

Downy woodpeckers scaled a nearby pine, claws scrabbling drily. A brown creeper alighted near the base of a trunk and began its inevitable upward spiral, hugging the bark, probing for insects. Chickadees, ever curious, alit nearby. Squirrels scampered past.

Now and then, a rifle popped in the distance. There would not, I thought, be many hunters nearby. Richard had only given a couple of people permission to hunt here and few others were likely to wander through. The property was tucked well back into the hills, with no roads nearby.

In midmorning, a shrew darted past, scurrying through the leaves. A few minutes later, a sleek, dark shape appeared—a mink, loping over tumbled stones that marked the perimeter of an old cellar hole. Richard had said that his neighbor's grandfather once lived in that house. Back then, there wouldn't have been many deer here, or even trees. The stone walls that ran through these woods would have divided pastures. The mink disappeared toward the wetland, returning, I presumed, from its nightly hunt.

Neither Richard nor I saw deer that day. Hiking back out along one of the ridges, though, we noted a sign that had not been there before first light. Even in the predawn dark, we would have seen it by flashlight: a fresh scrape, hoof marks plain in the scuffed soil.

That night, it rained. Dawn was mild and overcast. The woods were quiet, without even a single shot echoing among the hills.

Then, half an hour after sunrise, a rifle barked once. Richard's Savage, I felt sure.

At the shot, a rush of emotion surged through me. Jealousy? No, not quite. More like despair, the knowledge of failure.

Maybe I was inept. Maybe I was unlucky. Maybe I was like Uncle Mark's longtime hunting buddy and good-luck charm, Jay, who, Mark said, seemed to have a knack for bringing deer to those he hunted with. Mark told me he sometimes felt almost guilty for the success he enjoyed when they hunted together. Jay was a fine hunter, but he hardly ever got a deer when Mark was with him.

In any case, I knew that Richard had taken a deer and I felt certain that I would not. Mathematically, the odds were against it. This was not suburban Maryland or western New York, where I had heard you practically had to beat the deer off with a stick. In Vermont, fewer than one in ten rifle hunters tagged a deer each year. And the odds were even worse than that. Just as the area's whitetail population—ten or so deer per square mile—was concentrated in particular places rather than being distributed evenly across the landscape, hunting success was concentrated among certain hunters. The average success rate took into account the skilled, knowledgeable hunters who managed to kill a deer every single year. I was not reassured by the fact that it also took into account those who bought a combined hunting-and-fishing license but hunted deer very little, if at all. What were the chances for someone as clueless as I was? One in fifteen? I had heard of people hunting for ten, twenty, even thirty years and never dragging home venison.

This was pathetic. I aspired to commune with the land, meditating on the nature of life and death and suffering and sustenance and the cosmos, and I responded to my friend's success by spinning off into despair and statistics? What became of all the nonattachment and mindfulness I had been cultivating in the sixteen years since that retreat with Thich Nhat Hanh, the event that propelled me into veganism?

Forty-five minutes after the shot, Richard appeared.

"I need help dragging out a deer," he said.

Soon, we stood together, looking down at the buck. The antlers were slender, bearing six points, plus a stub where a seventh point had snapped off and worn smooth again. Richard had gutted the animal and dragged him some fifty yards before deciding to look for me. The body—solidly built, with plenty of fat reserves—pulled harder than he expected.

He showed me where it had happened. He had been sitting at the base of a tree, when a slight noise made him turn to his right. The buck had approached silently in the wet leaves and was only a few yards away. Slowly, Richard raised his rifle and turned. The buck spooked and leapt forward, but—strangely—didn't look at the hunter who sat so close. Within a few yards the deer paused, then continued walking slowly, his nose to the ground. Richard got his shot at twenty-five yards. The animal only went a few feet before dropping dead.

Even seeing the spot where it had happened, even seeing the dead animal in the flesh, I found his existence unlikely. Something that big and beautiful, in these woods, where I had been seeing little more than squirrels? The materialization of such a being seemed only slightly more probable than, say, that of a unicorn.

"Amazing, isn't it?" said Richard. "A living creature. Now meat."

I nodded.

"I wish you'd gotten him," he added.

I shrugged. Except for deer drives back in Wisconsin, I knew this was Richard's first time hunting whitetails with a companion. I would have been uneasy if I took a buck from his land and he did not.

Handing him my truck key, I suggested that he hike out with most of our gear and return with the plastic deer sled rolled up behind my front seat. I would stay and keep vigil, on the off chance that another buck came along.

For most of an hour, I sat. I watched the woods. I listened. And I glanced at the buck that lay nearby. He was, now, nothing more than a dead body. A carcass. Did I really want one of my own? Did I really want to snuff out the animating spirit of such a being? No, I thought. Not particularly.

My only visitor that hour was a raven. It glided directly overhead, skimming the tops of the tall white pines, croaking as it passed, perhaps already knowing that the buck's entrails lay nearby.

When Richard returned, we lashed the deer to the sled and started pulling. It was a hard drag, up and over the bony ridge, past the pool where the frogs, salamanders, and fingernail clams lived. When we reached the bottom of the front field, down beyond the house, we hoisted the deer up into the back of Richard's old truck.

At the Riverbend, we dropped the tailgate and hefted the buck onto the scale. "One sixty-three," said the young man doing the check-in. On the hoof, before Richard gutted him, the whitetail would have weighed about two hundred pounds. He might yield more than a hundred pounds of venison.

The following weekend, I returned to the Hundred Acre Woods alone. Having filled his rifle tag, Richard's hunting was over for the season. I retraced our drag path and found a new scrape within ten feet of where the buck had lain cooling while I watched over him. Down in the draw where Richard had shot the animal, I saw fresh deer tracks and noticed that the coyotes and ravens had been busy. All that remained of the entrails was the contents of the buck's stomach: a small pile of corn. He had been fattening himself in nearby fields.

For two hours, I sat in silence. Then, restless, I headed east, deeper into the woods. As I reached the tail end of a small ridge, I heard something. Hooves in dry leaves? I eased over the rise, trying to make my own footsteps sound like the rustlings of squirrels. A deer was trotting away, then another.

A minute later, the woods erupted. Leaves crunched and churned. Sticks snapped. Between the crowded trees I glimpsed deer sixty yards away, two of them, their bodies wheeling, their brows locked together. Two bucks fighting. The action was too fast and the cover too thick for me to see antlers, let alone take a sure, clean shot. I set down my pack and started moving toward them, but before I had taken five steps the tussle was over and both deer vanished. I stood there, heart pounding.

Another morning, half an hour after sunrise, a whitetail appeared near the same spot, straight ahead of me. Through my scope, I could see antler. The buck crossed a stream and moseyed up the slope, stopping now and then, passing within forty yards of me. But I couldn't be sure about the antlers: *spikes or forks?* A minute later, he got downwind of me, snorted in alarm, and was gone. Only then did my body start trembling.

Over Thanksgiving, Cath and I drove to New Jersey to visit her family. We returned to Vermont late Saturday, giving me one last day to rifle hunt. And hunt I did. I spent ten straight hours in the Hundred Acre Woods and saw not a single deer. By day's end, I was burned out. The optimism I had felt a few weeks earlier now seemed entirely unreasonable, and I began to wonder about the psychological health of putting so much energy into a pursuit that consistently proved my incompetence. I e-mailed Mark, just back from a successful hunt in Virginia, and shared my frustration and doubt. His reply assured me that even after four decades of hunting he could still relate to the feeling of futility. He had found no rhyme or reason to how long it took to get a deer, no evenhanded correlation between effort and success.

He had, however, noticed one curious irony: Sometimes, the less important it felt, the more likely it seemed that whitetails would appear. I was reminded of stories from Zen traditions, and of things my martial arts teachers had said back in high school and college. Mark knew that perseverance paid off. He would not succeed in the hunt by giving up and staying indoors. Yet trying too hard seemed to lower his chances. In fact, he tended to see deer more often and at closer range when he was just walking in the woods than when he was hunting. I wondered: If animals could sense predatory intent, picking up on its vibratory frequency, might not a hunter's desperation amplify the invisible ripples he or she sent radiating out among the trees?

I thought of Richard telling me how, when the leaves were dry and loud, he sometimes brought a book to the woods. He would sit reading and wouldn't pick up his .300 Savage until he heard hoof steps coming. Was that nonchalant attitude part of what brought those deer to the Four Directions Stand—four bucks, four years in a row?

Even if such a mind-set didn't improve my luck in the woods, it was worth cultivating. If I relaxed, I would enjoy the hunt more. That was vital, since I—unskilled and dependent on luck—might never succeed in the goal of taking a deer. In the interest of psychological self-preservation, I promised myself not to try so hard during the two weekends of December muzzleloader season. I would hunt just a couple hours here and there. I would do my best to ease back into not caring whether I saw deer.

I kept my promise. Opening weekend of black-powder season, I hunted a few hours near home. I didn't hope so hard. I didn't stay on high alert. I leaned back against a mossy boulder and admired the morning light, the glistening of maple twigs and balsam needles.

When half an inch of snow came, I returned to Richard's woods, hiking in after sunrise to look for tracks. They were there: two sets headed up past the ridgetop pool. With so little powder underfoot, the leaves frozen and loud, I had no prayer of sneaking up on that pair, so I backtracked. Sure enough, the hoofprints cut the long diagonal up through the small valley. The deer had passed right through the break in the ridge where Richard had killed the seven pointer a few weeks earlier: a place we had dubbed Seven Point Draw.

I sat exactly where Richard had been sitting that morning. After a few minutes, though, I felt uneasy. To my right, a spine of rock blocked my view. That was the direction from which Richard's buck and the two deer I had just backtracked had all come. So I moved a few yards and sat with my back to the stone.

Was that the faint sound of steps? Of hooves crunching dry leaves under the thin blanket of snow? I shifted position and half raised my .54-caliber caplock. Moments later, I saw deer some forty yards off, walking toward me among the pines. Two, three, four of them. I brought the rifle to my shoulder and eased back the hammer. The first in line was a doe. My tag was for a buck. The little parade had closed to less than thirty yards now, weaving through the trees. Heart pounding, I stared along the iron sights, watching for antlers. Was this the moment?

The lead doe was closer now. Looking past her, I could see that the second in line was also a doe. The third, also antlerless, looked like a six-month-old. And the fourth? Ah, another doe. There would be no shot today.

The lead doe stood broadside a dozen paces away, her breath pluming in the frosty air, her ears and great, dark eyes focused on me. All four deer paused, aware of my crouching form. Unsure what I was, they hesitated. They looked and listened. Then, slowly, they turned back the way they had come. Trembling, I sat and watched them go.

The final weekend of muzzleloader season, I returned again to the Hundred Acre Woods and startled two whitetails into flight as I hiked into Seven Point Draw. Once there, I sat down to wait. It was a cold morning, well below freezing, and bright sunlight streamed in among the pines, illuminating branches laden with fresh snow. All told, I reflected, it had been a good deer season. I had seen more whitetails than in my first two autumns combined and had managed not to take any stupid shots.

I didn't yet know this place half as well as Richard did, but here—as in the timberland behind our house—I felt a sense of belonging, a growing familiarity that encompassed both conscious knowledge and something less tangible: an impression, a grasp of how things connected and of how animals lived and moved on this land, an unsketched and perhaps unsketchable map. It reminded me of how I had felt about the water I fished as a boy.

Red squirrels leapt and chattered. Blue jays hopped among the snow-covered pine boughs. Ravens *quork-quorked* overhead. And, high up, long lines of late-season geese called out as they arrowed south. I thought of a line from Richard Nelson's *The Island Within*: "The exploration has turned inward, and I have slowly recognized that I am not an outsider here."

My sense of belonging had another dimension, too, one that surprised me. I had become part of a growing web of relationships with others who, like me, took guns to the woods, aiming to kill: a fraternity of kindhearted men found in the last place that I, as a profeminist vegan, would ever have imagined looking. For years, Mark and his Virginia hunting buddy, Jay, had been including me in much of their hunting-related e-mail correspondence. Recently, I had also started exchanging letters with Mark's uncle and hunting mentor—my great-uncle Al—an avid conservationist who lived in Oregon. This fall, I had hunted with both Mark and Richard. Before long, I hoped to hunt with a local man a year my junior, one of the only adults who had taken hunter education alongside me. And several new acquaintances, from the coast of northern New England to the foothills of the Blue Ridge Mountains in South Carolina, had suggested we hunt together someday.

Willie, too, remained part of that circle. Though he mostly fished, he had hunted as a boy and, shortly before his death, had mentioned that he might return to the woods someday. A month ago, just before rifle season, Cath and I had taken a weekend trip to southern Maine to see Beth. We brought along a welded sculpture Mark had made in Willie's honor: a miniature metal fishing pole less than two feet long, crafted from odds and ends.

The steel rod was slightly bent toward the tip, as if a fish had just taken the bait. A wire leader ran up through the guide rings and from it dangled a small, shapely fish, painted bright blue with a white belly. Mark had made the fish out of an old barbecue fork—the tang cut off short, a hole drilled for the fish's eye, the two tines twisted together to form the caudal curve and the widely forked tail. The fork made me think of the enthusiasm with which Willie sat down to every meal, and of the joy he took in presiding over the grill.

With Beth, we placed the rod at the head of his grave, planting the butt firmly in the earth, where the cemetery lawn met the woods. The fish danced above grass and oak leaves.

15

The Red Deer

We need another and a wiser and perhaps a more mystical concept of animals. . . . They are not brethren, they are not underlings; they are other nations, caught with ourselves in the net of life and time, fellow prisoners of the splendor and travail of the earth.

—Henry Beston, *The Outermost House*

In the predawn dark, my flashlight illuminated half a dozen large hoofprints in the freshly pawed earth. A big scrape.

A year had passed since I first hunted these woods with Richard. Over the summer, I had scouted here, sometimes alone, sometimes with our two-year-old black Lab, Kaia, the first dog either Cath or I had had in many years: an affectionate animal who kept us company, left her ominous canine scent around our gardens, and might become a hunting companion if I ever got serious about pursuing birds.

Now it was opening morning of rifle season. Near the scrape, a deer trail crossed the top of this little valley. Close by was a small cluster of maples where, in September, I had leaned pieces of fallen deadwood this way and that, fashioning a makeshift blind that would break up the outlines of a hunter's form, preparing a ground stand for Mark as he had once done for me. The second weekend in October, in bow season, my uncle had been here with me. He had lain in wait in that ring of maples, while I hunted a quarter mile farther down, near Seven Point Draw.

Now, in mid-November, I again headed down the small valley. Richard, tied up with another commitment, would not be in the woods today. As I approached the draw, I came to a place where several deer paths converged. My flashlight showed a second scrape. And a third. And a fourth. In his e-mailed report of a week earlier, Richard had written that there was "plenty of testosterone flowing in those woods this year." He wasn't kidding. The bucks were active.

I sat on a folding stool with my back to the trunk of a partly fallen spruce—windthrown, its top caught by another tree in mid-descent—and watched light come to the forest, glinting off the needles of the tall pines. After an hour, I heard something tromping around up on the ridge behind me: perhaps a deer, or a moose, or a hunter. There was no sense in trying to go have a look. The cover was too thick, the ground too thoroughly covered in dry, noisy leaves and branches. All I could do was wait, listen, and watch.

Scanning the woods below me, from the cleft of the draw on my left to the convergence of deer trails on my right, I knew the vantage point was good. I might not get an unobstructed shot, but deer would have trouble passing by unseen.

Sitting here on the second morning of Mark's visit in October, I had spotted two does at forty yards or more. Apparently at ease, they passed within fifteen paces of where I crouched, waiting for the moment when their attention would be focused elsewhere, the moment when one of them would pause and give me the opportunity to send a razor-sharp broadhead through her heart or lungs.

This time, I felt sure the arrow would fly true. I now wielded a compound bow with sights. It lacked the aesthetic charm of my longbow, but in target practice the shafts clustered together far more consistently and tightly, often touching.

The moment did not come. Both deer kept moving and, just before reaching Seven Point Draw, turned aside from the gentle, well-worn path and bounded effortlessly up the steep, thickly grown bank. Half an hour later, another doe had come through. She paused and looked away, offering the perfect broadside shot. But a pair of tiny fawns minced along behind her. I didn't even raise my bow.

It was good to know that I could get that close to deer when hunting from the ground. Though I knew that being in a tree stand probably increased my chances of success, it felt good to keep both feet on the earth.

Now, rifle in hand, I again sat and waited. A kinglet darted past. Chickadees flitted among nearby branches. Nothing more. After four hours, I grew restless and nearly headed home. But I knew I wouldn't get much time in the woods in the sixteen-day season, so I moved quietly through the draw where pine needles covered the ground, eased over the noisier maple-leafed shoulder of the ridge where I had watched the two bucks fighting a year earlier, and descended to the shaded softwood stand where I had watched a young buck cross the stream. I noted an active deer trail: a subtle furrow in the duff, hoofprints showing in places. Farther up the side of the ridge, I found a cluster of hoof-marked scrapes. For an hour I sat where a deer trail crossed an old stone wall. Finally, I came full circle to the ring of maples where Mark had hunted in October.

Now, in daylight, I saw that the big scrape I had found in the dark was only thirty yards from the crude blind I had constructed. Two more scrapes were even closer, one just five paces from where Mark had sat.

Inside the ring of young maples, I cleared out the dry, noisy leaves that had accumulated and then sat down. I liked the feel of the spot. But after another hour and a half, I had had enough for one day. I had been in the woods for more than eight hours and had seen neither hide nor hair of deer.

That evening, talking with Cath, I unraveled. I was doing it again, doing what I promised myself not to. I was trying too hard. And for what?

Was I hunting to procure local, wild meat and to confront what it meant to eat flesh? Well, that wasn't happening. Even if I did succeed someday, my hunting had proved a ridiculously inefficient way to obtain food. Over the past four years, I had invested hundreds of hours in the hunt: taking hunter education, reading about hunting, scouting the land, practicing with rifle and bow, and actually hunting. I had invested hundreds and hundreds of dollars, too: purchasing rifle, muzzleloader, longbow, compound bow, projectiles for each, tree stand, camo and blaze-orange clothing, and on and on. And I had not one pound of venison to show for it, except those given to me by Mark and Richard.

Was I hunting to commune with nature? Well, I wasn't getting any transcendental insights. I didn't come back from the hunt feeling all warm and fuzzy and one with everything. I came back feeling cold. If I wanted to go sit in the woods and meditate, I could do that anytime, without getting up at four in the morning and without toting a gun or bow. And if such attentiveness was my main goal, why not cultivate it in some other way? Why not become a birder or take up serious nature photography?

The more I talked, the deeper I spun into the vortex. All Cath could do was listen.

Was I hunting to develop my woodscraft? I supposed I had learned a few things. Hunting, like fishing, had sharpened my awareness, drawing my attention to details I would not have noticed before: to clipped twigs and seedlings where whitetails had browsed, to how deer tracks always crossed a hiking trail at a particular spot. I knew enough to pay attention to the direction of the breeze and to keep my hunting clothes from smelling too much like a human—most of the year, I kept them sealed in a plastic box with balsam sprigs and dry leaves from the forest floor. I knew that a grunting sound, or even a whistle, could stop a walking deer for a moment, giving a hunter a clear shot at a motionless target. But compared to hunters who had spent decades learning about woods and deer, I knew zilch.

I imagined that if I took a deer once, I would feel less pressure to succeed a second time. That would make the whole hunting experience more enjoyable. And yet, I said, reminding both Cath and myself of the obvious, I had never really wanted to kill a deer in the first place. If I felt that veganism could keep my body completely healthy and could truly prevent harm to animals and their habitats, I wouldn't be eating vertebrates at all, let alone wielding a deer rifle. I felt I ought to kill a deer, yes. Like feminist and vegan Carol Adams, I objected to the "absent referent"—the separation between meat eater and animal, between animal and meat. I felt obliged to meet the requirement suggested by Christopher Camuto in his book *Hunting from Home*: "I've long had an odd thought that no one who hasn't killed, skinned and butchered at least one animal on his or her own should be allowed to buy meat in a grocery store."

Over the past five years, though, I had already done some killing. I had caught and eaten trout from nearby streams and lakes. Twice, I had caught striped bass while fishing with Mark on Cape Cod, the second time using a rod of Willie's that Beth had given to me. I had shot at least two garden-raiding woodchucks, one of which ended up in the stewpot. And I had hunted, killed, and eaten a pair of snowshoe hares. What point was there in killing a whitetail, too? Was it just that a deer would provide substantially more food? Was I just trying to prove something to myself? Or was there more to it?

I'd had some exciting moments in the woods these past few years, especially my encounters with deer. But taking a life still did not appeal. For me, hunting would never be what Ortega y Gasset called a "case in which the killing of one creature constitutes the delight of another." Where killing and delight were concerned, Rachel Carson's words rang truer: "We cannot have peace among men whose hearts delight in killing any living creature."

But was I, after all, following the path the Spanish philosopher spelled out for the sportsman, seeking a deer's death as "the sign of reality for the whole hunting process"? Was it no more than some immature symbolic urge?

These doubts, I realized, had been with me for some time. I had been keeping them quiet, only half admitting them to myself, only partially sharing them with Mark, avoiding any mention of them to Cath. Even now, as I talked, I regretted subjecting her to my inner contortions.

Simply put, I was failing as a hunter—not only failing to bring home meat, but also failing to find meaning in the pursuit. If the hunt culminated in little more than exhaustion interspersed with mental and emotional chaos, what was the point in continuing? Maybe I would just stay home the next day. Better to spend Sunday morning doing something productive around the house than to waste several more hours sitting in the woods.

Later that evening, though, Richard called. He planned to hunt in the morning and asked if I would be coming. It would, I knew, be easier to sit in the woods if I had a companion nearby. Okay, I told him. I would be there, if only for the first few hours of the day.

As I drifted toward sleep, I considered the next morning's hunt. During our conversation, Cath had gently reminded me that my experience of hunting had everything to do with the set of my mind, heart, and soul. If I was going back to the woods, I needed an attitude adjustment. I thought back several years, to my earliest interest in the hunt. I remembered all my correspondence with Mark, all my questions, all his insights and helpful tips. I remembered the magic of receiving that old knife in the mail from him—with the gorgeous sheath he had stitched and painted with red buck and black hoofprints—and my confidence that it would bring me luck. I remembered the excitement of hunting with him for the first time, and my contentment when he got a deer and I was able to help with the butchering. I remembered the simple faith I'd had. My first deer would come in good time. I was in no hurry.

Though Richard had said I could have my pick of hunting spots, I decided I would not return to Seven Point Draw. It might be the most likely spot for seeing a buck, with deer trails funneling there as they did. But in the morning my focus would not be outward, on killing a deer. It would be inward, on returning to that quiet, open place. I would go back to the ring of maples where Mark had hunted in October.

Down in the basement, well before dawn, I pulled the old hunting knife from my pack. Richard had recently given me the tail from his seven-point buck, for tying trout flies. I plucked a few long, white hairs and tucked them into the knife sheath.

When I arrived at Richard's, he wasn't quite ready. He might be another fifteen minutes, he said. I should go ahead. He would be along soon and would probably sit up on the ridge near the Four Directions Stand.

I reached the ring of maples shortly before first light. Before I sat, I took out the knife and propped it against the base of a tree four feet in front of me. As the sky brightened, my eyes began to wander the woods. But they weren't needed there. With the leaves dry and frosty, my ears would tell me if anything moved. Instead, I looked at the knife, the rich orange-brown of the sheath, the long, white hairs sprouting from between blade and leather. The buck on the front, dyed red, seemed to stand among the maple leaves. The image could easily have taken form by flickering torchlight, in the caves of Lascaux in southwestern France, in ancient Europe, my ancestral homeland. But this was no pale imitation of some ancient hunting totem, European or North American. Painted for me by my uncle, this deer belonged in this place. The four of us—land, deer, uncle, and nephew—were linked.

Admiring the buck, thinking of Mark, my mind let go. Killing a deer didn't matter. Praying for a deer to appear didn't even matter. What mattered was sitting, listening, being there, attentive to the forest, grateful for the earth from which it sprang. What mattered was the rekindling of wonder.

For two hours, I sat. In the crisp leaves, red squirrels scampered, sounding huge.

To take the chill off, I poured myself a thermos cap of hot tea and sipped carefully. I had learned to breathe out, not in, as I was about to drink, to keep myself from inhaling steam that would tickle my throat and make me cough, disrupting the quiet of the forest.

I had just set down the empty cap when I heard the rhythm of steps in the leaves. Looking up the gentle slope among the trees, I saw a deer forty yards off and walking my way. A doe, surely. Then I got a good look.

Legal forked antlers. I hardly believed it.

But my body was in motion, easing forward off the folding stool, turning, finding some kind of stable position, half crouching, half kneeling. The buck was thirty yards away now, by that big scrape, his nose to the ground, reading scents among the maple leaves and pine needles.

I avoided looking at his head and eyes. Mark had told me how animals seemed to stay more relaxed if he didn't make direct eye contact. He guessed that deer could sense his gaze, the same way he sometimes felt the focus of someone's vision on him, even from hundreds of yards away.

I eased the safety off. The crosshairs trembled behind the buck's left shoulder.

There were branches in the way, two or three of them, not much thicker than my thumb. A bullet might pass between them. Or it might not. In my mind's eye, I saw the dark silhouette of the buck I had fired at two years earlier, the gouged earth where he leapt away, the torn wood where the bullet struck the spruce branch. I imagined this buck with a bullet, or fragments of a bullet, in his leg or gut. My trigger finger relaxed.

The buck's head came up fast. He had winded me, perhaps, or heard some slight rustle. I had missed my chance. In a moment, he would flee. I would not shoot at a running deer.

He dropped his head again, sniffed the ground, and licked his nose. Then he took a step. He was broadside to me. There was an open space among the branches. I barely heard the shot.

The buck jumped—a small, hunched movement—then leapt forward among the trees, running in a downhill arc. I stood up and absently remembered to chamber a second round. Something about his gait told me I wouldn't have to shoot again. In midrun, just twenty paces from me, he collapsed into the forest floor.

A wave of disbelief rolled over me as I walked toward him, rifle unloaded. His ribs heaved with a final, shuddering breath. I took the last few steps to where he lay and, from behind, touched the rifle muzzle to his eye. There was no reflexive flinch. He was gone.

Confident that neither hooves nor antlers would lash out in one last spasm, I crouched beside him, inhaled the musky odor of his body, and put a hand to his side.

If I ever succeeded in killing a deer, I had imagined that I, like Mark, would experience that flood of mixed emotions, sorrow and elation and awe and gratitude all jumbled together. But now that it had happened, now that this whitetail had gone down and stayed down, I didn't know what I felt. My feelings were obscured by shock: an invisible, impenetrable veil. Crouching there, I had no idea what gesture of gratitude or apology to make.

Finally, I whispered a few inadequate words, retrieved the sheathed knife from where it leaned against the maple, and unfolded my page of instructions on how to gut a deer. Tentatively, I made the first incisions through hair and hide, then through abdominal wall. The smells of the buck's blood and viscera mingled intensely with the musk of skin and hair. His entrails, jarringly hot against my hands in the freezing air, slid out, stomach full, liver heavy and dark, neat folds of intestines coming undone. I reached up inside him, cut the taut membrane of his diaphragm, and drew out the rest of his organs. His heart was torn in two.

When my clumsy field dressing was complete, I scrubbed my hands with maple leaves. Then I remembered that, by law, the first thing I should have done was tag the buck. I dug out my hunting and fishing license and there was the laminated funeral card: Willie looking up at me, smiling broadly. He would be proud of me, I thought. Mark, too, would be proud. But was I proud of myself?

It helped that it had been quick. Holding the deer's torn-in-two heart in my hand, I knew oblivion had come swiftly. It was the shot I had hoped for: no more than a few seconds of shock, no time for pain to take hold. It was easier than most other ways a deer's life was likely to end: in cold and starvation, across a car's front end, at the teeth of four-footed predators. Yet that swiftness did nothing to alter the raw fact. I had killed this graceful creature.

Now that I had taken his life, I wasn't sure I wanted it. Already I wondered: Was all this effort—the scouting, the hunting, and the long, grisly hours of butchering to come—really worth it? Now that the "absent referent" had become such a palpably present being, would I hunt again? A great hollow grief had begun to well up inside.

I knotted my tag to the buck's slender antlers with a scrap of old speaker wire. Then, leaving the gutted whitetail to cool in the frosty air, I gathered up pack and rifle and headed south along the ridge. Near the Four Directions Stand, I found Richard sitting on a fallen tree trunk, meditating on the forest, .300 Savage across his lap. I raised my hand for him to see, knuckle creases and fingernail edges still speckled with dried blood. Richard's brows lifted above deep-set eyes and a gentle smile spread across his angular face. He nodded.

"I heard the shot," he said.

Together we hiked back to his house where I dialed the old rotary phone and left a message for Cath. I shed rifle, pack, and outer layers—the effort of dragging would keep me warm—and fetched the thin plastic sled.

Back in the woods, Richard asked how it had happened. I showed him where I was sitting, where the buck was standing when I shot. Then we lashed the animal to the sled and dragged him up past the ridgetop pool.

Once, as we paused to catch our breath, I again told Richard how the buck had come walking, how he had raised his head as if in alarm, how he had taken that final step. Even with the deer there on the ground behind me, affixed to me by a drag rope, the event seemed implausible. I recounted the moment as though my speaking and Richard's hearing would make the bizarre occurrence more real, as though it would help me come to grips with what had happened.

"It's quite an experience, isn't it?" asked Richard.

I nodded.

We walked on, down the steep shale-studded slope and through the neighbor's sugarbush. As we approached the house—on a gentle downward slope now, so that I dragged the deer with no effort and Richard walked beside me—I told him how, the night before, I had recognized the need to shift my attitude, how the hunting knife had helped me refocus, how meditating on the spray of long white tail hairs and the red painted buck had returned me to that still, open place within. And then the buck had appeared, as if by magic.

Richard looked over at me and grinned. "That sounds kind of ooga-booga," he said. "You might want to be careful who you tell that story to."

I laughed.

True. It was probably crazy to think that my little ritual with the knife had conjured the deer. It wasn't a story I would want too many people to hear. Heaven forbid it should get into print.

On the other hand, perhaps that stilling of my mind—that cessation of striving—had quieted the invisible ripples I sent out into the forest. My presence in the woods still affected things, like a stone striking the surface of a pond, but perhaps I had become a smaller pebble.

Richard helped me heft the buck into the back of my pickup. It was time to head to the check-in station, then home, where the butchering would begin.

16
Reckoning

The paradoxes of life and death admit no ready solutions: they should not.
> —Mary Zeiss Stange, *Woman the Hunter*

Cath came out to the truck, her eyes full of compassion, both for the buck and for his ambivalent killer. Kaia sniffed at my pants curiously, smelling hair and blood, then backed off when I slid the deer to the ground. She had never been so close to any wild animal that large, dead or alive, and seemed unsure what to make of it.

It was strange: On the ground beside me lay one mammal I had shot and would soon eat. A few feet away stood another mammal I loved and fed, one whom Cath and I had welcomed into our family, extending the interspecies relationship that began tens of thousands of years ago, when wolves and humans first joined forces. Like Kaia, the deer deserved my care and compassion. Unlike Kaia, the deer was edible. An arbitrary distinction, perhaps—one I hoped I could live with.

By lunchtime, the buck hung upside down in our shed. A few drops of blood spattered the floor. I took the knife from my pack. I was not looking forward to this.

I could, of course, have maintained a sanitized distance. Once the deer was dead and gutted, I could have paid someone else to do the rest. Plenty of local people offered deer-cutting services. But that would have felt like a step back toward the comforting amnesia of the supermarket. Butchering was central to the entire killing-and-eating process.

Only half recalling how Mark had done it three years earlier, I began the skinning. Again I was struck by the completeness of the change. As soon as the hide was pulled back, the animal ceased to be an animal. No longer animated with spirit, no longer clothed in skin and hair, the deer became little more than muscle, fat, and bone. An inert carcass. Meat. Seeing this flesh in a plastic wrapper in the grocery store, most of us would find it hard to envision the actual animal, let alone imagine the steps required to complete its transmogrification.

I slid the razor-sharp blade under each scapula, freeing the forelegs. I separated head from neck. By the time I had severed the hip joints and freed the hindquarters, the meat was well chilled and I wedged the pieces into coolers to keep them from freezing solid overnight.

Then I carried my evening task back to the house and plunked it down on the kitchen counter: a hind leg, the thigh substantially thicker than my own. This was nothing like cleaning a fish or butchering a hare. On the check-in station scale, the buck had registered one hundred and twenty pounds. Alive—with all his organs intact, life pulsing through them—his weight would have matched mine.

I was standing there in the kitchen when Mark called from Virginia. I had left a phone message at Jay's house a few hours earlier, figuring I had missed them. He and Mark would have already left for the cabin along the Blue Ridge, where their annual hunt was about to begin. But Jay's wife had reached them by cell phone. Now, in early evening, Mark sat on the cabin's narrow front porch. He wanted to hear all about the morning's events. How, when, and where had it happened? Had the buck gone down quickly? The congratulatory excitement in his voice buoyed me up out of grief and shock.

After our conversation, I returned to the butchering, my hands slow and uncertain with the boning knife. My fingers slid under a leg muscle, separating it from the layer below. My knife snipped tendons and traced the curvature of bone. I added another slab of venison to a thirteen-by-nine glass pan, long used only for granola and vegetarian lasagna. I still wasn't sure how I felt about the killing.

Sixteen years earlier, the scene had been just like this. I had been standing at a kitchen counter, knife in hand. The creature on the cutting board had been trout instead of deer. With Thich Nhat Hanh's words on kindness reverberating inside, I had sworn off flesh foods.

Just a few weeks before this buck died, Nhat Hanh had posted a long letter on the website for Plum Village, his meditation center in southwestern France. In the letter, he asked all people to eat with mindfulness and compassion. He reminded us that tens of thousands of children die of malnutrition every day, while vast quantities of grain are fed to meat animals. He expressed concern over the livestock sector's impact on global forests and water supplies, and its contributions to climate change. "We are eating our own planet earth," he cautioned. Urging vegetarianism, Nhat Hanh encouraged us to look deeply into the meat we consume. In a plate of industrial sirloin or ground chuck, he asked us to see the suffering of starving children, and the pollution and degradation of the earth, not to mention the animal—once a living, sentient being.

This deep looking is a common theme in the Zen master's teachings. In his book *Peace Is Every Step*, he reminds us that all things are connected and interdependent, a principle he calls "interbeing." The paper upon which his book is printed, he notes, cannot exist without clouds: "Without a cloud, there will be no rain; without rain, the trees cannot grow; and without trees, we cannot make paper." Sunshine, too, he reminds us, is vital. And—wise teacher that he is—he reminds us of something else: "If we continue to look, we can see the logger who cut the tree and brought it to the mill to be transformed into paper." The killing and processing of trees is present in each page of his book. Even if we use some alternative fiber, such as kenaf, the making of paper requires sun, rain, earth, and plant, and also the humans who harvest and process the plant.

It was that kind of seeing that made me pick up a chain saw. In the framing and siding of our house and in the firewood that heated it, I saw the forest, cloaked in snowy stillness and dappled with summer sun. I saw the movements of water and nutrients in earth and tree. And I saw myself—the logger—and the mills to which Paul and I sold sawlogs and pulpwood.

It was that kind of seeing, combined with my body's needs, that led me away from veganism, dispelling my illusions about its moral purity. Like Nhat Hanh—who, in a passage entitled "Tangerine Meditation," reminds us not only to notice our food's taste and fragrance, but also to visualize "the blossoms in the sunshine and in the rain"—I saw beauty in my food. In salad greens, I saw the tiny, delicate leaves that first sprout from earth and seed. In strawberries, I saw the rain falling on Joey's fields a couple miles down the road, and tasted the sun that warmed and fattened the fruit.

But in those same crop fields, I also saw missing forests and prairies. In tofu, I saw the rifles and shotguns used to plug deer in soybean fields. In grains, I saw the birds, mice, and rabbits sliced and diced by combines. In cabbage, I saw caterpillars killed by insecticides, organic or not. In salad greens, I saw a whitetail cut open and dragged around the perimeter of a farm field, the scent of blood warning other deer not to eat the organic arugula and radicchio destined for upscale restaurants and grocery stores in San Francisco. In Joey's kale and berries, I saw smoke-bombed burrows.

Even in the vegetables from our garden—broccoli and green beans, lettuce and snap peas—I saw the wild grasses we uprooted, the earthworms we chopped with our shovels, the beetles I crushed between thumb and forefinger, the woodchucks I shot, and the dairy cows whose manure and carcasses fed the soil. In my own life and in the lives around me—heron and trout, hawk and hare, coyote and deer—I saw that the entire living, breathing, eating world was more beautiful and more terrible than I had imagined. Like Richard, I saw that sentient beings fed on sentient beings.

In this half-carved leg on the counter in front of me, I saw history: wolves and cougars, American Indians and colonists, forests and sheep, market hunters and conservationists. I saw a species of deer that had nearly been wiped off the continent.

I saw, too, that Cath and I would be eating more than this whitetail. We would also be eating everything the deer had eaten. We would be eating maple seedlings and cedar twigs. We would be eating clover from a hillside meadow and corn from the edge of a farm field. If I had shot this buck a few miles closer to home, we might even be eating hosta leaves and daylily buds from our own flower gardens.

I saw the woods and fields where this buck must have fed, and the stream where he must have paused to drink. I saw the scarred bark of maples and alders in the Hundred Acre Woods, old rubs that might have been made by this buck's sire. At the check-in station, a state biologist had examined the teeth and told me the deer was two and a half years old. He had been conceived three years ago, the same autumn I first hunted deer, perhaps the morning I picked up those orange plastic gloves, or the week I hunted with Mark on the Cape.

I saw the ring of maples. I saw the scrape thirty yards away. I saw the branches that might have deflected the bullet had I fired too soon.

I wondered what Thich Nhat Hanh would call the feeling that welled up in me as I stood here, separating flesh from bone. Would he acknowledge it as compassion? I wondered, too, how that other great Buddhist teacher—the 14th Dalai Lama of Tibet, who wrote the foreword to *Peace Is Every Step*—came to terms with his own flesh eating, how he integrated meat and mindfulness. There was, I thought, some strange poetry in the fact that Plum Village, Nhat Hanh's meditation center, lay just fifty miles from the caves of Lascaux.

The next morning, I stood again at the kitchen counter, steel mixing bowls arrayed around me, steak in one, stew meat in another. The thirteen-by-nine pan was piled with smaller pieces that I would put through the hand-crank grinder.

Gradually, my mind and heart had begun to settle into the task. There was a quiet rhythm to it, something meditative about the careful disassembly of bone, meat, and silver skin. Carried along by the movement of the knife, attentive to the interwoven structures of the deer's body, I thought of the way Paul had taught me to limb fir and spruce—the steady, flowing dance with chain saw and tree. The process, Cath suggested, was like canning vegetables: a small repetitive act done by these hands, a pattern within the larger patterns of the seasons, the patterns of all things that live and eat and die and feed one another.

Gardening and canning, like hunting and butchering, were ways of participating in the provision of our own sustenance. I knew that Cath would always grow carrots and salad greens, zucchini and snap peas, as well as all manner of flowers. Her gardening wasn't diminished by our purchase of vegetables and fruits, grains and beans, cheese and olive oil. She gardened to garden, as much for the moments savored and the connections grasped as for the nutrients ingested.

I was less sure about hunting. If the pursuit could not reliably provide a significant portion of our flesh foods—if we were going to be buying chicken anyway—I didn't know whether I would continue. I didn't know whether hunting would open some wider landscape of meaning for me, something beyond the occasional chance at a deer, and the deep sorrow that accompanied the kill.

In becoming a vegan, I had been mindful of my diet's consequences for the planet and for the beings who inhabit it. I aimed to confront those consequences head-on, to see them clearly, to choose the path of least harm. I sought a respectful, holistic way of eating and living, a kind of right dietary citizenship, my food choices shaped by ecological and animal-welfare concerns in much the way that early American vegetarianism was shaped by fears of animality, issues of social reform, and aspirations to masculinity and success. I was mindful, too, of my diet's inner consequences. Since I believed that killing animals was an unnecessary evil, integrity and alignment—a sense of values put into action—could only come from a meat-free diet.

In becoming a hunter, my outward aim had been the same: to be mindful of the consequences of my diet, and to confront one of those consequences—the death of animals—with my eyes open. Taking a life carefully and swiftly seemed the most conscientious path. I still sought a respectful, holistic way of eating and living, my decision to hunt shaped by the same concerns that shaped my veganism. My inner aim had also been the same. Having concluded that I needed some animal protein in my diet and that some harm to animals was inevitable in even the gentlest forms of agriculture, integrity and alignment could only come from taking responsibility for at least a portion of the killing.

Hunting, however, would not put me on a new high road to moral certainty. If this first experience of killing a deer was any indication, it would bring me face-to-face with ambiguity every time. Perhaps that was how it ought to be. I sliced off another chunk of deer and set it in a bowl.

Barring a concentrated effort at homestead-style self-sufficiency, Cath and I would never be growing or hunting most of our food, let alone all of it. We would never know exactly what impacts our eating had. And food, after all, was only part of the picture. Though Cath and I lived simply in comparison to many Americans, we still consumed far more than most of the other six and a half billion people on the planet. We weren't jet-setting around the world, but the gasoline we pumped into our car and pickup truck meant the drilling, shipping, transporting, refining, and occasional spilling of oil, not to mention the toxic byproducts of combustion. We recycled whatever we could, but the production of every manufactured item we bought—including rifle and garden fencing, freezer and canning pot, plates and forks, and the computer on which I now type these words—incurred ecological costs. We were part of industrial civilization.

Yet gardening and hunting reminded us that we were also part of nature. They gave us a felt sense of the elemental, inescapable relationships that sustained us. Between this deer and me there was no separation. The heavy scent of raw meat felt alien in my nostrils, yet the butchering seemed strangely familiar. The rhythm of the knife quieted my mind.

I turned over the leg, marveled at these powerful muscles and how they must have launched the buck in great leaps, and continued with the cutting. Seam by seam, layer by layer, I took the leg apart. Gradually, I began to feel that this animal and I and the hunt that brought us together were part of something fitting. When all seventy-plus pounds of venison were stashed in the freezer alongside blueberries, peas, and chickens, I returned to the woods, singing a song I had never heard, one without words. I left the scraps for the coyotes and ravens to find.

A week later, Richard shot a six pointer less than a hundred yards from the ring of maples. After Thanksgiving, he and a few other friends came for dinner. We feasted on venison scaloppine: tomato, garlic, parsley, mushroom, deer.

Epilogue
Mindful Eating

I n mid-December, I looked out our back window and saw a
whitetail bedded in the snow under a widely branching pine. I
watched through binoculars until the head turned and I could see
the round, foreshortened features of a young one—a small doe or
perhaps a button buck. The animal lay just thirty yards beyond
my archery target. It was the second-to-last day of Vermont's
final deer season, and my archery tag was valid for antlerless
deer. Stalking through the gently falling snow, I might get close
enough for a shot, but I was in no hurry to kill again so soon.
Instead, I watched, wishing the little one well in the cold, hard
months ahead.

Late that winter, nourished by venison stew, I dug out the old
brass buckle Mark had given me almost thirty years earlier, the
symmetrical cross in a near circle. When I started hunting, I had
purchased a length of thick, smooth leather from a local shoe-
repair shop, thinking I would make a new belt. Now I laid the
blank strap on the kitchen table. It took me weeks to see what
belonged there. With tools Mark had loaned me, I carved pairs
of maple leaves all around the belt, first defining their outlines,

then stamping the texture of their veins. Nestled between each pair of leaves, I fashioned a buck, his body curved and flowing, head turned to look back.

Carefully packaged and frozen, the venison kept well. In summer, Cath and I were still eating it: salad greens from the garden topped with thin slices of deer steak, lightly sautéed.

The next November, near dusk on opening day of rifle season, I followed a young buck through the forest. I had hunted the morning and early afternoon with Richard in the Hundred Acre Woods and decided to spend the last hour of light in timberland less than a mile from home. The young buck—a spikehorn, perhaps—ghosted away in the fading light. But he led me to a place I knew: a small stand of hemlocks I had found years earlier, in my first scouting forays. I couldn't have said why, then or now, but the place felt right.

A few days later, I returned. Just after first light, my second buck dropped where he stood, consciousness snuffed out in a flash.

The following autumn, another deer went down in nearly the same spot, my bullet through his heart. Grateful for the venison, and for my unlikely success a third year in a row, I knelt to lean a few small sticks against each other, then cloaked them with three fern fronds, still green in mid-November: a tiny, ephemeral shrine. When the field dressing was complete, I returned to the house to leave off rifle and pack. Soon, I would hike back into the woods and drag the animal home.

"How are you doing?" Cath asked, as we sat at the kitchen table sipping coffee.

I waggled one hand: *so-so.* "I'm in that zone."

She nodded. She had come to expect it.

It wasn't just the sudden disquiet of the kill itself: the unexpected opportunity, the prayer that my aim was true, the relief when the animal went down fast, the shock of the act. Nor was it the storm of uncertainty and grief that whirled through me after that first time in the Hundred Acre Woods. I felt clearer about my hunting now. Nor was it the terrible remorse I knew I would feel if I wounded an animal, causing suffering.

No, it was something else. It was a feeling for which I had no name. In a day or two, the sensation would crest like a great wave and begin to ebb slowly. Again and again, I would replay the kill in memory, trying to sift out something elusive, some meaning that lived just below the visible surface of the event.

Yes, it was something else. Some kind of soul-wrenching. Some altered state triggered by the encounter with animal and death. By my snipping of that thread of life.

Five weeks after my third buck fell, a doe stepped into the road. As I slowed the car, she trotted across and bounded into the woods. Cath and I both relaxed. We weren't going fast, but that had been close.

Then the second doe was there, very close, pausing at the edge of the road. I caught the flash of movement at the periphery of the headlights as she leapt forward. I went hard left. But she came in a blur. Cath and I heard the thud as the deer careened off the passenger side.

I stopped and backed up. The doe was lying in the road.

Done for, I thought.

Then she raised her head.

Oh, no. A sick feeling rose up inside. *Done for, but not dead.*

I had never hit a deer with a car before, and I was going to have to finish this one off, which would be illegal—or drive the half mile back home, call a game warden, and make the doe wait for mercy at the official hand of the law.

When Cath and I got out of the car, the doe stood up. Then, recognizing us as bipeds, she trotted off and disappeared into the woods. Examining the dented fender over the wheel, we realized it was more a case of deer hitting car than car hitting deer.

As we drove off, we agreed that we had all been lucky. It could have been far worse: for us, the doe, and the car.

Three hours later, I followed the doe's tracks by flashlight, figuring she would stop nearby if she was seriously hurt. In the snow, I found only hoofprints: no sign of a fresh bed. I prayed she had made it with nothing worse than bruises and a newfound respect for headlights, yet the incident still troubled me.

I knew, of course, that animals get maimed and killed by cars. As a volunteer firefighter, I had been on accident scenes. On one such scene, the driver had said she thought the deer ran away, but when I walked back down the highway in search of the missing front license plate, I saw the doe drag herself into the underbrush. I called the game warden and showed him where she had gone. I heard the gun's sharp report. The warden came back and told me what I already knew: She had been very badly injured.

I knew, too, that we maim and kill in a million other ways, our industrial, economic, and agricultural machinery incurring a massive debt in animal lives and, worse, in habitat. But I had always found such harm—regrettable and unintended—easier to accept than premeditated violence.

Now, thinking about the doe and the sick feeling that rose up as I saw her lying there in the road, I reconsidered. Did I really find it easier to accept these kinds of impacts? Did I really prefer the inadvertent, often-messy, often-unseen ravages I inflict on my fellow creatures as I go about the everyday routines of life? The answer, I realized, was no. If my existence was going to take a toll on other beings, I would rather exact that toll consciously, respectfully, swiftly—and for the specific purpose of eating. I could make a deeper peace with intentional harm, with the kill I had prepared for and chosen.

Hunting, of course, is not the only path to mindful eating.

Gardening reminds us to look deeply into our food, to contemplate our interactions with earth, plants, and animals, to see both the harmony and the harm. If gardening was impractical, if Cath and I lived somewhere like the Brooklyn apartment where I spent my last two years of college, then tending a few clay pots by a window could serve the purpose—our sense of interconnectedness awakened by touching soil, plucking basil, snipping leaves into simmering pasta sauce.

Learning about agriculture calls us to attention as well. Visiting a farm, talking with a farmer or compost producer, reading a magazine article about the growing of grains, beans, fruits, and vegetables—each of these brings our food into focus, cultivating awareness of the landscape changes wrought by crops and the constant impact on other beings.

We can, and sometimes do, visit the places where our poultry is raised. Meeting the people makes them more than faceless producers. Meeting the birds makes them more than food. Seeing them, and the conditions in which they live and die, helps us appreciate what it means to cook up a pan full of chicken marsala. If we were raising our own birds—for eggs or meat or both—that, too, would help us see more deeply, as we cared for them, got to know them, and confronted their deaths.

The particular practice does not matter. What matters is that deep looking. What matters is the kind of insight that can leap from here to there, from the simple fact of food on a plate to the ecological and ethical complexities of its origins. What matters is being able to walk into the grocery store, pick up a bag of apples or a loaf of bread, a bag of salad greens or a package of chicken legs, and imagine the mortality involved. What matters is seeing beyond the money I fork over in those trouble-free transactions of cash for food: at least guessing at the other costs incurred.

I do not need to weigh myself down with such awareness. As far as I can see, that brand of guilt serves no worthwhile purpose. But awareness encourages me to pause and reflect, to celebrate the food that reaches our plates, to respect the organisms we ingest and the people who bring them to our table, to say a few words of thanks before taking up fork or spoon.

And, for me, hunting helps. Year-round, it summons my attention, like the ringing of a prayer bell. In winter and spring, I can't slice stew meat or sauté backstrap without thinking of the animal I dragged home, recalling the specific impact my life had on that life. In late summer, as our venison dwindles, my attention turns again to the forest and I prowl along brooks and old stone walls, through stands of maple and hemlock, checking old deer trails for fresh sign. In autumn, I hike into the woods in the predawn dark, Orion high over one shoulder, frozen leaves underfoot. If I kill, I crouch beside the fallen whitetail to give thanks for all that sustains me, then make my way to the kitchen counter to complete the butchering: a meditation with meat and knife.

Notes

I could not have written this book were it not for the efforts of historians, anthropologists, biologists, ecologists, philosophers, poets, and other researchers and writers who preceded me. I am in their debt.

The opening epigraph is from Mary Midgley's *Animals and Why They Matter* (Athens, GA: University of Georgia Press, 1984), 27.

Chapter 1: No More Blood

It is difficult for me to imagine who I would have been as a kid—or who I would be as an adult—if I had not spent my boyhood summers almost entirely outdoors, wandering the woods, fishing for trout, catching tadpoles and bullfrogs. Interaction with the natural world is, I believe, vital to children's physical, emotional, mental, and spiritual health. I highly recommend Richard Louv's insightful exploration of this topic, *Last Child in the Woods: Saving Our Children from Nature-Deficit Disorder* (Chapel Hill, NC: Algonquin Books, 2005). Though ambivalent about hunting, Louv makes the case that "fishing and hunting remain among the last ways that the young learn of the mystery and moral complexity of nature in a way that no videotape can convey" (193). He takes his arguments a step further in *The Nature Principle: Human Restoration and the End of Nature-Deficit Disorder* (Chapel Hill, NC: Algonquin Books, 2011), contending that adults also need nature.

My brief discussions of the history and taxonomy of trout and salmon draw primarily on Robert J. Behnke's *Trout and Salmon of North America* (New York: The Free Press, 2002). Izaak Walton's description of carp as "the queen of rivers" comes from *The Compleat Angler* (1676; repr., New York: Wiley & Putnam, 1847), 147.

As noted on the copyright page, I am grateful for permission to reprint Wendell Berry's fine poem "The Peace of Wild Things."

This chapter's epigraph, from Ovid's *Metamorphoses*, can be found quoted in Howard Williams, *The Ethics of Diet: A Catena of Authorities Deprecatory of the Practice of Flesh-Eating* (1883; repr., Chicago: University of Illinois Press, 2003), 26.

Chapter 2: Man the Gardener

In my final two years of undergraduate work, completed at the New School for Social Research, I studied Mohandas K. Gandhi's moral and political philosophy under the guidance of the late feminist philosopher Sara Ruddick, and was particularly impressed by the twin commitments of Gandhi's lifelong quest for truth. On the one hand, he lived according to what he saw as the truth, which must, he wrote, "be my beacon, my shield and buckler." On the other hand, he had the humility and wisdom to recognize that his truth was incomplete, that it was only "the relative truth as I have conceived it." These lines are from Gandhi's aptly subtitled *An Autobiography: The Story of My Experiments with Truth* (1957; repr., Boston: Beacon

Press, 1993), xxviii. The line about "the life of a lamb" appears on page 235.

Discussion of vegetarianism in Greece, India, and Europe can be found in *The Ethics of Diet*, cited above, and also in Colin Spencer's *Vegetarianism: A History* (London: Grub Street, 2000). For a detailed exploration of the links between early European vegetarianism and Hindu traditions, see Tristram Stuart's *The Bloodless Revolution: A Cultural History of Vegetarianism from 1600 to Modern Times* (New York: W. W. Norton, 2007).

My primary source on the history of U.S. vegetarianism was Adam D. Shprintzen's "Abstention to Consumption: The Development of American Vegetarianism, 1817-1917" (PhD diss., Loyola University Chicago, 2011), which he generously shared and discussed in personal correspondence. The direct quotes drawn from Shprintzen's work are listed here, by opening words and page numbers in his dissertation: "an unwavering moral principle," 113; "a fascination with the possibilities," 218. Shprintzen's work was also my source for quotes from several other people and publications. These are listed here, with page numbers from Shprintzen's dissertation: Sylvester Graham, "the lower animals," 30; "dietetic intemperance and lewdness," 32; Charles Dickens, "breakfast would have been no breakfast," 51; *Scientific American*, "a good conceit," 106; *Saturday Evening Post*, "weak and cowardly," 107; *Water-Cure Journal*, "were there no hogs," 114; *American Vegetarian and Health Journal*, "a radical reform," 129; *Chicago Daily Tribune*, "leg breaking and ear twisting savagery," 290.

This chapter's epigraph is from the Book of Isaiah in the Hebrew Bible or Old Testament.

Chapter 3: Trouble in Eden

Howard Williams discusses Hesiod and "the peaceful spirit of agriculture" on page 2 of *The Ethics of Diet*. David Pimentel's study is described in his article "Soil Erosion: A Food and Environmental Threat," *Environment, Development and Sustainability* 8 (2006): 119-137. The U.S. Fish and Wildlife Service numbers on birds and pesticides were drawn from a two-page pamphlet issued by the Office of Migratory Bird Management, *Pesticides and Birds* (March 2000).

Several studies on the harm done to animals by grain harvesting are listed in a fact sheet by Champe Green, *Reducing Mortality of Grassland Wildlife During Haying and Wheat-Harvesting Operations* (Stillwater, OK: Oklahoma Cooperative Extension Service, 2007). For a related, intriguing, and controversial article based on Tom Regan's theory of animal rights, see Steven L. Davis, "The Least Harm Principle May Require That Humans Consume a Diet Containing Large Herbivores, Not a Vegan Diet," *Journal of Agricultural and Environmental Ethics* 16 (2003): 387-394.

Richard Nelson's *Heart and Blood: Living with Deer in America* (New York: Random House, 1997) is one of my favorite books on deer, not only because it is thoroughly researched and elegantly written, but because Nelson treats everyone—from animal-rights activists to trophy hunters—with respect. I have drawn quotes from his chapter on deer and agriculture, "The Hidden Harvest" (298-311). Thanks also to freelance writer Al Cambronne for discussing deer management and history with me.

In developing my historical sketch of the New England landscape, I consulted William Cronon's fascinating book, *Changes in the Land: Indians, Colonists, and the Ecology of New England* (New York: Hill and Wang, 1983), which includes his description of the precolonial coastal forest as "remarkably open" (25). I also drew on Tom Wessels's *Reading the Forested Landscape: A Natural History of New England* (Woodstock, VT: The Countryman Press, 1997) and Charles W. Johnson's *The Nature of Vermont: Introduction and*

Guide to a New England Environment (Hanover, NH: University Press of New England, 1980).

Wessels's *Reading the Forested Landscape* provides an intriguing introduction to the historical forces—from logging and agriculture to fires and hurricanes—that have shaped the region's forests. David Ludlum's remark about the "wool craze," from Ludlum's *Social Ferment in Vermont, 1791-1850* (New York: Columbia University Press, 1939), is quoted on page 57 of Wessels's book. The suggestion that New England's stone walls be considered "the eighth wonder of the world" appears on page 59.

I am grateful to Victoria Hughes and Marjorie Strong of the Vermont Historical Society for tracking down the Vermont Merino Sheep Association's *Spanish Merino Sheep: Their Importation* (1879), and helping me figure out what became of the several thousand animals William Jarvis brought over from Europe. Thanks also to Jennifer Donaldson of the Woodstock Historical Society for finding the local newspaper account of Alexander Crowell's slaying of the catamount, "Panther Hunt in Barnard," *The Standard* (Woodstock, VT), December 1, 1881.

This chapter's epigraph comes from Wendell Berry, *The Gift of Good Land: Further Essays Cultural and Agricultural* (New York: North Point Press, 1982), 281.

Chapter 4: An Animal Who Eats

The Dalai Lama, Tenzin Gyatso, mentions his dietary journey in *Freedom in Exile: The Autobiography of the Dalai Lama* (New York: HarperCollins, 1990). In light of my own certainty as a vegan, I was intrigued by his description of how, in his vegetarian phase, he felt "a sense of fulfillment from a strict interpretation of the rule" (179).

Henry van Dyke's discussion of "the enchantment of uncertainty" is from *Fisherman's Luck and Some Other Uncertain Things* (New York: Charles Scribner's Sons, 1899), 10.

This chapter's epigraph—from John Hersey's *Blues* (New York: Alfred A. Knopf, 1987), 9—is the Fisherman's initial reply to the Stranger, who has just expressed his distaste for "the fishing mystique: all that notion of the elegance and nobility of a brutal blood sport."

Chapter 5: Where the Great Heron Feeds

Speculations on aspens' chemical defenses are discussed in a number of articles, including Walter J. Jakubas and Gordon W. Guillon, "Coniferyl Benzoate in Quaking Aspen: A Ruffed Grouse Feeding Deterrent," *Journal of Chemical Ecology* 16, no. 4 (1990): 1077-1087.

I drew information on the global impacts of the livestock industry from Henning Steinfeld et al., *Livestock's Long Shadow: Environmental Issues and Options* (Rome: United Nations Food and Agriculture Organization, 2006). Some of this study's calculations and conclusions have been contested, especially those concerning greenhouse gases. It is important to recognize that the ecological impacts of livestock production vary greatly, depending on the methods employed; see, for example, the writings of Nicolette Hahn Niman, including *Righteous Porkchop: Finding a Life and Good Food Beyond Factory Farms* (New York: HarperCollins, 2009).

Jeremy Bentham's famous articulation of the question "*Can they suffer?*" comes from *An Introduction to the Principles of Morals and Legislation, Vol. II*, 2nd ed. (London: W. Pickering, 1823), 236.

For an excellent discussion of commercial fisheries, I recommend Paul Greenberg's *Four Fish: The Future of the Last Wild Food* (New York: Penguin, 2010).

Richard Nelson's line "The supermarket is an agent of our forgetfulness" appears in *Heart and Blood*, 281.

"Absent referent" is a term that originated in linguistics. Carol J. Adams uses it to make an important point about how we separate the idea of "meat" from the idea of "animal." The lines I quote in this chapter come from her book *The Sexual Politics of Meat: A Feminist-Vegetarian Critical Theory*, 10th anniv. ed. (New York: Continuum, 1990, 2000), 14.

The Dalai Lama's discussion of Tibetan Buddhists' "rather curious attitude" toward meat can be found in *Freedom in Exile*, 20.

Thomas Berry frequently used the word "autistic" to describe modern people's relational incapacity. In *The Great Work: Our Way into the Future* (New York: Bell Tower, 1999), 79, for instance, he wrote that his was "an autistic generation in its inability to establish any intimate rapport with the natural world."

William Cronon discusses the "dualistic vision in which the human is entirely outside the natural" in the book he edited, *Uncommon Ground: Rethinking the Human Place in Nature* (New York: W. W. Norton, 1995), 80-81. By setting "humanity and nature at opposite poles," he writes, "we thereby leave ourselves little hope of discovering what an ethical, sustainable, *honorable* human place in nature might actually look like."

Paul Shepard's line about large carnivores being inevitably "pursued by microbes, fungi, and plant roots" comes from his essay collection *Traces of an Omnivore* (Washington, DC: Island Press, 1996), 49. Val Plumwood's remarkable essay was originally published as "Being Prey," *Terra Nova* 1, no. 3 (1996): 32-44. Cleveland Amory's phrase "prey will be separated from predator" is from a 1992 interview with *Sierra* magazine, quoted in Nelson's *Heart and Blood*, 275.

This chapter's epigraph comes from Paul Rezendes, *Tracking and the Art of Seeing* (New York: HarperCollins, 1999), 20.

Chapter 6: Hunter and Beholder

The U.S. Fish and Wildlife Service's *2006 National Survey of Fishing, Hunting, and Wildlife-Associated Recreation* provided statistics on Americans' annual participation in fishing and hunting.

Susan Kent's observation concerning traditional societies' classifications of animals and fish appears in the book she edited, *Farmers as Hunters: The Implications of Sedentism* (Cambridge, UK: Cambridge University Press, 1989), 132, and was first brought to my attention by Mary Zeiss Stange's *Woman the Hunter* (Boston: Beacon Press, 1997), 45.

Estimates of U.S. per capita meat and fish consumption come from the U.S. Department of Agriculture's *Agriculture Fact Book 2001-2002*, 15.

The controversial idea that persistence hunting may have played a part in human evolution is sketched in Dennis M. Bramble and Daniel E. Lieberman's "Endurance Running and the Evolution of *Homo,*" *Nature* 432, no. 18 (2004): 345-352. It is also discussed in Christopher McDougall's *Born to Run: A Hidden Tribe, Superathletes, and the Greatest Race the World Has Never Seen* (New York: Alfred A. Knopf, 2009) and in Bernd Heinrich's *Why We Run: A Natural History* (New York: HarperCollins, 2001).

The 2001 shooting death of Deborah Prasnicki in Wisconsin was covered in national and regional news stories, including Meg Jones, "Trial Starts for Hunter Charged in Fatal Shooting," *Milwaukee Journal Sentinel*, March 27, 2003.

Jan E. Dizard's observation that "even hunters themselves are not all that trusting of other hunters" comes from his book *Mortal Stakes: Hunters and Hunting in Contemporary America* (Amherst, MA: University of Massachusetts Press, 2003), 162.

He notes that virtually none of the hunters he interviewed during his research would hunt with a complete stranger: "They would first want to know something about the person's temperament, judgment, and competency with a firearm. . . . If hunters are cautious about the company they keep while hunting, it is small wonder that nonhunters are concerned."

The line concerning the "many Tygers, monstrous and furious beasts" found in the New World comes from Job Hortop, *The Travails of an Englishman* (London: William Wright, 1591) and is quoted in Andrea L. Smalley's "'The Liberty of Killing a Deer': Histories of Wildlife Use and Political Ecology in Early America" (PhD diss., Northern Illinois University, 2005), which she generously shared with me.

In writing this chapter, I drew extensively from Daniel Herman's excellent *Hunting and the American Imagination* (Washington, DC: Smithsonian Institution Press, 2001). Direct quotes drawn from Herman's work are listed here, by opening words and page numbers in his book: "How was it that New England could be so full of game," 29; "lackluster hunters," 31; "They believed that Indians, like English aristocrats," 32; "the third stage," 42; "images of man fallen to a state of nature," 4; "take on the aura of the indigene," xiii; "a hunting people," x.

Herman's book was also my source for quotes from several others. These are listed here, again with page numbers from Herman's book: William Bradford, "hidious & desolate wildernes," 16; Lord Thomas Macaulay, "not because it gave pain to the bear," 30; Thomas Jefferson, "those who labour in the earth," 44; Charles Woodmason, "one continual Scene of Depravity of Manners," 39; James Fenimore Cooper, "driven God's creatures from the wilderness," 116; Henry William Herbert, "the demoralization of luxury," 174-175.

In personal correspondence, Herman suggested I consult Godfrey Hodgson's *A Great and Godly Adventure: The Pilgrims and the*

Myth of the First Thanksgiving (Cambridge, MA: Perseus Books, 2006) regarding the presence of venison, not turkey, at the first Thanksgiving.

Cotton Mather's diary entry about "making water at the wall" is quoted in Keith Thomas, *Man and the Natural World: A History of the Modern Sensibility* (New York: Pantheon Books, 1983), 38. The 1745 North Carolina law requiring hunters to tend corn hills is cited in Stuart A. Marks, *Southern Hunting in Black and White: Nature, History, and Ritual in a Carolina Community* (Princeton, NJ: Princeton University Press, 1991), 31. The phrase "the feathered lightning is no more" comes from Aldo Leopold's *A Sand County Almanac with Essays on Conservation from Round River* (New York: Ballantine Books, 1966), 118. Theodore Roosevelt's description of killing the bison comes from *The Wilderness Hunter* (New York: G. P. Putnam's Sons, 1893), 254.

This chapter's epigraph comes from Dizard's *Mortal Stakes*, 168.

Chapter 7: Double Vision

The mittens worn by Karen Wood the day she was killed have often been referred to as "white." In a detailed accounting of evidence introduced during the trial—Steve Kloehn, "Mittens, Rifle Entered into Evidence," *Bangor Daily News*, October 13, 1990—they are described as "large, cream-colored, knit mittens, with palms made of a dirty, buff-colored suede." Thanks to John Holyoke of the *Bangor Daily News* for locating this story.

The hunter-education text referred to in this chapter is the *New England Hunter Education Manual: Core Curriculum* (Seattle: Outdoor Empire Publishing, 2002).

Figures on injuries and fatalities come from multiple editions of *Injury Facts* (Itasca, IL: National Safety Council, 1999-2011) and from *What Are They Doing about Hunting Injuries?* (Albany, NY: New York State Department of Environmental Conservation, 2004).

My thanks to Pete Mirick of the Massachusetts Division of Fisheries and Wildlife for helping me track down data on the loss of open land in the state. The figures cited come from *Losing Ground: The Case for Land Conservation in Massachusetts* (Lincoln, MA: Massachusetts Audubon Society, 1991) and James DeNormandie and Claire Corcoran, *Losing Ground: Beyond the Footprint* (Lincoln, MA: Massachusetts Audubon Society, 2009).

Facts on Missouri and Arkansas conservation funding come from *Promises Made, Promises Kept: Celebrating 25 Years of 'Design for Conservation'* (Jefferson City, MO: Missouri Conservation Commission, 2002) and *Keeping Arkansas Natural Forever: Amendment 75: Promises Kept* (Little Rock, AR: Arkansas Game and Fish Commission, 2002).

Abraham Kaplan's law of the instrument "Give a small boy a hammer" comes from his book *The Conduct of Inquiry: Methodology for Behavioral Science* (San Francisco: Chandler Publishing, 1964), 28.

The quote concerning hunters' lack of commitment to "hunting as a management tool" comes from Daniel J. Decker and Nancy A. Connelly's "The Need for Hunter Education in Deer Management: Insights from New York," *Wildlife Society Bulletin* 18, no. 4 (1990): 447-452.

Figures on public opinions of hunting for meat, sport, and trophies come from an unpublished survey about various hunting and fishing issues: *Sportsmen's Attitudes* (Harrisonburg, VA: Responsive Management, 2006). The Stephen Kellert study referred to is "Attitudes and Characteristics of Hunters and Antihunters," in *Transactions of the Forty-third North American Wildlife and Natural Resources Conference* (Washington, DC: Wildlife Management Institute, 1978), 412-423.

This chapter's epigraph comes from Michael Pollan, *The Omnivore's Dilemma: A Natural History of Four Meals* (New York: Penguin Press, 2006), 336.

Chapter 8: A Hunter's Prayer

In writing this chapter, I drew on José Ortega y Gasset's prologue-turned-book, *Meditations on Hunting* (1942; repr., Belgrade, MT: Wilderness Adventures Press, 1995). Most of the direct quotes come from page 105. The remainder are listed here: "exemplary moral spirit," 97; "Paleolithic man," 57; "represent the most primitive human species" and "the slightest hint of government," 76; "Today's best-trained hunter" and "eternal troglodyte," 115.

Edward Abbey's criticism of Ortega y Gasset comes from the essay "Blood Sport" in *One Life at a Time, Please* (New York: Henry Holt, 1978), 39. The quote from Robert Kimber concerning "utilitarian" hunters comes from his book *Living Wild and Domestic: The Education of a Hunter-Gardener* (Guilford, CT: The Lyons Press, 2002), 45-46.

A Hunter's Heart: Honest Essays on Blood Sport, ed. David Petersen (New York: Henry Holt, 1996) helped me begin to explore my mixed feelings about hunting. I quote several lines from Richard Nelson's introduction "Finding Common Ground": "Inupiaq men lived to hunt," 8; "hunting was entirely evil," 1; "twisted together with them," 2. I also refer to Ann S. Causey's essay "Is Hunting Ethical?," 80-89, and Mary Zeiss Stange's "In the Snow Queen's Palace" (adapted from "Little Deaths," *Sports Afield*, November 1994), 108-112. The other quotes drawn from *A Hunter's Heart* are from Mike Gaddis, "Taking a Life" (originally published in *Audubon*, November 1990), 121, and George N. Wallace, "If Elk Would Scream" (originally published in *High Country News*, October 14, 1983), 96.

In this chapter, I paraphrase several arguments made by Mary Zeiss Stange in *Woman the Hunter* (cited above); the line "for the same inner reasons" appears on page 8. I also quote Marti Kheel, "License to Kill: An Ecofeminist Critique of Hunters' Discourse," in *Animals and Women: Feminist Theoretical Explorations*, ed. Carol J. Adams and Josephine Donovan

(Durham, NC: Duke University Press, 1995); the quotes drawn from Kheel's essay are "to camouflage and to legitimate," 87, and "quest to establish masculine identity," 110.

The quotes and paraphrases from Susan Morse come from personal conversations and from an interview conducted by James Ehlers, "Return of the Cougar: It's Time for the East to be Wild," *Outdoors Magazine* (March 2002): 30-32.

I discuss Ted Kerasote's essay "Restoring the Older Knowledge," which appears in *A Hunter's Heart*, and quote directly from it: "the disciplined, mindful, sacred activity," 293; "the world that feeds us," 294. I also refer to Kerasote's *Bloodties: Nature, Culture, and the Hunt* (New York: Random House, 1993); he discusses the central European model of hunter education on page 218, and mentions his attempt to "outwit" the pain caused by his eating on page 232. In personal correspondence, Kerasote generously shared his thoughts on the origins of "sport" in agrarian societies, and on the ancient concept and word as antecedents of their modern counterparts.

Linda Hogan's essay "The Feathers" appears in her book *Dwellings: A Spiritual History of the Living World* (New York: Simon & Schuster, 1995) and ends with the phrase "simple powers, strange and real," 20.

Thomas Berry's line "For too long we have been away somewhere" was originally published in his book *The Dream of the Earth* (San Francisco: Sierra Club Books, 1988) and appears in *Learning to Listen to the Land*, ed. Bill Willers (Washington, DC: Island Press, 1991), 255.

This chapter's epigraph comes from Barry Lopez, *Arctic Dreams* (New York: Charles Scribner's Sons, 1986), 413.

Chapter 9: Healing Ground

The line "Ah, how good it feels! The hand of an old friend" is from Henry Wadsworth Longfellow's play *John Endicott* and appears in

Longfellow's Poetical Works (London: George Routledge and Sons, 1883), 502. The quote concerning "the apostolic injunction to 'rejoice'" is from Clive Staples Lewis, *The Problem of Pain* (New York: Macmillan, 1944), 61.

Valerius Geist's line comes from his article "Threats to Wildlife Conservation," *Deer and Deer Hunting* (February 1987): 31, and is quoted in Nelson's *Heart and Blood*, 279. Thanks to C. Brickman Way for finding that magazine issue at a flea market and thinking of me.

The line "those ranks of trophy heads" appears in C. L. Rawlins's "I Like to Talk about Animals" in *A Hunter's Heart*, 90.

This chapter's epigraph comes from John Burroughs, "The Gospel of Nature," in *Time and Change: The Writings of John Burroughs, Part Sixteen* (1912; repr., Whitefish, MT: Kessinger Publishing, 2004), 245.

Chapter 10: Into the Woods

In sketching the history of white-tailed deer, I relied on *White-tailed Deer: Ecology and Management*, ed. Lowell K. Halls (Harrisburg, PA: Stackpole Books, 1984), especially Richard E. McCabe and Thomas R. McCabe's chapter "Of Slings and Arrows: An Historical Retrospection" and George Mattfeld's "Northeastern Hardwood and Spruce/Fir Forests." The McCabes' quote "The whitetail rarely was hunted" appears on page 72. I drew additional historical data—as well as information on human-deer conflicts, deer population growth, and the ecological impacts of overabundant deer—from Richard Nelson's *Heart and Blood*.

For a detailed introduction to the shifting fortunes of various Massachusetts wildlife species over the past few centuries—including large mammals and grassland birds—see Debra Bernardos et al., "Wildlife Dynamics in the Changing

New England Landscape," in *Forests in Time: The Environmental Consequences of 1,000 Years of Change in New England*, ed. David R. Foster and John D. Aber (New Haven: Yale University Press, 2004), 142-168.

Leopold's line "just as a deer herd lives in mortal fear of its wolves" is from *A Sand County Almanac*, 140.

The Public Trust Doctrine and North American wildlife conservation model are discussed by Valerius Geist, Shane P. Mahoney, and John F. Organ in "Why Hunting Has Defined the North American Model of Wildlife Conservation," in *Transactions of the Sixty-sixth North American Wildlife and Natural Resources Conference* (Washington, DC: Wildlife Management Institute, 2001), 175-185.

Concerning historical views of hunters, I drew primarily on Herman's *Hunting and the American Imagination*; Elisha Jarrett Lewis's words on the "pot hunter" are quoted on page 154. I also drew on Louis S. Warren, *The Hunter's Game: Poachers and Conservationists in Twentieth-Century America* (New Haven, CT: Yale University Press, 1997).

This chapter's epigraph comes from *A Sand County Almanac*, xviii-xix.

Chapter 11: Kinds of Killing

Joseph Campbell's words on "the essence of life" are drawn from his book *The Hero's Journey* (New York: Harper & Row, 1990; Novato, CA: New World Library, 2003), 13; citation refers to the New World edition.

Leopold's thoughts on "sportsmanship" and "gadgetry" are from *A Sand County Almanac*, 212-216. David Stalling's essay, "Space Ace Technology, Stone Age Pursuit" (originally published in *Bugle*, Winter 1995) appears in *A Hunter's Heart*, 182-190.

Thomas Berry reportedly expressed his thoughts on "the great conversation" while talking with high school students. His words are transcribed in Rich Heffern's "Prophet for the Earth: An Exploration of the Thought of Fr. Thomas Berry," *Eco Catholic* (blog), *National Catholic Reporter*, January 4, 2011, http://ncronline.org/blogs/eco-catholic/prophet-earth-exploration-thought-fr-thomas-berry: "We are talking to ourselves. We are no longer talking to the rivers and forests, we are no longer listening to the winds and the stars. We have broken the great conversation. By breaking that conversation, we have shattered the universe. All the disasters that are happening now are a consequence of this spiritual autism." A very similar passage appears in Berry's *Befriending the Earth: A Theology of Reconciliation Between Humans and the Earth* (Mystic, CT: Twenty-Third Publications, 1991), 20.

Philip J. Deloria's line about "the dispossession and conquest of actual Indian people" comes from his book *Playing Indian* (New Haven, CT: Yale University Press, 1998), 182.

Robert Kimber's thoughts on animals, gifts, and "property rights" are from *Living Wild and Domestic*, 79.

This chapter's epigraph comes from Nelson's *Heart and Blood*, 286.

Chapter 12: Fickle Predators

Ted Kerasote's description of the mother elk's response to the death of her calf is from "A Killing at Dawn," *Audubon* 102, no. 2 (2000): 38-41. Kerasote offers other intriguing thoughts on anthropomorphism and interspecies communication in his book *Merle's Door: Lessons from a Freethinking Dog* (New York: Harcourt, 2007), 10.

Regarding the history of deer populations and modern hunting seasons in Vermont, I relied on Marc Boglioli's *A Matter of Life and*

Death: Hunting in Contemporary Vermont (Amherst, MA: University of Massachusetts Press, 2009).

I also relied on archival materials and historical data helpfully provided by John Hall, Lilla Stutz-Lumbra, Chris Saunders, and John Buck of the Vermont Fish and Wildlife Department, including Leonard E. Foote's *A History of Wild Game in Vermont*, 3rd ed., rev. (Montpelier, VT: Vermont Fish and Game Service, 1946).

Louis Warren's line "How one hunted and what one killed" comes from *The Hunter's Game*, 14.

This chapter's epigraph comes from a column by Pulitzer Prize winner William A. Caldwell—"Hawk and Hare Are One," *Bird Watcher's Digest* (September 1978): 61-62—in which he contemplates life, death, and predation. The column's title is an abbreviation of a line by Gary Snyder, "The hawk, the swoop, and the hare are one," from *Earth House Hold* (New York: New Directions Publishing, 1957), 92.

Chapter 13: Blood Trails

The quotes referred to by Marti Kheel in "License to Kill" are from Paul Shepard, *The Tender Carnivore and the Sacred Game* (New York: Charles Scribner's Sons, 1973), 173, and Ortega y Gasset, *Meditations on Hunting*, 101.

The Connecticut and Maryland wounding-rate studies referred to are discussed by Howard J. Kilpatrick and W. David Walter, "A Controlled Archery Deer Hunt in a Residential Community: Cost, Effectiveness, and Deer Recovery Rates," *Wildlife Society Bulletin* 27, no. 1 (1999): 115-123, and M. Andy Pedersen, Seth M. Berry, and Jeffrey C. Bossart, "Wounding Rates of White-tailed Deer with Modern Archery Equipment," *Proceedings of the Annual Conference of the Southeastern Association of Fish and Wildlife Agencies* 62 (2008): 31-34.

David Petersen discusses the humaneness of bowhunting, and relates several anecdotes of people being hit by broadheads, in his book *Heartsblood: Hunting, Spirituality, and Wildness in America* (Washington, DC: Island Press, 2000), 172-174.

Leopold's passage on the "peculiar virtue in wildlife ethics" is from *A Sand County Almanac*, 212.

This chapter's epigraph is from Susan Ewing, "To Each Her Own," in *Heart Shots: Women Write about Hunting*, ed. Mary Zeiss Stange (Mechanicsburg, PA: Stackpole Books, 2003), 73.

Chapter 14: Hunting with the Buddha

Richard Nelson's line "the exploration has turned inward" is from his book *The Island Within* (San Francisco: North Point Press, 1989; New York: Vintage Books, 1991), 172; citation refers to the Vintage edition.

This chapter's epigraph is from Kimber's *Living Wild and Domestic*, 148.

Chapter 15: The Red Deer

Christopher Camuto's line "I've long had an odd thought" comes from his book *Hunting from Home: A Year Afield in the Blue Ridge Mountains* (New York: W. W. Norton, 2003), 288.

Ortega y Gasset's "case in which the killing of one creature" is from *Meditations on Hunting*, 101. Rachel Carson's "We cannot have peace among men" is from an undated letter, Rachel Carson to Fon Boardman, Beinecke Rare Book and Manuscript Library, Yale University, New Haven, CT.

This chapter's epigraph comes from Henry Beston, *The Outermost House: A Year of Life on the Great Beach of Cape Cod* (New York: Doubleday, 1928; New York: Penguin, 1976), 25; citation refers to the Penguin edition.

Chapter 16: Reckoning

In this chapter, I refer to a letter written by Thich Nhat Hanh, "Letter from Thây," October 17, 2007, http://www.plumvillage. org/letters-from-thay/27-letter-from-thy.html. Nhat Hanh's words on paper, clouds, rain, and loggers are from *Peace Is Every Step: The Path of Mindfulness in Everyday Life* (New York: Bantam Books, 1991), 95. His words on tangerine blossoms are from page 21 of the same book.

This chapter's epigraph comes from Stange's *Woman the Hunter*, 189.

Acknowledgments

My deepest thanks:

To Catherine Cerulli, for all the forms your love takes, for embracing my transformation, for believing in my writing before I did, for doing more than your share on the home front when I was glued to my desk, and for your keen editorial eye.

To Mark Cerulli, Jay Mason, Richard Czaplinski, Rob Bryan, Steve Wright, Damien Middelton, Ryan Johns, Tom Cady, and Drew Lanham, for accompanying me on the first legs of my journey into hunting, for helping me see what the pursuit could mean.

To Jan Clausen and Jane Lazarre, for encouraging my writing almost twenty years ago, and Ted Gup, for doing so more recently; and to Stephen Long, Jason McGarvey, and Nathan Kowalsky for providing the first opportunities to bring parts of this story to the printed page.

To my agent, Laurie Abkemeier, for having the skill, insight, good humor, and raw tenacity necessary to shepherd this book— and this author—through the wilderness of publishing; to my editor, Jessica Case, for being so enthusiastic about bringing this project to fruition, for doing everything possible to make it a success, and for offering many helpful questions and suggestions along the way; to everyone else at Pegasus Books who helped create this book; and to everyone at Open Road Media who published the digital versions and helped spread the word.

To Catherine Cerulli, Mark Cerulli, and Richard Czaplinski, again, and to Eric Nuse, Beth Segers, Mary Colleen Sinnott, Susan Morse, Daniel Herman, Adam Shprintzen, Ted Kerasote, Mary Zeiss Stange, and Marc Boglioli for reviewing portions of this manuscript and offering constructive comments.

To all my friends and family, for supporting this book even when it was only a glimmer of an idea, for asking questions and offering reflections, for helping me understand what this story was about; and to all the readers of my blog, for commenting on my posts and engaging each other in spirited and civil debate, for opening my eyes to new perspectives and challenging me to reconsider my own.

To the places that have shaped my life and to the creatures who have nourished me, body and soul.

About the Author

TOVAR CERULLI has worked as a logger, carpenter, and freelance writer. In 2009, he was awarded a graduate school fellowship by the University of Massachusetts, where his research has focused on food, hunting, and human relationships with the natural world. He lives in Vermont with his wife, Catherine, their Labrador retriever, and an eclectic mix of cookbooks. Visit him at www.TovarCerulli.com.